FINS DE SIÈCLE/NEW BEGINNINGS

THE DOLPHIN

General Editor:
Dominic Rainsford

31

FINS DE SIÈCLE / NEW BEGINNINGS

Edited by
Ib Johansen

AARHUS UNIVERSITY PRESS

Printed in Denmark by Narayana Press
ISBN 87 7288 382 0
ISSN 0106 4487

AARHUS UNIVERSITY PRESS
Langelandsgade 177
DK-8200 Aarhus N, Denmark
Fax (+45) 8942 5380
www.unipress.dk

73 Lime Walk
Headington, Oxford OX3 7AD
Fax (+44) 1865 750 079

Box 511
Oakville, Conn. 06779
Fax (+1) 860 945 9468

Editorial address:
THE DOLPHIN
Department of English
University of Aarhus
DK-8000 Aarhus C, Denmark
Fax (+45) 8942 6540

This volume is published with financial support from the Aarhus University Research Foundation and The Danish Research Council for the Humanities

Cover illustration by Dominic Rainsford after Odilon Redon

Contents

Ib Johansen
Introduction 7

Part One: AD 1000 15

Richard North
Anglo-Saxon and Scandinavian Attitudes to 999/1000 AD 17

Part Two: The 1890s 39

Per Serritslev Petersen
Fictional Constructions of Female Vampirism in the Nineteenth-Century *Fin-de-Siècle* Crisis of Masculinity and Its Modernist Aftermath: Bram Stoker, Joseph Conrad, D. H. Lawrence 41

Michael Böss
Root Music: Occult Notions of Identity in W. B. Yeats and Contemporary Social Criticism in Ireland 71

Robert Rix
Salomé and the *fin du globe*: Oscar Wilde's Decadent Tragedy 94

Part Three: 1890s/1990s 125

Ib Johansen
American Specters: Two Versions of Ghostliness in American *fin-de-siècle* Culture 127

Part Four: Approaching 2000 in Literature 161

Norman Ravvin
The Apocalyptic Predicament: Timothy Findley's Predetermined Novel 163

Sylvia Mikkelsen
Feminist Aesthetics at the Threshold of the New Millennium: The Questioning of 'Feminine Essentialism' from Emily Dickinson to Julia Kristeva 177

Part Five: The 1990s/2000: Interdisciplinary Approaches 191

Cheralyn Mealor
In the Meantime: Nation in New Labour's Millennium Countdown 193

Jan Ifversen
Globalization – A Catch-all Concept for the End of the Millennium 215

Jamsheed Shorish
Fear Amidst Plenty: The Duality of Economic Optimism at the Close of the 20th Century 240

Anjum P. Saleemi
Linguistic, Mental and Biological Laws 255

Part Six: The 1990s/2000: Ends, Idiocy, Beginnings 265

Graeme Thomson
No Ground to Stand On 267

Notes on Contributors 290

Introduction

Ib Johansen

The articles collected in the present volume focus on *three* different *fins de siècle* as well as on two different *fins de millénaire* - beginning with the end of the first millennium AD (Richard North) and ending up with the 1990s, with special reference to the politics and/or poetics of *the postmodern condition*, characterizing in structural terms the said decade (Graeme Thompson). In some of the articles presented here, however, the *new* millennium also becomes an important - implicit or explicit - thematic preoccupation, insofar as the sense of an ending is intermittently replaced by other - more forward-looking - reflections (for example, Sylvia Mikkelsen's article 'Feminist Aesthetics at the Threshold of a New Millennium'). Apart from this we notice that the articles in the present anthology here cover a very wide area of topics, adopting in their approach to this new version of *la querelle des anciens et des modernes* (or the struggle between the Old and the New) a number of different methodologies, as well as taking up a great variety of *discursive genres*. All these turnings in the widening gyre of the new millennium - frequently hovering between apocalyptic gloom and utopian leanings - are definitely characterized by their very *heterogeneity*, possibly provoking in this respect a kind of *embarras de richesse* in their readers. But according to William Blake, '[t]he road of excess leads to the palace of wisdom' ('Proverbs of Hell'), and perhaps this exuberance is precisely one of the essential characteristics of the period(s) the articles in question reflect (on).

According to Frank Kermode, 'the most famous of all predicted Ends is AD 1000. It is now thought that earlier historians exaggerated the "Terrors" of that year, but it need not be doubted that it

Fins de Siècle/New Beginnings, ed. Ib Johansen, *The Dolphin* 31, pp. 7-13.

ISBN 87 7288 382 0; ISSN 0106 4487.

produced a characteristic apocalypse-crisis'.[1] However, Richard North in his article in the present volume, 'Anglo-Saxon and Scandinavian Attitudes to 999/1000 AD', argues that at least in Northern Europe (in England and in Scandinavia) this so-called 'apocalypse-crisis' did not manifest itself in very obvious ways, whereas the one example of an apocalyptic vision of the world belonging to the said period and discussed at some length by North, the Old Icelandic poem *Voluspá* (my transcription), on the other hand clearly demonstrates that to the Icelandic poet and his audience, 'Christianity in the second millennium would be the natural sequel to polytheism in the first; the year 1000, like the Day of Judgment, would mark the transition' (according to North, such beliefs can possibly be associated with the evangelistic fervour of missionary preachers in Iceland and elsewhere at the end of the tenth century).

In my article 'American Specters' I point out how there are, in postmodernist fiction, quite a few examples of 'an obsessive emphasis on endangered and/or extinct species' (note 81). In Per Serritslev Petersen's article in the present volume, 'Fictional Reconstructions of Female Vampirism in the Nineteenth-Century *Fin-de-Siècle* Crisis of Masculinity and Its Modernist Aftermath: Bram Stoker, Joseph Conrad, D. H. Lawrence', male anxieties are foregrounded with an emphasis on a similar perspective, e.g. when this scholar reaches his 'philosophical conclusion' at the end of the essay, referring at this point to 'the increasingly *endangered* species of masculine men – postmodernized, postfeminized, *post* everything good and brave', inhabiting 'our current 20th-century *fin-de-siècle*' world (first italics mine). The crisis of masculinity is thus emphatically linked up with sexual politics – or with 'the terror regime of the New Woman' (Serritslev). But it also appears to be influenced by the more or less sinister apocalyptic atmosphere of the new *fin de siècle*, or as it is pointed out by Harold Bloom in his *Omens of Millennium* (1996): 'Approaching the Millennium, we encounter numerous omens that will be variations upon the ancient image that, more than any other, breaks down the orthodox antithesis between God and man [...]. The angelic world, whether it be metaphor or reality, is a giant image in which we may see and study ourselves, even as we move towards what may be the end of our time.'[2] Serritslev's female vampires (whether they be metaphor or reality) appear to belong to a similar archetypal realm as the angels mentioned above by Bloom - but in this case they are definitely associated with the *symbolism of evil*. However that may be, Serritslev's *thematic* readings could arguably be problematized (or even de-constructed?) by being transferred to a different theoretical register: if, for instance, Dracula and his female consorts were submitted to a Marxist or a (post)feminist approach.

Michael Böss's article 'Root Music: Occult Notions of Identity in W. B. Yeats and Contemporary Social Criticism in Ireland' is less pessimistic than Serritslev's essay in its outlook on the cultural situation in contemporary (i.e. late twentieth-century) *Ireland*, where a number of connections are established between Yeats's visionary poetics on the one hand and on the other hand the 'occult politics' of a cultural commentator like John Waters (who has written, among other things, a book focusing on the Irish rock band U2, *Race of Angels: Ireland and the Genesis of U2*). According to Böss, Waters's *organicistic* approach to Irish politics 'resembles the more extreme versions of cultural nationalism which could be found all over Europe in the first half of the twentieth century, for example in the writings of W. B. Yeats'. Even if we are not, literally speaking, in the neighbourhood of *Blut und Boden*, we are nevertheless reminded, for example, of Heidegger's extraordinary emphasis on *Erde* ('earth') precisely in the 1930s (editor's comment) ...

Robert Rix's erudite approach to Oscar Wilde's *Salomé* in '*Salomé* and *la fin de globe*: Oscar Wilde's Decadent Tragedy' establishes a number of thematic and structural links between Wilde's play and late nineteenth-century aesthetic culture (the Decadent movement). And Rix argues - convincingly as far as I can see - that the self-conscious *ethos* and poetology of the drama turns it into 'a tragedy wrapped in the attire of dark satire', showing 'the pursuit of a Decadent life as abortive and finally wrong', inasmuch as its *Faustian* theme becomes rather conspicuous in that connection ('much of Wilde's writing [...] deals with how souls are sold to sin and the tragedy in trying to repurchase the mistaken bargain').

My own article, 'American Specters', focuses on two different versions of ghostliness in American *fin-de-siècle* culture, in Henry James's classic novella *The Turn of the Screw* and in William S. Burroughs's *Ghost of Chance*. My aim is to demonstrate to what extent *spectrality itself* has become one of the major philosophical issues of the late twentieth century (e.g., in Derrida, Rabaté, and Aris Fioretos), and how this quasi-omnipresent thematic preoccupation with ghosts has also invaded the field of (decadent and/or post-modernist) *fiction*.

Norman Ravvin's article 'The Apocalyptic Predicament: Timothy Findley's Predetermined Novel' focuses on the forementioned Canadian novelist's *Not Wanted on the Voyage* (1985) – a novel that rewrites *the story of the Flood* (a theme likewise taken up in Julian Barnes's *The History of the World in 10½ Chapters*); this is a radical revisionary gesture on Findley's part, insofar as the Biblical account is deconstructed by the author in an altogether thoroughgoing manner, for '[u]nlike Melville's Ahab, whose monomania confronts and is informed by a world where Hebrew and Christian values intermingle, Findley's imaginative world strives to purge itself of all things Jewish, much as the apocalyptic books of *The New Testament* were written to dramatize an ongoing battle between these two cultural forces' (Ravvin). Noah is characteristically turned into a rather nasty character in Findley's novel, just as it happens to be the case in Alicia Ostriker's *The Nakedness of the Fathers*, where 'our father [i.e. Noah, dead drunk] woke up and began screaming, cursing me. / You'll be black, he screamed. The sweat stood out on his forehead. You'll never get anywhere. Your children will be slaves and servants.'[3]

In Sylvia Mikkelsen's article 'Feminist Aesthetics at the Threshold of the New Millennium: The Questioning of "Feminine Essentialism" from Emily Dickinson to Julia Kristeva' various feminist approaches to 'Amherst's Madame de Sade' (to adopt an epithet coined by Camille Paglia) are taken up and discussed in a critical perspective. Sylvia Mikkelsen likewise establishes a (French) connection between Emily Dickinson and Marguerite Duras, insofar as the psychic space of 'unresolved quasi-sexual tensions between Dickinson's artist-self and femininity resembles the psycho-drama which fuelled the imagination of [...] Duras', and the critic finishes her article with a *hope for the new millennium*, i.e. that 'the future "sisters" of Emily Dickinson, Marguerite Duras and Sylvia Plath will also appeal to the reader's hermeneutical and existential openness to new and alien experiences and ideas, including psychosexual transactions and constructions beyond the stereotypes of feminine and feminist essentialism'.

Whereas the main emphasis of the articles discussed until now has been on *literature* (fiction and poetry), Cheralyn Mealor in her article 'In the Meantime: Nation in New Labour's Millennium Countdown' foregrounds some of the cultural and ideological implications of the construction of the controversial Millennium Dome, at Greenwich. Mealor's cultural critique is mainly aimed at 'the appropriation of the millennium in New Labour rhetoric, which has consistently attempted to rouse national pride in order to promote its One Nation vision of New Britain'. Mealor argues that the construction of the Dome is yet another example of the (British) *Empire Striking Back* (!). Instead of paying homage to such ideological fetishes, 'it is necessary explore the multiple, disjunctive temporalities within the nation that do not conform to the symbols of contemporaneity set up by the nationalist time-frame, and which contest the historicist view of the nation as a self-identical, united subject progressing towards its destiny along the line of homogeneous time'. As it has been argued by Walter Benjamin in his 'Theses of the Philosophy of History' (1940), universal history (or historicism) operates on the basis of a purely *additive* method: 'it musters a mass of data to fill the homogeneous, empty time'; by way of contrast, Mealor's approach to the political topic she has taken up is precisely *to read its hidden agenda*, to pursue other tracks than those that are laid down for us, if we follow invariably 'the line of homogeneous time'. For as it is pointed out by Blake in his 'Proverbs of Hell': 'Improve[me]nt makes strait roads, but the crooked roads without Improvement, are roads of Genius'.

The two subsequent essays, Jan Ifversen's 'Globalization – a Catch-All Concept for the End of the Millennium' and Jamsheed Shorish's 'Fear Amidst Plenty: The Duality of Economic Optimism at the Close of the 20th Century', both of them foreground *interdisciplinary issues*. Whereas Ifversen focuses on cultural analysis in his approach to the rather slippery concept of *globalization* – discussing among other things Benjamin Barber's 'conceptual couples McWorld and McJihad' – Jamsheed Shorish takes up some of the *economic* issues associated with our millennial anxieties (epitomized by the notion of the so-called 'Y2K Bug'), arguing in this connection that '[t]he divergence of opinion regarding the millennium change is perhaps one of the more overt symptoms of a long-standing illness in economic analysis'.

Anjum P. Saleemi's article, entitled 'Linguistic, Mental and Biological Laws', likewise offers an interdisciplinary approach to its topic; and in this connection Saleemi argues that the 'relationships between brute physicality, the biological, and mental events and entities have become extremely important issues that are being subjected to rigorous investigation at the turn of the millennium'. The old mind–body is here reinterpreted in the light of new insights that have emerged in recent years within the field of linguistics or language theory (Chomsky, Searle, *et al.*), and what Saleemi envisages is the possibility of a unified theory (such as modern cosmologists, incidentally, are also concerned with) – or what he terms 'a holistic ontological view'. However, Saleemi ends up with leaving the entire question *open*, quoting in this context Searle's observation that 'the brain is only the size of a soccer ball, but it remains the biggest black hole in the science of human scientific endeavour, and likely to remain so for a long time to come'! Are we going to find the truth, the whole truth, and nothing but the truth behind this sinister *event horizon* – or are the stakes too high? Is it (in the long run, i.e. after two, five, or one hundred thousand years) still impossible for us to *connect*?

Finally, Graeme Thompson offers a series of lyrical meditations on the *fin-de-millénaire* in his article 'No Ground to Stand on'. Thompson's text moves rather freely forward and backward between various discursive genres and registers, 'deterritorializing' his own theoretical discourse in an attempt to re-construct *the music of chance* (to use terms borrowed from Deleuze, Guattari, and Paul Auster). Things definitely fall apart in this philosophical *quatuor pour la fin du temps* (or should we call it an *entretemps* or a *contretemps*?). However that may be, Thompson makes use of a number of different media in his essay, referring to film, music, philosophy, and literature, and he gradually builds up a mosaic of *quotations*, where it is occasionally difficult to pinpoint exactly *when* the quotation stops and the critic's 'own' discourse takes over. But all this is in accordance with the (narrative) (meta)logic of postmodernism (or poststructuralism) itself, for here everything has *always been said already*. In the beginning was the Word, but at the end of the second millennium AD what is left is perhaps only Lucky's *word salad* (in *Waiting for Godot*) – or Eliotesque fragments flying in the air, unable to establish or substantialize the Great Code or Sacred Canon any longer. The rest is silence ... or perhaps another (meta-) language(?).

Notes

1. Frank Kermode, *The Sense of an Ending* (New York: Oxford UP, 1967) 9.
2. Harold Bloom, *Omens of Millennium: The Gnosis of Angels, Dreams, and Resurrection* (London: Fourth Estate, 1996) 10-11.
3. Alicia Ostriker, *The Nakedness of the Fathers: Biblical Visions and Revisions* (New Brunswick, NJ: Rutgers UP, 1994) 44.

Part One
AD 1000

Anglo-Saxon and Scandinavian Attitudes to 999/1000 AD

Richard North

The year 1000 arrived unheralded in mainland Scandinavia, where there was virtually no calendrical means of perceiving that this year could mark the passing of one era and the start of another. Nor was millennium the cause of any numerological fanfare in England, where *The Anglo-Saxon Chronicle* records for this year no celebration of any kind, literary or religious. It is in Iceland around 1000, instead, that one might talk of there being an attitude to the end of the common era. Iceland is the (unlikely) place where Anglo-Saxon and Scandinavian attitudes to the millennium, insignificant in themselves, fused to create a unique Christian-heathen apocalypticism which comes the closest to corresponding with our own. How this fusion came about, I shall now attempt to show.

In England there is no political record about an imminent Apocalypse or Revelation in the Christian calendar for 1000, unless, perhaps, one include under this heading Archbishop Wulfstan's one surviving use of numerology in his sermon *Secundum Marcum*:

Nu sceal hit nyde yfelian swyðe, forðam ße hit nealæcð georne his timan, ealswa hit awriten is 7 gefyrn wæs gewitegod: *Post mille annos soluetur Satanas*. Þusend geara 7 eac ma is nu agan syððan Crist wæs mid mannum on menniscan hiwe, 7 nu syndon Satanases bendas swyðe toslopene, 7 Antecristes tima is wel gehende, 7 ðy hit is on worulde a swa leng swa wacre.

Now things must of necessity become very bad, because it is fast approaching his time, just as is written and was formerly prophesied: 'After a thousand years

Fins de Siècle/New Beginnings, ed. Ib Johansen, *The Dolphin* 31, pp. 17-38.

ISBN 87 7288 382 0; ISSN 0106 4487.

Satan will be let loose' *[based on Rev. 20: 7]. A thousand years and more has now passed since Christ was among men in human form, and now Satan's bonds are very frayed, and the time of Antichrist is very close, and so the longer the world goes on the weaker it is.*[1]

No date is known for this sermon, but it is a reasonable guess that Wulfstan delivered it not long after 1002, after (or perhaps even to inaugurate) one of his consecrations either as Archbishop of York (1002-23) or as Bishop of Worcester (1002-16) in the same year.[2]

There is no like sense of a numbered millennial watershed elsewhere in Old English literature. The *Chronicle*'s entry *sub anno* 1000 (E) is short and sardonic: it indicates that the king of this time, Æthelræd (ruled 978-1016), took his navy up to Cumbria to raid the Viking settlements in this remote region, while the enemy he was presumably trying to find, the Danish fleet that had devastated most of England for the previous ten years, took shelter in Normandy nearly a thousand miles the other way. There is a hint in this *Chronicle* entry that this king, whose name *Æßel-ræd* means something like 'good idea', was living up to his nickname *un-ræd*, which means 'no idea'. There was no political reason to aggrandize this year. The Anglo-Saxons around the year 1000 were demoralized and fast losing control of their country. The war with Denmark had started with a raid in 885, a few years before Sveinn Haraldsson became king of Denmark in *c.* 887. In 991 there was another recorded (Norwegian) raid on Maldon, a royal mint town on the River Blackwater in Essex. There is a well-known commemorative work, now called *The Battle of Maldon*, probably written in 991 or 992, in which the East Saxons' loss of the flower of their army and their best general, Earl Byrhtnoth, is presented as a moral victory. What this heroic poem, albeit now minus its opening and closing lines, does not say is that King Æthelræd then paid £10,000 to the victorious Viking army in addition to their spoils from Maldon, and a further £22,000 in 994 when he signed a non-aggression treaty with a group of Vikings whose leaders were King Sveinn 'Forkbeard' Haraldsson of Denmark (ruled 987-1014) and Óláfr Tryggvason, soon to be king of Norway (ruled 995-1000). Contrary to what Æthelræd hoped, the Danes and other Vikings did not go away, but they attacked and invaded England from then on every two years or so, often under King Sveinn's leadership. Old English prose, otherwise known as the West Saxon literary standard, was reaching its zenith with the West Saxon Ælfric, a pupil of the tenth-century Benedictine Reform, who issued the first and second series of *Catholic Homilies* in 990-92 and *Lives of the Saints* in 992-98. Works of Latin and Old English prose and verse from this and earlier centuries were even then being copied and recopied into costly new books, of which the bare handful that now survives bears witness to these decades as an age of great wealth and learning. That this was not an age of English generalship, however, is clear in the fact that Æthelræd lost his kingdom in 1016 to the son of the Danish invader, Canute Sveinsson (ruled 1016-35). The sum which King Canute, or 'Cnut' to call him by his Old English name, awarded himself from English coffers in 1018, two years after his coronation, came to £72,000, plus another £10,500. Altogether, from the start of Æthelræd's reign (978-1016), the English are thought to have paid over to the Danes a grand total of at least £219,500, effectively financing their own occupation and the dismemberment of the royal line of Alfred (ruled 871-99). There was no way to foresee this disastrous outcome back in the year 1000, but it is possible that the strain of the long war with Denmark at the time is one reason why the end of the first millennium in England slipped by without record of any religious observance in the *Chronicle.*

The Anglo-Saxon Chronicle is the name for a set of West Saxon annals which is written in six vernacular (A-F) and at least two Latin versions, and which claims to date from 60 BC and in some cases extends till the mid twelfth century. This *Chronicle* was sometimes written close to the events, sometimes not. Not only British history but also English literature is lucky to have its six versions of the vernacular *Chronicle*, for there is no such record for the Scandinavians of the same period. What passes for native history in Scandinavia in and around the year 1000 was first written down about seventy years later, in Latin and by a German canon named Adam of the cathedral church of Hamburg-Bremen.[3] Adam of Bremen, as he is called, makes no special mention of the first millennium. Nor do the later histories, annals and chronicles of Denmark and Norway that were written in Latin in the twelfth and thirteenth centuries. The exception to this rule is the medieval literature of Iceland.

Iceland is a far-away place, but its literature, which was written virtually all in the Old Norse vernacular from the twelfth century onwards, rivals any in medieval Europe. Icelanders had reason to celebrate the year 1000 for the simple reason that this was the first year of their official status as Christians. The oldest surviving record of their conversion is a historical work called *Íslendingabók* ('The Book of Icelanders'), which was written in *c.* 1125 by Ari Þorgilsson, a priest from the west of Iceland. Ari was one of the first of his country to write in his own language, and the trouble he took over his book is evident from the fact that it survives in a second draft and was finished in a careful, slightly laborious, style. Ari points his whole work towards the Icelandic conversion, and his attention to the year 1000, the round number of the moment of his nation's salvation, may be clear from the fact that he divides his work into ten chapters (with the conversion in ch. 7 and the history of Icelandic bishops to his day in chs. 8-10). In fact, Ari's work is polished: he gives dates or relative chronology wherever possible, and his citation of living informants connecting him and us to the events of a century earlier is modelled on that in Bede's 'History of the English Church and People' (*c.* 734). In an age when it is often impossible to distinguish factual history from legendary fiction, Ari emerges as a fairly trustworthy narrator. All the more interesting, then, to note that when Ari dates the potential salvation of Icelandic souls 'one hundred and thirty years after the killing of Edmund [870], and a thousand after Christ's birth by the common count' (ch. 7), he makes no reference to an aspect of Christianity with which we are culturally familiar: the idea of a Christian Apocalypse.

In our time the Apocalypse (or Parousia, Revelation, Last Days, End Time, Rapture, whatever we call it) is to varying degrees on the minds even of the most secular people in countries in which Christianity is the leading religion. The numerical roundness of '2000', or the technical succinctness of 'Y2K', hints at the arrival of change, even if this turnaround will not bring about the world's complete end. There appear to be some protestant sects in which Christ's Second Coming is tied to a date ending in three noughts.

Other branches of Christianity shy away from predicting a date, but it is still clear that the End of the world is expected by many believers. Christianity has always posited an End, one which even resonates today in the wider secular world, where many have their minds fixed on the techno-apocalypse of mass computer failure. At least the thought of this potential chaos might remind us of the specific fear which we think our ancestors had about the Apocalypse at the end of the first millennium. In so far as there was any time-keeping in the 'Dark Ages', was it not the Church, the purveyor of apocalyptic fantasies, that kept the calendar? Is the Revelation of John not printed at the end of every bible, in which ch. 20, vs. 1-3, in particular, seems to foretell the End after a thousand years?

The narrator of the Revelation of John, allegedly St John as the title claims, begins his text as a pastoral letter to seven churches around the Aegean. Thereafter he recounts a divinely inspired vision in which the future Day of Judgement is revealed to him in an often incoherent form. Seven churches; the Lamb with seven horns and seven eyes; the seven seals which are broken by the Lamb to reveal the Last Days; the seven angels blowing trumpets to reveal the means of the world's destruction; seven visions, through which the birth of Jesus and His combat with Satan are mystically portrayed with reference to the Devil as a 'Dragon' which the archangel Michael throws down to hell; seven bowls of plagues before the Whore of Babylon, whose seven hills recall Rome; then more visions. At the climax, in Rev. 20:1-3, the narrator says (appropriate text drawn from the *Revised English Bible*):

> I saw an angel coming down from heaven with the key to the abyss and a great chain in his hand. [2]He seized the dragon, that ancient serpent who is the Devil, or Satan, and chained him up for a thousand years; [3]he threw him into the abyss, shutting and sealing it over him, so that he might not seduce the nations again till the thousand years were ended. After that he must be let loose for a little while.[4]

After reading these verses, in which the number 1000 makes such a striking counterpoint to the number seven, we might be justified in assuming that people a thousand years ago believed the world would end at the start of the year 1000. But this assumption is wrong; at least it is, if it is thought that the Church officially encouraged this belief. It did not; in fact, from the fourth century on, the Church discouraged this type of numerology, which is known as 'millenarianism' or 'chiliasm'. The Church discouraged the literal, rather than figurative or symbolic, interpretation of this number in Rev. 20. The relative quiet of official religion in Europe on the matter of Apocalypse in 1000 may come as a surprise; but I shall have to consider it briefly before I make any attempt to throw light on the attitudes of Anglo-Saxons or Scandinavians to the end of the first millennium.

It is not easy even to sketch the theological background to Christian apocalypticism. Norman Cohn pioneered the view that the Apocalyptic has worked as a social stimulant or consolation at various times of social crisis or upheaval.[5] Bernard McGinn's qualification of Cohn is that 'Apocalypticism was a way in which contemporary political and social events were given religious validation by incorporation into a transcendent scheme of meaning'.[6] Thus it would seem that Archbishop Wulfstan of York (d. 1023), whose *Secundum Marcum* McGinn does not cite in his book, could use the fear of an imminent Apocalypse as a means of controlling his flock. Wulfstan was a public speaker and ecclesiastical politician who drafted Æthelræd's law-codes in 1008 and revised them ten years later for King Cnut. In writing the *Institutes of Pollity*, in particular, Wulfstan attempted to clarify the roles of Church and State and expressed traditional views about the three estates of society; these views are also clear in his vested self-interest, by which he held the bishopric of Worcester (1002-16) for fourteen years alongside the archbishopric of York (1002-23); and in the twenty or so sermons attributed to him, the most famous of which is his *Sermo Lupi ad Anglos quando Dani maxime persecuti sunt eos* of *c.* 1014 ('Sermon of the "Wolf" to the English when the Danes most greatly persecuted them'). Wulfstan was no anarchist nor mystical leader, then, but in ten of these sermons it is clear that he was ready to cajole, to frighten and even to calm his congregations with the theme of Antichrist and the apocalypse. At the start of *Sermo Lupi*, for example:

Leofan men, gecnawað ßæt soð is: ðeos woruld is on ofste, and hit nealæcð ßam ende, and ßy hit is on worulde aa swa leng swa wyrse, and swa hit sceal nyde for folces synnan ær Antecristes tocyme yfelian swyße, and huru hit wyrð ßænne egeslic and grimlic wide on worolde.

My dear people, acknowledge this as the truth: this world is hastening, and it is drawing near to the end, and so the longer the world goes on the worse it is, and thus, through the sins of the people, things by necessity must get really bad before the coming of Antichrist, and then, indeed, it will be terrifying and cruel far and wide throughout the world.[7]

Wulfstan rewrote this sermon a couple of times from 1014 onwards, some years after the end of the first millennium. Wulfstan was a chiliast, according to his earlier work, *Secundum Marcum*, in which he quotes from Rev. 20:7; but it is worth noting that he begins this homily with a longer passage from Mark 13 and otherwise Matthew 24-25 and Luke 21, each of which predicts the Second Coming without the inference of a fixed date. By citing the Antichrist so many times without a date Wulfstan seems to have responded to a millenarianism within his audience. However, the fact that his *post mille annos* occurs but once in his homilies, may show that he was unwilling to endorse all this Christian subculture as his own.

The Revelation of John, in which the number 1000 is contained (in ch. 20), was probably written in *c.* 90 AD in Asia Minor but by an author other than the Apostle. It was conceived within a tradition of biblical prophecy of which the most important older instances are the Book of Daniel 11-13 (written at the time of a Greek-Syriac tyranny over Israel in *c.* 168 BC); St Paul's 1 Thessalonians 4:13-5:11 and 2 Thessalonians 2 (*c.* 51 AD); and the 'Little Apocalypse' from the above synoptic gospels of the end of the first century. In these texts the Day of Judgement is prophesied at an undisclosed time after the blowing of a heavenly trumpet, the Lord's descent from heaven and the resurrection of the dead. To this orderly view of the future the lurid imagery of Revelation offers a startling contrast. Its combination of Judaic symbolism, Babylonian mythology and contemporary political reference make it, in McGinn's words, 'the most powerful apocalyptic work ever written'.[8] In Revelation, within the time this work was written, the

'Whore of Babylon' was probably taken to be Rome, the persecutor of Christians everywhere; the Antichrist, or Beast, one of two, was Nero (ruled 54-68), or later Domitian (ruled 81-96); the thousand years was initially thought to refer to the kingdom of God on earth, which Jesus would inaugurate upon His Second Coming and in which He would live with the resurrected Saints, and at the end of which the souls of the unsaintly dead would be judged.

In due course, when the Second Coming did not arrive within the period hoped for by first- and second-century worshippers, the more modest eschatology was influenced by two major literary sources: the so-called Sibylline Books, of which fourteen survive, written by Jews and Christians with Classical models from the mid-second century onwards; and by Revelation itself in favour of various types of chiliasm (the belief in the kingdom of a thousand years). Bishops Papias (early second century) and Irenaeus, who ended as bishop of Lyons in Gaul 178-200, were prominent adherents of this numerological doctrine. Another chiliast, Tertullian of Carthage (*c.* 160-*c.* 200), identified the force inhibiting or restraining the Antichrist, which is cited in 2 Thessalonians 2, with the Roman empire. The Roman presbyter Hippolytus, who died in 235, was concerned to show that the world would not end in *c.* 300. His contemporary, the Latin Syrian poet Commodian of the mid-third century, interpreted two Antichrists in Revelation, one of them a revived Nero, the other a Persian emperor. In the early fourth century the Roman convert Lucius Lactantius established this doctrine of two Antichrists followed by Jesus' thousand-year reign. The anti-Roman bias within these interpretations, however, began to change on the accession of the emperor Constantine I (ruled 306-37), who legalized Christianity in the empire in 324. Henceforth it would be less simple for chiliasts to identify the empire with Babylon, and more so to justify first the Roman emperor, then later the Vatican Papacy, with the Kingdom of God on earth to which Revelation refers in ch. 20. St Augustine, who inclined to chiliasm in his youth and yet rejected it after the Gothic sack of Rome in 410, confirmed in his book 'The City of God' (*De civitate Dei*) that Rome henceforth stood for a spiritual, not earthly, city of God; the corollary was that literal readings of Revelation were to be abandoned; that the Second Coming might arrive at any moment, rather like one's own apprehension of grace; and that the struggle between Lamb and the Antichrist in Revelation should now be read as symbolic of the choice we all face between good and evil. Tyconius, a North African like Augustine (*c*. 330-90), further pursued Augustine's attack on apocalypticism with entirely figural readings in his 'Commentary on Revelation' (*c*. 385). Other Patristic writers added their weight, but it was chiefly these two latter Fathers founded the orthodox view of the Last Days in the Roman Church which has persisted until the present. This view rejects any form of chiliasm or belief in the thousand-year reign of Christ. Where the doctrine of chiliasm survived, it did so at a mystical or subcultural level, with the addition of an important change: since Rome was now Christian and could be regarded as the embodiment of the thousand-year reign which begins with Jesus' birth, the chiliasts of later centuries could generally take the date for the Second Coming as being in the year 1000. This date, too, can be read in Rev. 20, if Satan's chaining is made to take place at his failure to devour the infant Jesus earlier in Rev. 12:1-6; in this case, Satan's ascent from the abyss in Rev. 20:3, 'for a little while' as the narrator says, would represent his role in Armageddon prior to the Day of Judgement.

Mostly, however, from the fifth century onwards, the doctrine of the thousand years was disregarded as a historical hindrance to the thief-in-the-night Second Coming disclosed in 1 Thessalonians 5:2 and indicated in Mark 13:33-7. Chiliasm would have survived only in the popular religious subculture. Thus, for example, it was St Augustine's sanctioned view of sudden and unexpected grace which influenced Pope Gregory the Great as he wrote to King Æthelberht of Kent at the outset of the Roman mission to Anglo-Saxon England in 601: 'we also wish Your Majesty to know, as we have learned from the words of Almighty God in Holy Scripture, that the End of the present world is already near and that the unending kingdom of the Saints is approaching'. Gregory's letter defines the orthodox view of the Apocalypse up to and beyond Archbishop Wulfstan at the other end of the Anglo-Saxon period in the first half of the eleventh century. Bede was faithful to this orthodoxy, as was every other ecclesiastical commentator whose works have survived. By the time of *The Seafarer* (a poem possibly composed in the eighth century although written down in one copy in the Exeter Book towards the year 1000), the doctrine of the imminent Second Coming is a standard part of the devotional aesthetic (ll. 48-52):

> Bearwas blostmum nimað, byrig fægriað,
> wongas wlitigiað, woruld onetteð;
> ealle ßa gemoniað modes fusne
> sefan to siße, ßam ße swa ßenceð
> on flodwegas feor gewitan.

Groves take on blossoms, villages grow beautiful, fields become dazzling, the world hastens on; all these things urge travel on the eager senses of the heart of that man who thus intends to set out on the sea-roads far and wide.

The spring-time imagery in this passage recalls Bede's hymn (before 735) *De die iudicii* ('On the Day of Judgement'), in which an apparently lyrical summer scene is swiftly transformed into the crooked weather of the Last Days:

> While I sat sad and alone under the covering of a shady tree among the flowering grasses of the fertile earth with the branches echoing on every side from the wind's breath, I was suddenly disturbed by a bitter lament and I sang these mournful verses because my mind was sad.[9]

Bede's poem was rendered into Old English in the late tenth century in the so-called *Judgement Day II* (preserved in a mid-eleventh-century manuscript: CCCC 201) in which the later poet, a clumsy adaptor, omits Bede's word *maestus* ('sad'), while at the same time he adds streams, a grove, a glade, a plain and some clouds.[10] That he makes these changes may show, if anything, a weakening of the apocalyptic strain in his Christianity. The poet of *The Seafarer*, in comparison, is in a different mental universe and one closer to Bede's. His poem is of a man's voluntary search for extremity on the deep in order to move closer to God; the pleasures of the spring surroundings are enjoyed by him, but still rejected as inferior to those he will taste in heaven, once he has made the sea-crossing (as it were) to the world of God. The apocalyptic theme is for the present moment subsumed in this theme; and it is worth noting that the half-line *woruld onetteð* at *Sea*

49, which means something like 'the world hastens on', conveys both the image of the merry pace of May and the sinister idea of the world's decline, two for us opposed things in one expression, yet for the poet a fusion without antagonism: for him, the imminent End of the world is truly a matter for rejoicing. This phrase is, in any case, almost identical in meaning to that frequently employed by Wulfstan three centuries later: *ðeos woruld is on ofste* ('this world is hastening'). Some of Wulfstan's homilies are preserved in the same mid-eleventh-century manuscript that contains the laboured Old English translation of Bede's poem.[11] In this respect, the Apocalypse was rarely out of the minds of Anglo-Saxons from one end of their period to the other.

One of Wulfstan's sources for *Secundum Marcum* was the *Libellus de Antichristo* ('Book of Antichrist') written in *c.* 950 by his older contemporary the monk Adso of Montier-en-Der (910-992). Adso says that the Antichrist

> will destroy the Law of the Gospel, call the worship of demons back into the world, seek his own glory, and call himself almighty God. This Antichrist will have many ministers of his own evil: many of them have already gone forth into the world, such as Antiochus, Nero and Domitian. In our own time we know there are many Antichrists.[12]

This extract illustrates the political uses to which the later Christian apocalyptic was put. Adso's work leads towards the story of the conversion of Iceland in *c.* 999, to the extent that directly or indirectly it influenced the missionaries who proclaimed the gospel there. This moment occurred not long after Adso's death and while Wulfstan was still bishop of London; and I shall suggest that the sibylline poem *V¡luspá* was composed in Iceland as a result (this long anonymous poem is quoted in the prose Edda of Snorri Sturluson, 1230s, and is preserved in Codex Regius (AM 2365 4to, 'the poetic *Edda*', *c.* 1280) and in Hauksbók, *c.* 1300). In the rest of this essay I shall use the Christian Apocalyptic based ultimately on the Revelation of John in an attempt to show a relationship between Adso of France, Wulfstan of England, the Icelandic conversion and the poem *V¡luspá*.

To judge from Ari's *Íslendingabók*, in conjunction with other references, it seems that the official mission to convert the Icelanders began in 997 (the same year Sveinn Forkbeard was sending his fleet against England). Sveinn's former ally, the former Viking Óláfr Tryggvason, who had probably helped to kill Byrhtnoth in Maldon in 991, but whom King Æthelræd sponsored in baptism three years later in 994, was now king of (most of) Norway with his base in the Trondheim region. Óláfr on arrival there in 995 had converted many Norwegians at the point of the sword; his clergy in 997 were probably mostly Anglo-Saxons and Germans; one of these clerics, a certain Þangbrandr, sported a militancy that was too much even for Óláfr. Whether it was to save the souls of new pagan subjects in the western Atlantic, or to get this Flemish or Saxon lay preacher off his hands, Óláfr sent Þangbrandr to Iceland. Þangbrandr returned empty-handed in 998, having 'killed one or two men', in Ari's restrained terms. In fact, it was no secret that Þangbrandr's obsessive violence had turned half of Iceland against him. As if facing Antichrist in each heathen that crossed his path, he fought one duel after another as he worked his way from the east coast to the west. According to a late thirteenth-century work, *Kristni saga* ('The Saga of Christianity'), Óláfr made another abortive attempt, after Þangbrandr, to convert the Icelandic heathens through a man named Þormóðr from England (who was probably a Dane). But at any rate, the mission failed; in his rage, King Óláfr began to round up the sons of Icelandic chieftains who were then in Norway. Their fathers sent a chieftain named Gizurr Teitsson to negotiate for their release (herein Gizurr's family, which provided Iceland with its first line of bishops, consolidated its chiefly power). In exchange, Gizurr reinstituted the Christian mission in the summer of 999 in Iceland, bringing the confrontation which Þangbrandr had engendered to a head in the General Assembly; the mood was tense and both sides heavily armed; in the end, the lawspeaker solved the crisis, after a communion with pagan gods, by converting all Icelanders to the faith so long as three items of the old pagan religion could continue (exposure of unwanted children; the eating of horseflesh; private sacrifice). By an act of parliament Iceland had now entered the community of civilized nations subject to the Pope in Rome.

There are several things to be pointed out in this story, virtually all of which derives ultimately from Ari. One is that Þangbrandr, originating from either Flanders or Saxony, was brought up in one of these regions presumably in the 960s or 970s and potentially close to the late Carolingian ambience of Adso of Montier-en-Der. Adso had already dedicated his book on the Antichrist to Gerberga, who was both the wife of Louis IV of West Francia (ruled 936-54) and the sister of Emperor Otto I of Saxony (ruled 936-73). Otto I sponsored the mission which converted Haraldr 'Bluetooth' Gormsson, Sveinn's father and the last pagan king of Denmark in *c.* 960. Less successfully, Otto had also tried to convert Earl Hákon, Óláfr's apostate forerunner in Trondheim. In the light of this royal Saxon's missionary zeal, it seems likely that it was the spirit of Adso's injunctions about innumerate Antichrists that propelled Þangbrandr to antagonize the heathens in Iceland, rather than to convert them:

> In our own time we know there are many Antichrists. Any layman, cleric, or monk, who lives in a way contrary to justice, who attacks the rule of his order of life, and blasphemes the good, he is an Antichrist, a minister of Satan.[13]

In this light, Þangbrandr's technique with the Icelanders could be called apocalyptic rather than missionary.

What evidence there is that Revelation might have provided Þangbrandr with his theme, is contained in the *Apologeticus*, a defence of monastic rights that was written in 995 by Abbo (*c.* 945-1004), a Benedictine reformist and later abbot of Fleury; and in two places within *Njáls saga*, a late classical saga that was written by an unknown author in Iceland probably *c.* 1290.

Firstly, in *Apologeticus*, Abbo of Fleury says that his abbot, Richard, had heard that the 'Lotharingians', that is those people living in the upper and lower Rhineland, believed that the world would end in the year 1000. 'The rumour had filled almost the whole world', Abbo says (McGinn 1998: 89). In their original form, these words are testimony to the widespread popularity of chiliasm not long before the millennium and again in a German-speaking province not far from the area in which Þangbrandr had originated.

Secondly, in *Njáls saga*, there is a traditional story about Þangbrandr, newly arrived in Iceland, singing mass one autumn morning for the Archangel Michael (ch. 100). When Hallr of Síða, his host, asks to be put into the protection of the Archangel, Þangbrandr consents, on condition that Hallr and all his household are baptized. Michael was popular in the north as the conveyor of souls to heaven. But it is also true that three of Michael's four instances in all the bible concern his role in the Apocalypse (the exception is Jude 9): in Dan 10:13 and 12:1, Michael fights against the Antichrist from whom he protects man at the end of history; in Rev. 12.7, when the war breaks out in heaven, Michael duels with Satan the dragon and throws him down into the pit. With its reference to Archangel Michael, this story makes a connection between Þangbrandr and the preaching of the Christian Apocalypse, notably of Revelation. Thirdly, also in *Njáls saga*, Þangbrandr disputes with Steinunn, a woman poet who tries to convert him to paganism. 'have you heard that Þórr challenged Christ to a duel and Christ did not dare to fight him?', she asks; Þangbrandr replies that he has heard 'Þórr would be nothing but dust and ashes if God did not permit him to live' (ch. 102). Compare Rev. 13:3-8, in which the Dragon, i.e. the Devil, confers his power on the Beast, i.e. the Antichrist:

> The whole world went after the beast in wondering admiration, [4]and worshipped the dragon because he had conferred his authority on the beast; they worshipped the beast also. 'Who is like the beast?' they said. 'Who can fight it?' [5]The beast was allowed to mouth bombast and blasphemy [...] [7]It was also allowed to wage war on God's people and to defeat them, and it was granted authority over every tribe, nation, language and race. [8]All the inhabitants of the earth will worship it [...]

Verses 4-5 show the way in which Þórr could be presented as the Antichrist, or as the beast for which Christ is the only capable opponent. Particularly verses 7-8 recapture the way in which Þangbrandr describes Christ's sufferance of Þórr as his opponent. These parallels are perhaps a third reason to associate Þangbrandr with the preaching of Revelations.

If we put these three details together, it seems likely that Þangbrandr's violence came about as a result of his preaching of Revelation to the Icelanders in the years 997-8. His would have been a literal interpretation. As we have seen, Abbo of Fleury recalls the widespread popularity of such unofficial readings of the Apocalypse: when he was young, perhaps in *c.* 970, Abbo heard a preacher in Paris cathedral saying that 'as soon as the number of a thousand years was completed, the Antichrist would come and the Last Judgement would follow in a brief time'.[14]

Is there any evidence that material from Revelation influenced the composition of the sibylline poem *V¡luspá*? We must first ask what was the structure of the older Norse apocalypse. Our guide to this structure is contained in the work *Gylfaginning* ('The Beguiling of Gylfi'), which Snorri Sturluson, an antiquarian, lawspeaker, politician and landowner, wrote probably as the third stage of his prose *Edda* in the 1230s. Snorri bases most of his native pre-Christian end-time mythology on his version of *V¡luspá*. There is little sibylline material outside *V¡luspá*, unless we count 'The short *V¡luspá*' (st. 29-44 of the probably thirteenth-century 'Lay of Hyndla' or *Hyndluljóð*), a smaller poem which clearly imitates *V¡luspá*. The remaining references to Ragnar¡k, as the Norse apocalypse is known, are to be found scattered all over the poetic corpus, whether these be in the anonymous balladic works of the poetic *Edda*, or in Skaldic (i.e. occasional) verse the names of whose authors survive. In the latter case, the various details about Ragnar¡k contained in Skaldic kennings, or in verbal periphrases, tend to substantiate what is said in *V¡luspá*. The gods make mistakes of ever more serious kinds, gamble for their survival more recklessly each time, and finally go down fighting in Ragnar¡k, their own Armageddon, in a last stand against a horde of giants and monsters from the east.

In the case of Eddic verse, the probably mid-tenth-century poem *Vafßrúðnismál* ('The words of Vafßrúðnir') conveys an attitude to the apocalypse which would be hard to find in any Christian vernacular: 'Tell me Gagnráðr,' says the giant Vafßrúðnir, whose hall the god Óðinn has entered in disguise as Gagnráðr so as to test his wits against the giant, 'if you wish to venture your skill in my house, what is the name of that plain on which Surtr and the sweet dear gods will meet for battle?' Óðinn's answer shows no sign of awe, curiosity or concern: '"Combat-riding" is the name of that plain on which Surtr and the sweet dear gods will meet for battle; a hundred leagues it is in each direction, that is the plain ordained for them.' Óðinn's priority for correct detail is typical of this poem, in which the poet or poets have catalogued their mythology within the narrative frame of a wisdom contest. But if this poem is anything to go by, it seems to reveal a general lack of emotion in the poet's society concerning Ragnar¡k. To judge by *Vafßrúðnismál*, the End of the world is expected with an equanimity almost as if this were not a catastrophe on a linear scale but the reflex of a cyclical process previously based on the works of the seasons or on the rise and fall of the year. *V¡luspá*, too, has been judged to contain traces of this once presumably seasonal cycle, although there is no doubt that the pathos and grandeur with which the eschatology of *V¡luspá* has been developed make this poem quite superior to anything else in its genre. This development could not have come about without Christianity. In the words of Ursula Dronke, the latest editor of *V¡luspá*, the poet of *V¡luspá* 'has external effects in his poem that could come from eschatological homilies or apocalyptic visions of sinners in hell'.[15] As Dronke has pointed out, also in another study on this poem, this poet displays the neutrality of sheer bad luck where the Norse gods are concerned, even while he presents the End of man's world as a moral catastrophe. No Christian-Judaic apocalyptic scheme could have sanctioned the objectivity of the divine theme in combination with the horror with which the human condition is here revealed. Where the apocalypse is concerned, in this way, the poet of *V¡luspá* sought to blend his own traditions with those of Christianity.

This was clearly the impulse of the Norwegian poet Eilífr Goðrúnarson (best known for his *Þórsdrápa* ('Þórr's Commemorative Lay', *c.* 985), a rich and psychologically complex heathen work without much trace of Christian influence). The poem is unfortunately lost in which Eilífr composed on a Christian theme. Only two lines survive:

> Setbergs kveða sitja   sunnr at Urðar brunni,
> svá hefr ramr konungr remðan   Róms banda sik l¡ndum.

They say He sits in the south by the well of Fate: thus has the powerful king of Rome empowered Himself in the lands of the stronghold of the bonds [:gods]

To Eilífr, Christianity is now identified with 'fate', a physical law, one which is even stronger than the Norse gods in their last Scandinavian redoubts. The gods must obey this law to the extent that they eventually die in battle against the giants at the End of their world. In this light, Eilífr has decided to treat Christianity as if it were synonymous with the Norse Apocalypse. His fragment is dated for these reasons to just before the millennium.

Not all Norse or Icelandic poets were as reflective as Eilífr or as enlightened as the author of *V¡luspá*. The opposing satirical strain is evident in a verse which is said to have been declaimed by Hjalti Skeggjason in the Icelandic assembly in 998, a year before the showdown there between Christians and pagans. Hjalti, a young Christian perhaps of Byronic sensibility, was outlawed as a result of his poem, which survives in no more than a line:

Vil ek eigi goð geyja; grey ßykki mér Freyja.

I don't want to blaspheme the gods (/ the god to bark); Freyja seems a bitch to me.

In this line, Hjalti first appears to claim piety, then rapidly undermines his claim by dissecting the elements of the Icelandic compound *goðgá*, which usually means 'blasphemy', in such a way that the second element of this word means 'barking'; the noun *goð* is syntactically ambiguous, for it can be plural ('gods', in which case the verb *geyja* means something like 'to barrack') or singular ('god', in which case there is an accusative and infinitive construction and Freyja is portrayed as a bitch with many dogs). Hjalti's portrait of Freyja resembles an image of Wulfstan's from a different context, one found again in *Sermo Lupi* (c. 1014):

And scandlic is to specenne ßæt geworden is to wide, 7 egeslic is to witanne ßæt ofte doð to manege, ße dreogað ßa yrmße, ßæt sceotað togædere 7 ane cwenan gemænum ceape bicgað gemæne, 7 wið ßa ane fylße adreogað, an æfter oðrum, 7 ælc æfter oðrum, hundum geliccast, ße for fylße ne scrifað.

And it is shameful to speak of what has happened too widely, and terrible to know what often too many men do, who carry out such a miserable crime as when they club together and buy a woman in common in one common purchase and with that one woman carry out filth, one after the other, and each man after the other, most like dogs, that have no care for filth.[16]

That is to say, Hjalti has referred negatively to the sanctioned promiscuity of Freyja, goddess of love and fertility, by using the language of contemporary Christian preachers of whom Wulfstan was a typical example.

A later, probably Christian, strain of this type of satire may be seen in the poem *Lokasenna* ('Loki's tirade'), which Dronke edits in the same volume as *V¡luspá* (1997) and which seems to have been composed in the poet-conversion era, perhaps the mid-eleventh century. It is the technique of the poet of *Lokasenna* to mock the gods for the human characteristics they have acquired after 'millennia in human hands'.[17] But, again with Freyja, the poet's language also reflects that of Christian homilists. Loki attacks Freyja (stanza 30):

Þegi ßú, Freyia, ßik kann ek fullgerva –
era ßér vamma vant.
Ása ok álfa, er hér inni ero,
hverr hefir ßinn hór verit.

Hold your tongue, Freyia, I'm fully familiar with you – in you there's no shortage of sins. Of the Æsir and elves who are here indoors each one has been your bed-fellow.[18]

That the poet of *V¡luspá* used Christian sermons for his picture of human infamy is evident from various words and phrases. Witness his image of hell (st. 38/1-6):

Sá hón ßar vaða ßunga strauma
menn meinsvara ok morðvarga,
oc ßannz annars glepr eyrarúno.

She saw there wading onerous streams men perjured and wolfish murderers and the one who seduces another's close-trusted wife.[19]

Particularly the phrase *menn meinsvara ok morðvarga* ('men perjured and wolfish murderers') appears to be modelled on the Old English *mansworan and morßorwyrhtan*, which survives not only in

Wulfstan's *Sermo Lupi*, but also, in variant forms, in his *De fide catholica, Sermo de baptismate, De regula canonicorum* and *Sermo ad populum.*[20] Witness, also, the *V¡luspá*-poet's image of family feud and incest (st. 44/1-6):

Brÿðr muno beriaz ok at b¡nom verða[z],
muno systrungar sifiom spilla.
Hart er í heimi hórdómr mikill

Brothers will fight and kill each other, sisters' children will defile kinship. It is harsh in the world, whoredom rife.[21]

The fratricide recalls Wulfstan's *ne byrhð broðor ofßrum* ('no brother will help another') and like phrases in *Secundum Marcum, Secundum Lucam* and *Sermo Lupi.*[22] The whoredom in *V¡luspá*, like Loki's allegation that each god has been Freyja's *hór* ('bed-fellow') in *Lokasenna*, is also reminiscent of Wulfstan's language in his passage which includes perjurers in *Sermo Lupi*:

Her syndan mannslagan 7 mægslagan 7 mæsserbanan 7 mynsterhatan; 7 her syndan mansworan 7 morßorwyrhtan; and her syndan myltestran 7 bearnmyrðran 7 fule forlegene horingas manege.

Here there are slayers of men and slayers of kinsmen, slayers of mass-priests and haters of monasteries; are here there are perjurers and murderers, and here there are whores and child-murderers and many foul fornications.[23]

It is known how Wulfstan varied and repeated words, phrases, sentences and even paragraphs from one sermon to another; and also how other preachers imitated his idiosyncratic style. Dronke alludes to other potential areas of Christian loan in *V¡luspá*, in particular to the *Cantus Sibyllae* which was made part of the Christmas Office from the ninth to eleventh centuries in England; and even to the recently discovered *Prophetiae Sibyllae magae* out of the Sibylline Oracles. These sibylline texts are generically closer to *V¡luspá*, as Dronke has shown.[24]

On the other hand, it is the Revelation of John which provides some more striking, and so far unrecognised, parallels with *V¡luspá*. In Dronke's translation of this poem (with my amendments in bold print):

The aficionado of *fin-de-siècle* masculine romance must undoubtedly have appreciated this sublime synthesis of high Victorian duty and the pornographic thrill of what Bram Dijkstra terms ritual rape.[14] A nice gloss on the phallic connotations of this scene is provided by another, equally popular late-Victorian masculine romance, H. Rider Haggard's *She* (1887). When, in the heart of African darkness, the cannibalistic Amahagger people are at the point of killing Leo, the handsome masculine English hero, and the Amahagger girl Ustane, who has fallen in love with Leo, throws herself on his prostrate body in order to protect him, the exasperated Amahagger chief commands: 'Drive the spear through the man and woman together [...] so of a verity they shall be wed'.[15] Besides, the more sophisticated aficionado would also have appreciated the ironic reversal of masculine and feminine stereotypes in the decapitation business: the severed head is no longer that of a *male* victim as in the biblical Judith and Salome stories (popular motifs in *fin-de-siècle* art and literature, witness, for instance, Oscar Wilde's *Salomé*), but rather a *female* Medusa head.

Arthur has staked his manly claim, and Lucy, his vampiric shrew of a New Woman, has been definitively tamed , the triumphant victory of Victorian masculinity and patriarchy being celebrated *Over her Dead Body*, to quote the title of Elizabeth Bronfen's book, subtitled *Death, Femininity and the Aesthetic*.[16] The crudely male-chauvinist subtext of phallic penetration and (ex)termination is, of course, glossed over by the manifest text of masculine romance, in terms of which the staking and decapitating of Lucy represents a heroic act of manly altruism, which saves a fallen woman's soul and returns it to God.

If vampy-naughty Lucy was really asking for her vampirization and 'final solution', her virtuous friend Mina arguably deserves a better fate in our masculine romance, for the latter has been capable of negotiating much more successfully the conflicting demands of Victorian femininity and modernized/professionalized womanhood (she is a schoolteacher complete with typewriter). 'Ah, that wonderful Madam Mina!', Van Helsing enthuses. 'She has man's brains – a brain that a man should have were he much gifted – and a woman's heart' (302). At an early stage in the story, Mina has reassured herself and the reader about her true feminine credentials when, in her diary, she makes a point of distancing herself from the overweening feminism-cum-libertinism of the New Woman, who, she imagines

> will some day start an idea that men and women should be allowed to see each other asleep before proposing or accepting. But I suppose that the New Woman won't condescend in future to accept; she will do the proposing herself. And a nice job she will make of it, too! There's some consolation in that. (119)

Albeit a 'wonderful' specimen of modern womanhood, Mina is still only a woman and as such too weak to resist the animal magnetism of the Transylvanian demon-lover when it is her turn to be vampirized: 'I was bewildered,' Mina later confesses to her male friends, 'and, strangely enough, I did not want to hinder him [that is, Dracula]' (370). While Mina is 'in a half swoon', Dracula first has *his* fill of blood from her, and then, opening a vein in his chest with his long, sharp nails, he forces Mina to drink his blood in order to contaminate her, thus making her his vampiric companion and helper, 'flesh of my flesh; blood of my blood; kin of my kin' (370). *Post factum* (or, subtextually speaking, *post coitum*) the poor woman can only bewail her tragic fate: 'What have I done to deserve such a fate, I who have tried to walk in meekness and righteousness all my days' (371). But the sadistically masculinist author insists on having even this paragon of feminine virtue vampirized *qua* woman, and she is literally branded as unclean with a mark of shame when Van Helsing, in a belated attempt to protect her against Dracula, touches her forehead with a 'piece of Sacred Wafer': 'There was a fearful scream which almost froze our hearts to hear. As he had placed the Wafer on Mina's forehead, it had seared it – it had burned into the flesh as though it had been a piece of white-hot metal' (381).

So God Himself insists on stigmatizing the poor woman: 'Even the Almighty', Mina wails, 'shuns my polluted flesh!' But must our wonderful Madam Mina, to quote Van Helsing's eulogistic phrase, really bear the red mark of shame upon her forehead until Judgment Day? And must she – after Dracula has given her what Van Helsing calls the 'vampire's baptism of blood' (414) – become a real vampire like Lucy? And will her loving husband, Jonathan

Harker, have to follow her into 'that unknown and terrible land' (383) because he has made up his mind that she should not go there alone? Or must he kill her in order to 'set free [her] immortal soul' (424), as she makes him promise her? Of course not. The story is, after all, a masculine *romance*, so poetic justice will be done to this wonderful woman in the end.

The scene of Mina's happy ending is in Transylvania, a 'world of dark and dreadful things' (459), where Van Helsing and his group of Anglo-American vampire-hunters (now also including Mina's husband) catch up with Dracula, who has fled England to retreat to his Transylvanian lair. Close to the Castle of Dracula the vampire-hunters attack the group of gypsies that are carrying and protecting the box within which Dracula is lying in his 'vampirecological' earth. After some desperate fighting, the box is captured and Jonathan, Mina's husband, can now cut Dracula's throat with his big kukri knife while Morris, the American, plunges his bowie knife into the vampire's heart. Morris, however, is fatally wounded, but before the Texan gentleman expires, he can point his finger at Mina's forehead and proclaim: 'Now God be thanked that all has not been in vain! See! the snow is not more stainless than her forehead! The curse has passed away!' (485).

Mina has been restored to her former feminine perfection and deservedly so. Unlike Lucy, she never possessed the demonic potential for New-Woman vampirism, the kind of aggressive female eroticism or 'voluptuousness' that may seduce, corrupt and ultimately destroy even the best of men. The prototype of this demonic female sexuality will be found in the Transylvanian heart of darkness itself, within the Castle of Dracula, appropriately situated in a land 'so wild and rocky, as though it were the end of the world' (468). At the very beginning of the story, Jonathan (Mina's fiancé at this early stage) pays a visit to the Castle of Dracula where he has to assist the vampire in buying his London real estate. One night he encounters three female vampires with 'brilliant white teeth that shone like pearls against the ruby of their voluptuous lips' and experiences 'some longing and at the same time some deadly fear' (53). He cannot help feeling 'a wicked, burning desire that they would kiss [him] with those red lips', and when one of them bends over him, Jonathan is an easy victim:

There was a deliberate voluptuousness which was both thrilling and repulsive, and as she arched her neck she actually licked her lips like an animal, till I could see in the moonlight the moisture shining on the scarlet lips and on the red tongue as it lapped the white sharp teeth. [...] I closed my eyes in a languorous ecstasy and waited – waited with beating heart. (54)

Jonathan is saved by Count Dracula's timely intervention: 'This man belongs to me!' (55). The count does not want him vampirized by his womenfolk until he has pumped him for all the information he needs for his real-estate transactions abroad. *Pace* Queer Theory and its various attempts to appropriate *Dracula*,[17] the Count has no *homosexual* interest in Jonathan, and he promises his lascivious girls that they can 'kiss him at [their] will' (55) when he has done with him. Even a dedicated vampirologist like Van Helsing finds it hard to resist the erotic charm of these female vampires when, at the end of the story, he enters the Castle of Dracula to (ex)terminate them in their vampire-sleep. Van Helsing is, after all, only a man of flesh and blood, so when he confronts the vampires, one after the other, he almost loses his nerve:

She lay in her Vampire sleep, so full of life and voluptuous beauty that I shudder as though I have come to murder. [...] Yes, I was moved – I, Van Helsing, with all my purpose and with my motive for hate – I was moved to a yearning for delay which seemed to paralyse my faculties and to clog my very soul. [...] She was so fair to look on, so radiantly beautiful, so exquisitely voluptuous, that the very instinct of man in me, which calls some of my sex to love and protect one of hers, made my head whirl with new emotion. (475-76)

However, in Stoker's late-Victorian masculine romance a man can still be expected to do what a man has got to do. Eventually, Van Helsing braces himself and finishes his 'butcher work' within the Castle of Dracula (477). Subtextually, the threat of the New Woman's monstrous sexuality, her so-called viraginity, with its fatal unmanning potential, has once again been successfully negotiated over the dead bodies of women demonized or stigmatized as vampires.

Joseph Conrad's *Heart of Darkness*: Modernity and the Fascination of the Vampiric Abomination

Only a couple of years separate Stoker's Transylvanian heart of darkness from Conrad's Congo in the serialized version of *Heart of Darkness* (1899), one of the canonical works in the *fin-de-siècle* literature of European *Kulturpessimismus*. From a vampirologist's point of view, the most interesting character in Conrad's text is Kurtz, the so-called hollow man, for here, I suggest, we may also have a case of the modern male victimized by a female vampire, namely, in Kurtz's case, by his African mistress, his *Vénus noire*, whom even Marlow, Conrad's sober master narrator, portrays with unstinted admiration and fascination as 'a wild and gorgeous apparition of a woman', 'savage and superb, wild-eyed and magnificent'.[18] For Marlow the black vampire-woman epitomizes the African wilderness, whose 'colossal body of the fecund and mysterious life seemed to look at her, pensive, as though it had been looking at the image of its tenebrous and passionate soul' (226). Marlow's portrait of Kurtz's African demon-lover is inscribed in the romantic and post-romantic tradition of European exoticism-cum-eroticism, which Mario Praz has explored so thoroughly in *The Romantic Agony* (1970). Exoticism and eroticism, Praz notes, have always gone hand in hand, because 'a love of the exotic is usually an imaginative projection of sexual desire'.[19] By way of illustration, Praz quotes, for instance, the French novelist Eugène Sue's portrait of Cécily, the diabolical creole in *Les Mystères de Paris* (1843):

> cette grande créole à la fois svelte et charnue, vigoureuse et souple comme une panthère, était le type incarné de la sensualité brûlante qui ne s'allume qu'au feux des tropiques. Tout le monde a entendu parler de ces filles de couleur pour ainsi dire *mortelles* aux Européens, de ces vampires enchanteurs qui, enivrant leur victime de séductions terribles, pompent jusqu'à la dernière goutte d'or et de sang...[20]

Or, in my English translation:

> this impressive creole, at once supple and fleshy, was the incarnation of that fiery sensuality which ignites only when exposed to the fires of the tropics. Everyone has heard of these coloured girls as being, as it were,

fatal to European males, of these beguiling vampires who, while inebriating their victim through terrible acts of seduction, drain him of his last drop of gold and blood...

If Kurtz's African woman represents *le type incarné de la sensualité brûlante qui ne s'allume qu'aux feux des tropiques*, Kurtz himself – that is, 'the original Kurtz' (237) – is claimed, by various people in the book, to epitomize European civilization and enlightenment, his mother being half-English, his father half-French. Consequently, the International Society for the Suppression of Savage Customs had entrusted this original Kurtz with 'the making of a report, for its future guidance' (207). The result is described by Marlow as a beautiful piece of writing, of 'unbounded power of eloquence – of words – of burning noble words', but, at the end of his 'moving appeal to every altruistic sentiment', Kurtz had written a kind of postscript: 'Exterminate all the brutes!' (208). This postscript was evidently added after his fatal encounter with the African heart of darkness, whose 'whisper had proved irresistibly fascinating' (221). For the original Kurtz turned out to be hollow at the core, lacking 'restraint in the gratification of his various lusts' (221). The African wilderness had 'caressed' him, 'it had taken him, loved him, embraced him, got into his veins, consumed his flesh, and sealed his soul to its own by the inconceivable ceremonies of some devilish initiation' (205). When meeting him at the Inner Station, Marlow is struck by 'the composed languor of his expression', which is 'not so much the exhaustion of disease'. No, this shadow of Kurtz looks 'satiated and calm, as though for the moment it had had its fill of all the emotions' (224-25). Despite the characteristic opacity of Conrad's diffusely metaphorical style, the eroticized language does suggest that Kurtz's satiation and exhaustion derives primarily from the gratification of his various sexual/sensual lusts, and that the prime agent of his gratification is the African vampire-woman, who has *caressed, embraced, taken* and *loved* him, *got into his veins*, and pumped him dry, body and soul, *jusqu'à la dernière goutte*.

Kurtz's vampirized *body* is irredeemably lost in the African heart of darkness and appropriately buried in some 'muddy hole' (240). Marlow is the self-appointed saviour of his *soul*, but, alas, he does not share Van Helsing's steely Victorian determination. For Marlow and his author are much closer to Modernism than to Victorianism. Philosophically ambivalent about Kurtz's existential mission and crisis in Africa, Marlow can both denounce Kurtz as a hollow sham and pay homage to him as 'a remarkable man', a Faustian or Nietzschean *Freigeist* beyond good and evil, an existential hero of tragic modernity, whose vision had dared 'to embrace the whole universe, piercing enough to penetrate all the hearts that beat in the darkness' (241), and, finally, 'condemning, loathing all the universe' in the famous last words, 'The Horror! The Horror!' (246). The so-called unforeseen partnership between Kurtz and Marlow, a kind of philosophical *entente cordiale*, represents another fictional articulation of the radical nihilism that Conrad himself had expressed, in no uncertain terms, in some of his letters to Cunninghame Graham.[21]

Marlow is equally ambivalent about his allegiances to Kurtz's two women, the black vampire-woman, who evidently triggers off Marlow's own 'fascination of the abomination' (140), and the white Intended in Brussels, 'a soul as translucently pure as a cliff of crystal' (242). Exotic-vampiric sexuality and sensuality are ironically juxtaposed to the purity and spirituality of stereotyped Victorian womanhood. On the one hand, Marlow clearly despises the innocence-cum-ignorance of conventional Victorian womanhood ('It's queer', Marlow notes *en passant*, 'how out of touch with truth women are' (149)), but, on the other hand, he cannot help worshipping, like one of Stoker's chivalrous Victorian gentlemen, at the feet of the Intended as the sublime incarnation of Victorian femininity, to whom he feels obliged to lie about Kurtz and his African heart of darkness – 'bowing my head before the faith that was in her, before the great saving illusion that shone with an unearthly glow in the darkness, in the triumphant darkness from which I could not have defended her – from which I could not even defend myself' (249).

Unlike *Dracula, Heart of Darkness* is not a masculine romance that successfully negotiates or contains the crisis of masculinity at the turn of the century when, in Yeats's famous words, things fell apart and mere anarchy was loosed upon the world. At the end of the story, Marlow, a radically disillusioned convalescent after his

African ordeal, has returned to Europe, where he finds himself in an existential no-man's-land or waste land, a patient etherized, like Eliot's Prufrock, upon the operating table of modernity. However, Marlow's evident fascination with the vampiric abomination of the African woman and his unforeseen partnership with Kurtz *in extremis* suggest that his philosophical options also included Yeats's 'rough beast', the radical primitivism of K. K. Ruthven:

> The Savage God Yeats identified is in many ways the epitome of a particularly intense form of primitivism that developed towards the end of the nineteenth century, merged with current anarchism, and culminated in a desire to destroy European civilization. Here we have something far more radical than the cultural primitivism which Lovejoy and Boas define as mere 'discontent of the civilized with civilization'.[22]

After all, as Marlow points out, modern man is still capable of responding to the noises of prehistoric man, be they ever so ugly: 'The mind of man is capable of anything – because everything is in it, all the past as well as all the future' (186). Faced with modern civilization and its discontents (to quote the title of Freud's famous diagnostic text), Kurtz and, by implication, Marlow were ready to opt for Ruthven's radical primitivism, regressing into the dark heart of African Mother Nature, *Magna Mater, la Vénus noire,* giving in to the fascination of vampiric abomination, sacrificing Victorian manhood in the womb/tomb of *wild* and *gorgeous* black sex. As Camille Paglia argues in her *Sexual Personae*: 'In the beginning was nature'; '[s]ex is a subset to nature' and 'the natural in man'; hence, '[s]exuality and eroticism are the intricate intersection of nature and culture'. Sex, 'abdominal, abominable, daemonic', has been seen, Paglia concludes, throughout the history of civilization, as a descent from Apollonian sky-cult to Dionysian earth-cult,[23] a descent, one might add, epitomized in the masculine *fin-de-siècle* nightmare of the New Woman-Vampire.

Legacies of the *Fin-de-Siècle* Vampire-Woman in D. H. Lawrence's Fiction

Conrad's African heart of darkness is also one of D. H. Lawrence's mythopoeic sites of radical primitivism, exoticism, and vampirism.

In *The Rainbow* (1915), Ursula, who is the protagonist in the last *fin-de-siècle* generation of Lawrence's three-generation Brangwen saga, represents the New Woman, emancipated in terms of religion, education, class, and sexuality. As typical Lawrentian protagonist, Ursula is engaged in an on-going quest for existential authenticity, exploring 'the illimitable endless space for self-realization and delight for ever'.[24] Disillusioned with her college studies and 'the light of science and knowledge' (488), Ursula turns to the darkness of sex and eroticism as her new space of self-realization, and she welcomes back her ex-lover Skrebenski, who has served, for a couple of years, in the British army in Africa. As a lover, Skrebenski proves a potent African tiger at the beginning of their renewed relationship, 'splendid and royal' (495), and he tells her about his exotic Africa, 'the strange darkness, the strange, blood fear', 'the negro, with his loose, soft passion that could envelop one like a passion', 'the hot, fecund darkness that possessed his own blood'(496). As a result, Ursula finds herself submerged in a 'sensual sub-consciousness', in which she mocks her college professors, who believe that it is better to be 'stiffened, neutralized men' than 'the dark, fertile beings that exist in the potential darkness' (499).

Ursula and Skrebenski become engaged, but soon the demonic New Woman in Ursula starts rearing her vampiric head in their relationship. After a few days of happiness in Paris, Skrebenski experiences 'the first deadly anguish, the first sense of the death towards which they were wandering' (507). He feels his manhood 'cruelly, coldly defaced' (519) by Ursula, who has reduced him to 'the stripped, rudimentary, primal man' (514) and found him wanting as such. Like Kurtz, albeit in a different, more Nietzschean sense, Skrebenski is hollow at the core, his male core: his 'soul could not contain her in its waves of strength, nor his breast compel her in burning, salty passion' (530). In the climactic scene on the Lincolnshire coast, Skrebenski's vampiric emasculation is consummated under the 'dazzling, terrifying glare of white light' (531) from a full moon, with which Ursula has merged so completely that Skrebenski hears her voice like a 'ringing, metallic voice, like the voice of a harpy' (531).[25] Like one of the many man-slaughtering sphinxes in *fin-de-siècle* art – indeed, one painting, by the American artist Elihu Vedder, is entitled 'Sphinx of the Sea-Shore'[26] – Ursula now engages in her own sea-shore act of vampirizing Skrebenski with a demonic 'strength of destruction':

> she fastened her arms round him and tightened him in her grip, whilst her mouth sought his in a hard, rending, ever-increasing kiss, till his body was powerless in her grip, his heart melted in fear from the fierce, beaked, harpy's kiss. The water washed again over their feet, but she took no notice. She seemed unaware, she seemed to be pressing in her beaked mouth till she had the heart of him. (532)

After they have made love, Skrebenski appears to lose consciousness, and when he surfaces again, he sees Ursula's face lying 'like an image in the moonlight, the eyes wide open, rigid', 'the unaltering, rigid face like metal in the moonlight' (532). Again he is presented as the victim of vampiric penetration, 'as if the knife were being pushed into his already dead body' (532). He runs away from Ursula, leaving 'the horrible figure' (533) on the sands. By now Skrebenski, once a potent African tiger, has had his fill of *Vénus noire*: 'She was the darkness, the challenge, the horror. He turned to immediate things. He wanted to marry quickly, to screen himself from the darkness, the challenge of his own soul. He would marry his Colonel's daughter' (535).

Within the ambivalent universe of Lawrence's anxious masculinity, Skrebenski is both treated as the victim of New-Woman vampirism and, at the same time, written off as an existential wimp, who scuttles back to the securities of bourgeois civilization instead of facing, with his primal woman Ursula, the challenge of his own dark male soul. This ambivalence is typical of Lawrence's radically dialogic or (to use his own terminology) allotropic imagination,[27] and it also affects the characterization of Ursula, who is presented both as the vampiric New Woman, whose aggressive sexuality emasculates the modern male (Skrebenski in this case), and, at the same time, as her author's *alter ego* in her ongoing existentialist quest for authenticity. Lawrence's radical ambivalence or 'dialogism', as far as his female protagonist is concerned, also comes out, with a vengeance, in the last chapter of *The Rainbow*. After her showdown with Skrebenski, Ursula has returned home to Beldover where she realizes that she is pregnant. If she was doubtful before whether she wanted to marry Skrebenski, there is no doubt in her mind now that she must 'go out to him [in India], and marry him [she does not know that he has already married the Colonel's daughter], and live simply as a good wife to him' (536). Taking leave of her vampiric-demonic persona, Ursula now aspires to become Stoker's or Van Helsing's wonderful Madam Mina: 'I swear to you', she writes in her letter to Skrebenski, 'to be a dutiful wife, and to serve you in all things' (537). She feels acute remorse for her former 'wicked, perverse behaviour' and decides to abolish her Lawrentian quest for self-realization *in extremis*:

> She had been wrong, she had been arrogant and wicked, wanting that other thing, that fantastic freedom, that illusory, conceited fulfilment which she had imagined she could not have with Skrebenski. Who was she to be wanting some fantastic fulfilment in life? Was it not enough that she had her man, her children, her place and shelter under the sun? (536-37)

At the very end of *The Rainbow*, Ursula, in another dialogic/allotropic *volte-face*, discards her Victorian angel-in-the-house persona and returns to that of the intrepid New-Woman quester, landing herself upon the shore of 'the unknown, the unexplored' (546) and glimpsing, in a rainbow, a new world 'built up in a living fabric of Truth' (548).

In *Women in Love* (1920), the sequel to *The Rainbow*, Ursula finds her New Man, or, at least, a Lawrentian male *alter ego*, namely Birkin. This Lawrentian New Man is duly fascinated by the African heart of darkness, a fascination comprising an aesthetic interest in 'negro statues, wood-carvings from West Africa'[28] as well as ultra-primitivist speculations about the 'African process of purely sensual understanding', garnished with 'mindless, dreadful mysteries, far beyond the phallic cult' (331). However, he chickens out of confronting the ghost of Ursula's New-Woman vampirism in the chapter entitled 'Moony'. Ursula is again associated with the demonic power of the full moon, whose reflection in a pond Birkin is cursing and continually destroying by throwing stones at its 'white-burning centre' (324). As vampiric New Woman, Ursula is here identified with Cybele, the 'accursed Syria Dea' (323), that is, the Asiatic goddess or *Magna Mater*, whose male devotees, to quote Robert Graves's *The Greek Myths*, 'tried to achieve ecstatic unity with her by emasculating themselves'.[29] At this stage, Birkin – somewhat anticlimactically, considering his fascination with African primitivism – wants 'happy stillness', 'gentle communion' and 'no passion' (329) in his relationship with Ursula. Although she contemptuously calls him a Sunday School teacher, he insists on a 'non-Dionysic' relationship:

> 'I don't mean let yourself go in the Dionysic ecstatic way,' he said. 'I know you can do that. But I hate ecstasy, Dionysic or any other. It's like going round in a squirrel cage. I want you not to care about yourself, just to be there and not to care about yourself, not to insist – be glad and sure and indifferent.' (328)

As Lawrence's *alter ego,* Birkin, however, is spared the ordeal of sexual vampirization in *Women in Love.* His friend Gerald is not that lucky in his relationship with Ursula's sister Gudrun, another New Woman, whose feminist emancipation and sophistication are reinforced by her also being a *fin-de-siècle/ l'art-pour-l'art* artist. As modern vampire-woman, Gudrun identifies with Cleopatra, the classic *femme fatale,* whom she sees as, essentially, an erotic *artist* because she 'reaped the essential from a man, she harvested the ultimate sensation, and threw away the husk' (546). As eroticist-artist *à la* Cleopatra, Gudrun has to ask herself: 'what was the lover but fuel for the transport of this subtle knowledge, for a female art, the art of pure, perfect knowledge in sensuous understanding' (547). At the end of *Women in Love,* Gerald becomes the tragic victim of Gudrun's decadent vampirism. He is the eponymous hero (or, rather, anti-hero) of the chapter entitled 'The Industrial Magnate', and as Machine God or *Deus ex Machina,* he epitomizes the hubris of modern technological civilization. As Gudrun's lover Gerald is doomed because, like Kurtz in *Heart of Darkness* and Skrebenski in *The Rainbow,* he is hollow at the core, the existential core of his modernized manhood being nothing but 'the great dark void which circled at the centre of his soul' (405). This *dark void* is easily penetrated and dominated by the fatal eroticism of his vampire-woman, and Gerald soon realizes, as he confesses to his friend Birkin, that there is 'something final' about his relationship with Gudrun:

'[...] Gudrun seems like the end, to me. I don't know - but she seems so soft, her skin like silk, her arms so heavy and soft. And it withers my consciousness, somehow, it burns the pith of my mind.' He went on a few paces, staring ahead, his eyes fixed, looking like a mask used in ghastly religions of the barbarians. 'It blasts your soul's eye,' he said, 'and leaves you sightless. Yet you *want* to be sightless, you *want* to be blasted, you don't want it any different.' (535-36)

When Gudrun meets, in the Tyrolese Alps where she is holidaying with Gerald, the German artist Loerke, who represents the state of the art as far as *fin-de-siècle* decadence is concerned, she is ready to throw away the husk of her vampirized lover, that is, Gerald. By now she is utterly bored with Gerald's *borné* Englishness and his fake Don-Juan masculinity, for '[n]othing [she tells herself] is so boring as the phallus, so inherently stupid and stupidly conceited' (563). After almost strangling Gudrun in front of his rival Loerke, Gerald is suddenly overcome by a 'revulsion of contempt and disgust' (573). For Gerald the moment has come when death is seen as the only escape from the *malaise* of modernity in general and his victimization by the vampiric New Woman in particular, and, overpowered with 'a sleep-heavy iciness' (575), he heads for the white alpine no-man's-land to commit suicide.

Pussum, who is introduced in Chapter Six of *Women in Love*, is a more explicitly decadent version of Lawrence's erotic-vampiric New Woman. As a cynical upper-class whore in *fin-de-siècle* London bohemia, Pussum corresponds to the New-Woman stereotype that Dijkstra, in *Idols of Perversity* (1988), characterizes as 'a polyandrous predator indiscriminately lusting after man's seminal essence'.[30] In Pussum, a delicately decadent eroticism, 'unfolded like some red lotus in dreadful flowering nakedness' (123), seems to merge with the dark African sensuality of Birkin's primitivism, the '[p]ure culture in sensation, culture in the physical consciousness, really ultimate *physical* consciousness, mindless, utterly sensual' (133). The male victim of this vampire is the young bohemian Halliday, whom Pussum intends to capture and 'have complete power over' (135), even though Birkin as *Salvator Mundi*, as we see later in the chapter entitled 'Gudrun in the Pompadour', attempts to save Halliday from total emasculation and corruption in the vampiric 'Flux of Reduction' (474), that is:

> using sex [as Birkin lectures him in the messianic letter that is quoted and ridiculed by Halliday and his bohemian friends in the Pompadour café] as a great reducing agent, by friction between the two great elements of male and female obtaining a frenzy of sensual satisfaction – reducing the old ideas, going back to the savages for our sensations, always seeking to *lose* ourselves in some ultimate black sensation, mindless and infinite – (475-76)

Birkin is here pleading for what could be called his (and Lawrence's) holistic-allotropic philosophy, a conception of life as basically a psychodynamic dialectic of alternating regressive and progressive moves. At the beginning of *Women in Love*, Gudrun uses the French phrase *reculer pour mieux sauter* to account for her own need to go back to her existential roots in childhood before taking another leap forward in her adulthood (56). But Halliday's problem is, as diagnosed by Birkin, that, instead of oscillating dialectically between *reculer* and *sauter*, between regression and progression, he is stuck in a purely regressive groove, as it were. Fascinated and victimized by Pussum's erotic vampirism, Halliday is reduced to what R. D. Laing, in *The Voice of Experience*, has called *extreme regression*, a psycho-pathological condition in which a person's intellectual and emotional life has 'run into total impasse.[31] In his letter to Halliday, Birkin reminds his bohemian friend that his regressive flux of reduction should, eventually, lead to a leap of progressive commitment in life: 'if, Julius [Halliday], you want this ecstasy of reduction with the Pussum, you must go on till it is fulfilled. But surely there is in you also, somewhere, the living desire for positive creation, relationships in ultimate faith, when all this process of active corruption, with all its flowers of mud, is transcended ...' (475).

In *Women in Love* it is the aristocratic lady Hermione Roddice who impersonates the Lawrentian version of the New Woman as *psychic* vampire, that is, the modern female intellectual that, in Auerbach's words, saps the male's psychic energy, or, in Eliot's/Prufrock's phrase, fixes the male in a formulated phrase and leaves him sprawling on a pin, wriggling on the wall. As psychic vampire, Hermione can be seen as the Apollonian counterpart of Ursula's more Dionysian or 'Cybelean' womanhood. Hermione herself notes that Ursula is 'more physical, more womanly' (138), and Birkin, Hermione's discontented lover in the first part of *Women in Love*, soon realizes that Ursula is 'like a strange unconscious bud of womanhood', and that he is 'unconsciously drawn to her' (148). In contrast to Ursula, Hermione is all consciousness, all intellect: 'she was a woman of the new school, full of intellectuality, and heavy, nerve-worn with consciousness' (62), a '*Kulturträger*, a medium for the culture of ideas' (63). In fact, Hermione is ridiculed and humiliated, throughout the novel, as the New-Woman intellectual, the psychic vampire of modern feminism:

Knowledge [Birkin argues in one of his numerous attacks on Hermione's intellectualism] means everything to you. Even your animalism, you want it in your head. You don't want to *be* an animal, you want to observe your own animal functions, to get a mental thrill out of them. It is all purely secondary - and more decadent than the most hide-bound intellectualism. What is it but the worst and last form of intellectualism, this love of yours for passion and the animal instincts? Passion and the instincts - you want them hard enough, but through your head, in your consciousness...' (91)

As a result of her perverse intellectualism, Hermione lacks a robust female self: 'she had no natural sufficiency, there was a terrible void, a lack, a deficiency of being within her' (63-64). It is this existential deficiency that constitutes her as a psychic vampire, *for ever craving for her man*: when he, Birkin, was there, 'she felt complete, she was sufficient, whole' (64). Even his potential absence torments her, and she always seems to await him 'in a faint delirium of nervous torture' (69). Birkin instinctively reacts against Hermione's psychic vampirization, perceiving her 'rapt face' as 'the face of an almost demoniacal ecstatic' (69). He is leaving her for Ursula, and it is Hermione's subconscious realization of Birkin's desertion and her equally subconscious hatred for her ex-lover that, for once, sets her free from the prison-house of her intellectualism, her tormenting self-consciousness, and transforms her, momentarily at least, into an *unconscious, physically* aggressive vampire-woman, who must have her primitive revenge on her faithless male. In the execution of that revenge, Hermione will 'know her voluptuous consummation' (163), smashing Birkin's head with the blue ball of lapis lazuli that has so far only served as a paper-weight on her desk:

> Her heart was a pure flame in her breast, she was purely unconscious in her ecstasy. She moved towards him and stood behind him for a moment in ecstasy. [...] Then swiftly, in a flame that drenched down her body like fluid lightning and gave her perfect, unutterable consummation, unutterable satisfaction, she brought down the ball of jewel stone with all her force, crash on his head. (163)

Ironically and logically, it is a *book*, a thick volume of Thucydides, that Birkin, the male intellectual, but also the self-confessed primitivist, uses to ward off the second blow of the female intellectual's *paperweight*, thus saving himself or, to be more precise, his head or brain, from being fatally emasculated. As physical, as distinct from psychic, vampire, Hermione is furthermore demonized in being *left-handed*, which Birkin realizes 'with horror' (163). Still, Lawrence is generous or dialogic enough to allow Hermione, in a subsequent interior monologue, to articulate her New-Woman rationalist-feminist critique of Birkin and his allotropic ego:

> Rupert [Birkin] – he had now reacted towards the strongly female, healthy, selfish woman [that is, Ursula] – it was his reaction for the time being – there was no helping it at all. It was all a foolish backward and forward, a violent oscillation that would at length be too violent for his coherency, and he would smash and be dead. There was no saving him. This violent and directionless reaction between animalism and spiritual truth would go on in him till he tore himself in two between the opposite directions, and disappeared meaninglessly out of life. It was no good – he, too, was without unity, without *mind*, in the ultimate stages of living; not quite man enough to make a destiny for a woman. (378)

To switch from the psychic to the purely physical or sexual vampire once more, we may finally consider Bertha Coutts, the gamekeeper's wife in *Lady Chatterley's Lover* (1928). This Bertha – who is undoubtedly related, in terms of literary genealogy, to another vampiric Bertha in English fiction, namely Bertha Mason, Rochester's mad wife in Charlotte Brontë's *Jane Eyre* – is Lawrence's most venomous representation of the New Woman as an aggressively vampiric-phallic female. Bertha's husband Mellors *alias* Lady Chatterley's potent lover, is another Lawrentian *alter ego*. Battling against the money, the machine, and 'the insentient ideal monkeyishness' of the modern world, Mellors claims to stand for the touch of bodily awareness and tenderness, so all he really needs in life is a good woman like Connie *alias* Lady Chatterley, who will always be *with him*, sexually or otherwise, always tender and aware of him: 'Thank God', he congratulates himself while making love to her, 'she's not a bully, nor a fool. Thank God she's a tender and aware woman'.[32] But before he met Mrs, sorry, Lady Right, young Mr Mellors had, alas, stumbled into Miss Wrong, that is, Bertha Coutts, a young woman with 'a sort of sensual bloom', a woman 'who *wanted* [him] to fuck her', which, initially, made him 'as pleased as punch' (209). After the honeymoon, however, Bertha Coutts turned out to be the kind of selfish New Woman that also liked to fuck her man, that is, fuck him *her way*. So she started bullying her husband in the marital bed, insisting on having her own clitoral orgasm and not always being *with him*. Mellors is still seething with anger and disgust when, years later, he tells Connie about the perversities of his wife's sexual vampirism and egoism:

> But when I had her, she'd never come off when I did. Never. She'd just wait. If I kept back for half an hour, she'd keep back longer. And when I'd come and really finished, then she'd start on her own account, and I had to stop inside her till she brought herself off, wriggling and shouting, she'd clutch with herself down there, and then she'd come off, fair in ecstasy. And then she'd say: That was lovely. Gradually I got sick of it: and she got worse. She sort of got harder and harder to bring off, and she'd sort of tear at me down there, as if it was a beak tearing at me. By God, you think a woman is soft down there, like a fig. But I tell you the old rampers have beaks between their legs, and they tear at you with it till you're sick. Self! Self! Self! all self! tearing and shouting! They talk about men's selfishness, but I doubt if it can ever touch a woman's blind beakishness, once she is gone that way. (210)

In his vampirization/pathologization of the New Woman's sexuality (complete with 'beakish' *vagina dentata*), Mellors seems to be in complete agreement with the notorious Italian criminologist Cesare Lombroso and his disciple Gugliemo Ferrero, who, in *The Female Offender* (1895), had argued that female sexuality, once unleashed, could only be disastrous because the sexual impulse itself was a male prerogative. In fact, active enjoyment of sex could awaken an inherent criminal instinct in woman.[33] But to return to *Lady Chatterley's Lover*: young Mellors had, alas, been incapable of disciplining *his* female offender, so he had had to leave his wife, opting for celibacy, convinced that 'there was no real sex left: never a woman who'd really "come" naturally with a man' (212). Mellors, however, eventually becomes a gamekeeper and Lady Chatterley's lover: this is the closest Lawrence gets to writing the masculine romance of modernity.

In Lawrence's post-War world of sexual politics, Lady Chatterley's tender femininity is clearly the exception that proves the rule, the rule being increasingly the rampant sexual and intellectual vampirism of the New Woman. The masculine-cum-feminine happy ending of *Lady Chatterley's Lover* is also exceptional in so far as Lawrence's fictional constructions and negotiations in the ongoing sex war have typically produced blatantly misogynist endings. One of Lawrence's so-called savage pilgrimages went to Mexico, and the Mexican heart of aboriginal, neo-Aztec darkness and Mexican *machismo* in particular provided Lawrence with various radical solutions to his New-Woman Question. Within western civilization, American as well as European, there appeared to be no effective way of taming the vampiric shrew of modernity (even though clitoridectomy *was* performed extensively in the 1890s, especially in the United States),[34] but let the New Woman go to Mexico and see what happens.

Three examples from Lawrence's Mexican pilgrimage in 1920s will suffice. In *The Plumed Serpent* (1926), Lawrence has his Irish-American female protagonist Kate visit Mexico and, after some mental and ritual acculturation, marry the Indian general Cipriano, who teaches her true feminine submission and makes her prefer the 'soft, heavy, hot flow' of vaginal orgasm to the 'seething electric female ecstasy' of clitoral orgasm, 'the beak-like friction of Aphrodite of the foam'.[35] In 'None of That', another New Woman, rich, American Ethel Cane, visits Mexico, challenges Mexican *machismo* with her American feminism and 'terrible American energy',[36] falls for a Mexican version of Nietzsche's superman, a '*schwarze Bestie*' (223), namely the brutal bull-fighter Cuesta, who instinctively recognizes Ethel as the American version of the vampiric New Woman: 'What does she want? She hates a man as she hates a red-hot iron. She is as easy to embrace as an octopus, her gate is a beak. What man would put his finger in that beak? She is all soft with cruelty towards a man's member. A white devil, as sacred as the communion wafer!' (227).

Cuesta tames this American shrew by having her gang-raped by his men. Ethel commits suicide as a consequence, but she still leaves Cuesta half-a-million dollars. Last, but not least: in 'The Woman Who Rode Away', another emancipated American woman, the thirty-three-year-old wife of a fifty-three-year-old owner of some silver mines in Mexico – middle-aged hubby still admiring 'to extinction' his 'dazzling Californian girl from Berkeley'[37] – rides away, bored with her marriage and overcome by 'a foolish romanticism', feeling it was 'her destiny to wander into the secret haunts of these timeless, mysterious, marvellous Indians of the mountains' (42). These noble savages, however, capture, imprison, strip, and sacrifice the white woman on the altar of their sun god, the sacrificial ritual closely resembling that of Stoker's ritual termination-cum-penetration of Lucy the vampire. The old Indian priest, with his flint knife, 'would strike, and strike home, accomplish the sacrifice and achieve the power', the power being '[t]he mastery that man must hold, and that passes from race to race' (71). But long before the hour of her sacrificial slaughter, the New Woman Who Rode Away has learnt her lesson in her Indian prison camp:

> Her kind of womanhood, intensely personal and individual, was to be obliterated again, and the great primeval symbols were to tower once more over the fallen individual independence of woman. The sharpness and the quivering nervous consciousness of the highly-bred white woman was to be destroyed again, womanhood was to be cast once more into the great stream of impersonal sex and impersonal passion. Strangely, as if clairvoyant, she saw the immense sacrifice prepared. (60)

Amor Fati Vampirici: An Elegiac Fin-de-Siècle Coda

From Stoker's *Dracula* to Lawrence's *Lady Chatterley's Lover*, we have witnessed how, in various mythopoeic hearts of Transylvanian, African, Mexican or plain Sylvan darkness, more or less heroic champions of traditional masculinity have organized and implemented, more or less successfully, their ritual slaughters of the *fin-de-siècle* female vampire, the New Woman, who, like a second Eve, was held responsible for the fall of not only her own true femininity, but also that of true masculinity. A rough female vampire-beast had, indeed, slouched to Bethlehem to be born, and the big question was, as Yeats put it in another poem, 'A Prayer for my Daughter' (1919), how feminist hatred could be driven hence and the female soul recover its 'radical innocence'. Well, masculinist mythopoeia won't do the trick alone: as Keats had to confess in his Nightingale Ode, mythopoeic imagination cannot cheat so well as she is famed to do. If he is lucky, the modern heterosexual male may, perhaps, avoid sharing the ignoble fate of poor Mr Prufrock, for ever sprawling on the psychic pin of the New Woman in her intellectual *salon*, but I am afraid he will still have to resign himself, somehow or other, to his modern predicament, that is, the terror regime of the New Woman, with what could be called a stoical *amor fati vampirici*. A case in point, culled from the less mythopoeic, more realistic drama of the mid-century Angry Young Men: Jimmy Porter, the male protagonist of John Osborne's *Look Back in Anger* (1956), feels that he is being devoured whole, like 'some over-large rabbit', every time he makes love to his modern vampire-wife Alison, who, he claims, has 'the passion of a python'.[38] Since Jimmy is unable to join the gay Michelangelo Brigade – as a hetero, he considers himself 'a sort of right-wing deviationist' (36) – he is obliged to draw the following philosophical conclusion at the end of the play, a conclusion which, I fear, in our current 20th-century *fin de siècle* still holds true for the increasingly endangered species of masculine men – postmodernized, postfeminized, *post* everything good and brave:

Why, why, why, why do we let these women bleed us to death? Have you ever had a letter, and on it is franked "Please give Your Blood Generously"? Well, the Postmaster-General does that, on behalf of all the women of the world. I suppose people of our generation aren't able to die for good causes any longer. [...] There aren't any good, brave causes left. If the big bang does come, and we all get killed off, it won't be in aid of the old-fashioned, grand design. It'll just be for the Brave New-nothing-very-much-thank-you. About as pointless and inglorious as stepping in front of a bus. No, there's nothing left for it, my boy, but to let yourself be butchered by the women. (84-85)

Notes

1. Carol Churchill, *Cloud Nine* (London: Pluto, 1979) 29.
2. Churchill 3.
3. Elaine Showalter, *Sexual Anarchy: Gender and Culture at the* Fin de Siècle (London: Virago Press, 1992) 38.
4. Nina Auerbach, *Our Vampires, Ourselves* (Chicago: U of Chicago P, 1995) 101.
5. D. H. Lawrence, *Studies in Classic American Literature* (Harmondsworth: Penguin, 1983) 76.
6. Friedrich Nietzsche, *The Gay Science*, trans. Walter Kaufmann (New York: Vintage, 1974) 333.
7. D. H. Lawrence, *Fantasia of the Unconscious and Psychoanalysis and the Unconscious* (Harmondsworth: Penguin, 1977) 69.
8. Quoted in Auerbach 105.
9. Rebecca Stott, *The Fabrication of the Late-Victorian* Femme Fatale (London: Macmillan, 1996) 12.
10. Linda Dowling, 'The Decadent and the New Woman in the 1890s', *Nineteenth-Century Fiction* 33 (1979): 435, 438.
11. Bram Stoker, *Dracula* (Harmondsworth: Penguin, 1993) 78. Subsequent references are cited parenthetically in the text.
12. Sigmund Freud, *Civilization, Society and Religion* (Harmondsworth: Penguin, 1991) 55.
13. Bram Dijkstra, *Evil Sisters: The Threat of Female Sexuality and the Cult of Manhood* (New York: Alfred A. Knopf, 1996) 94.
14. Dijkstra 119.
15. H. Rider Haggard, *She* (Harmondsworth: Penguin, 1994) 105.
16. See Elizabeth Bronfen, *Over Her Dead Body: Death, Femininity and the Aesthetic* (Manchester: Manchester UP, 1992).
17. See, for instance, Christopher Craft's '"Kiss Me with Those Red Lips": Gender and Inversion in Bram Stoker's *Dracula*', *Representations* 8 (Fall 1984), reprinted in *Dracula* (New York: Norton, 1997), and Andrew Schopp, who endorses Craft's thesis that homoerotic desire, in *Dracula*, is continually displaced by monstrous heterosexuality: 'Dracula's heterosexual feeding [...] represents a displacement of homoerotic desire' ('Cruising the Alternatives: Homoeroticism and the Contemporary Vampire', *Journal of Popular Culture* 30.4 [Spring 1997]: 235). As Bram Dijkstra correctly notes, Dracula 'dem-

onstrates a very myopically heterosexual bent' (*Idols of Perversity: Fantasies of Feminine Evil in Fin-de-Siècle Culture* [New York: Oxford UP, 1988] 344).

18. Joseph Conrad, *Heart of Darkness and Other Tales* (Oxford: Oxford UP, 1999) 225-26. Subsequent references are cited parenthetically in the text.
19. Mario Praz, *The Romantic Agony* (London: Oxford UP, 1970) 207.
20. Praz 207.
21. See, for instance, the letter to Cunninghame Graham, dated 14 January 1898: 'The attitude of cold unconcern is the only reasonable one [that is, to the inherent absurdity of the human condition]. Of course reason is hateful – but why? Because it demonstrates (to those who have the courage) that we, living, are out of life – utterly out of it. The mysteries of a universe made of drops of fire and clods of mud do not concern us in the least. The fate of a humanity condemned ultimately to perish from cold is not worth troubling about. If you take it to heart it becomes an unendurable tragedy. If you believe in improvement you must weep, for the attained perfection must end in cold, darkness and silence. In a dispassionate view the ardour for reform, improvement for virtue, for knowledge, and even for beauty is only a vain sticking up for appearances as though one were anxious about the cut of one's clothes in a community of blind men' (*The Collected Letters of Joseph Conrad*, ed. F. R. Jack and L. Davies, Vol. 2 [Cambridge: Cambridge UP, 1986] 16-17).
22. K. K. Ruthven, 'The Savage God: Conrad and Lawrence', *Critical Quarterly* 10.1-2 (1968): 39.
23. Camille Paglia, *Sexual Personae: Art and Decadence from Nefertiti to Emily Dickinson* (Harmondsworth: Penguin, 1992) 1, 56.
24. D. H. Lawrence, *The Rainbow* (Harmondsworth: Penguin, 1989) 489. Subsequent references are cited parenthetically in the text.
25. It is worth noting, perhaps, that the New Woman as aggressive phallic-metallic demon-lover seems to have become naturalized or legitimized in today's (or yesterday's) *fin-de-siècle* sex culture, at least in its glossy *Cosmopolitan* manifestation. According to feng-shui expert Kathy Colman, a woman's birth year corresponds to one of five feng-shui elements, and if your element happens to be *metal*, your sexual energy will be articulated as follows: 'You have a powerful erotic energy and you enjoy being in control. You love being on top and tying him up. And you don't mind arousing yourself while he watches. You like challenging positions and your surroundings must be dramatic, inspiring and convey something taboo' ('Find Your *Sexy* Element', *Cosmopolitan* [London] March 2000: 112). Ursula, alas, was born a century too early to escape her Lawrentian fate of being stigmatized and demonized as *metallic* harpy or vampire.
26. See Bram Dijkstra's description of the painting in *Idols of Perversity*: 'Elihu Vedder's "A Sphinx of the Sea-Shore" shows a young woman with long red hair, wide open eyes, and a half-open mouth, a face distorted by elemental passion, nestling her cat's body flat against the soil. She is surrounded by the wreckage of ships, half-buried skulls, the skeletal remains of an arm and a hand still reaching for her from the sand. Like a cat playing heedlessly

with the body of a mouse, she holds a man's skull between her forepaws, nestling it against her bosom, her nails digging into its bone' (328).

27. While the concept of the dialogic imagination, of course, derives from Mikhail Bakhtin, the term *allotropic* is launched by Lawrence himself in a letter to Edward Garnett (dated 5 June 1914), in which he introduces his modernist psychology of the allotropic (that is, radically unstable, dynamic) ego: 'You mustn't look for the old stable ego of the character. There is another ego, according to whose action the ego is unrecognizable, and passes through, as it were, allotropic states which it needs a deeper sense than any we've been used to exercise, to discover are states of the same single radically unchanged element' (*The Letters of D. H. Lawrence*, ed. George J. Zytaruk and James T. Boulton, Vol. 2 [Cambridge: Cambridge UP, 1981] 183).
28. D. H. Lawrence, *Women in Love* (Harmondsworth: Penguin, 1989) 127. Subsequent references are cited parenthetically in the text.
29. Robert Graves, *The Greek Myths*, vol. 1 (Harmondsworth: Penguin, 1962) 117.
30. Dijkstra, *Idols of Perversity* 334.
31. R. D. Laing, *The Voice of Experience* (London: Allan Lane, 1982) 158.
32. D. H. Lawrence, *Lady Chatterley's Lover* (Harmondsworth: Penguin, 1990) 290. Subsequent references are cited parenthetically in the text.
33. See Dijkstra, *Idols of Perversity* 158-59.
34. See Dijkstra, *Idols of Perversity* 178.
35. D. H. Lawrence, *The Plumed Serpent* (Harmondsworth: Penguin, 1990) 459.
36. D. H. Lawrence, *The Woman Who Rode Away and Other Stories* (Harmondsworth: Penguin, 1995) 215. Subsequent references are cited parenthetically in the text.
37. Lawrence, *The Woman Who Rode Away and Other Stories* 40. Subsequent references are cited parenthetically in the text.
38. John Osborne, *Look Back in Anger* (London: Faber, 1960) 37. Subsequent references are cited parenthetically in the text.

Root Music: Occult Notions of Identity in W. B. Yeats and Contemporary Social Criticism in Ireland

Michael Böss

In 1994, the Irish-American journalist Richard Conniff visited Ireland. Afterwards he claimed that the Republic is modernising at such a rate that it will soon have forfeited a unique cultural heritage. Ireland, he thought, is becoming a country resembling any other country in the western world instead of remaining true to its original, authentic self.[1]

There is a time-honoured tradition for such an allegation by a foreign observer. It goes back a hundred years and to another fin-de-siècle. At the time of the last turn of the century, the perception that an authentic Irish culture and way of life were disappearing as a result of modernising changes in society was widespread among non-Irish intellectuals who were suspicious of the effects of the growing materialism and rationalism of their own age and society. Some of them went on their own spiritual 'pilgrimages' to the west of Ireland, especially to Atlantic islands, where they expected to meet people who were leading lives, they thought, that were simpler and truer than their own.

Such nostalgia for a supposedly more holistic way of life was shared by many Irish urban intellectuals and writers, for example W. B. Yeats. Like many of his friends in London, Yeats deeply resented what he saw as the effects of modern mass society. His Celticist project and occultist worldview, I will argue, was one of the ways in which he tried to reconcile the contradictory values of his own age; but also of his own mind. For in spite of his rejection of the 'filthy modern tide', Yeats was, fundamentally, a very modern man, who, like modern people today, longed for alterna-

Fins de Siècle/New Beginnings, ed. Ib Johansen, *The Dolphin* 31, pp. 71-93.

ISBN 87 7288 382 0; ISSN 0106 4487.

tives to modernity and had visions of unity to put up against the fragmentation and incoherence that he perceived around and in himself.

The assumption of my argument in this essay is that occultism may serve a 'healing' function in periods characterised by rapid cultural and social transformation. The structure of my argument is as follows: First, I want to demonstrate that for all the contradictions and variables of Yeats's life and writings, his occultist beliefs constituted a constant. Then I will show that Yeats's occultism represents and anti-modern worldview which has equivalents in Ireland today. I will use the social and cultural criticism of the Irish journalist and writer John Waters as an example. By analysing the ideological deep structure of three of Waters's books, I intend to establish a number of parallels between his own and Yeats's occultist notions of individual and national identity. I will end by briefly indicating the sinister potential implications of such notions.

Yeats, the Modern

Yeats's personal life and preoccupations mirror a modern sensibility and mind to a striking degree. Yeats was never a traditionalist in any sociological sense of the word. Take, for example, his lack of a sense of rootedness in a particular landscape, culture and community. This lack caused him to spend a whole lifetime trying to recuperate and invent such roots. But in vain, for Yeats never felt at rest in any of the worlds between which he was constantly moving to and fro, physically and mentally. He was an existential nomad. A man divided within himself. A man with many masks, as Ellmann has said.

And in spite of his declared anti-modern stance, Yeats far from rejected modernity wholesale. What characterised his view of the modern, rather, was ambivalence. A good example is his attitude to science. In 1913, in a letter to his father, he airs his long-held belief that certain people can become mediators between the world of men and the world of spirits. Many people today would see this as evidence of premodern irrationality. Yet, towards the end of the letter, Yeats writes:

I have had wonderful 'psychic' evidence of late. A charming girl I know, very simple and pious, a girl of good family, has developed automatic writing of the most astounding type. She only knows English and a little French but writes, in her mediumistic state, Greek, Latin, Italian, Chinese, Provencal, Hebrew, Italian and other languages; she answers mental questions in Greek. The case cannot be published but I am examining it carefully with the help of British Museum language experts and writing a report as elaborate as if for publication. Various spirits have also written through her hand and given their names and the dates of their deaths, etc. ... I am now elaborating a curious theory of spirit action which may I believe make philosophic study of mediums possible. I am really absorbed in this for the moment.[2]

We notice here Yeats's enthusiasm about the prospect of having alleged spiritual communication explained and tested by scientific ('philosophic') theory and experiment. He reconciles the potential conflict between science and supernaturalism by telling his father that he is on the verge of discovering 'a curious new theory of spirit action', i.e. a synthesis of the two. It was in order to be able to form such a synthesis that he was drawn towards a monist and occult view of the world.

Also Yeats's politics were characteristically modern in all their ambivalence and complexity. Throughout his life, he constantly vacillated between Parnellian and Georgian Ireland, between democratic Whiggism and Anglo-Irish elitism, between nationalist communalism and liberal individualism. Again, occult convictions, such as his belief in the existence of a spiritual link between Celtic cottage and Anglo-Irish manor, served him to reconcile and heal such otherwise conflicting social and ethnic polarities.

It may of course be argued that Yeats's vision of a future Irish state held together by a sense common identity and solidarity across social and ethnic barriers represented a budding modern conception of civic nationality. The problem with Yeats's political vision was, however, that once he started to feel the defeat of his own class and ethnic group, he grew more and more reluctant to submit it to – modern – democratic rules of the game. Hence, his elitism and flirtation with 'Italian philosophy', i.e. the social holism (corporatism) of Mussolini and Blueshirt fascism.

Yeats's elitism, however, was not only the product of his disenchantments with political reality in independent Ireland. It had been founded early in his life as I will now demonstrate in my analysis of 'Speaking to the Psaltery', one of the essays from *Ideas of Good and Evil.*

The Music of the Human Voice

William Butler Yeats was not a man with an ear for music. He did not like song, for example. But he did know how to appreciate and use the phonological and physical qualities of language for aesthetic purposes. At times he wrote poems which, when recited, are pleasing to more than the ear. But it is hard to blame his sisters for asking him to stop when, during evenings at home, he began to intone his very own 'music' from a corner of the sitting-room. On such occasions, William often decided to withdraw to the kitchen with a reading lamp in his hand. Here he could continue his voice experiments without being hissed at.

Young Yeats was developing the idea that the human voice could be trained to express the essence of personality; an essence which he sometimes called 'passion', sometimes 'music', and which, in time, he came to regard as a form of cosmic energy, especially after he came under the influence of occult philosophies in the early 1890s. From this period on, he saw this energy, manifesting itself most notably in sexuality and artistic creativity, as running from the wellspring of energy of the total universe. As on so many other occasions in his life, it took a woman to help him nourish first intuitions into thought.

In 'Speaking to the Psaltery', Yeats describes some experiences he has just had with one of his woman friends, Florence Farr. Farr was an actress, she was beautiful, and Yeats had a sexual affair with her at that time; even more important, there was a spiritual relationship between them. She shared his interest in occultism and he saw her as a kind of soul mate that had taken the strains off his inhibited self. Yeats later wrote to her:

> You cannot think what a pleasure it is to be fond of somebody to whom one can talk – as a rule any sort of affection annihilates conversation, strikes one with silence like that of Adam before he had even named the beasts. To be moved and talkative, unrestrained, one's own self, and to be this not because one has created some absurd delusion that it is all wisdom,

as Adam may have in the beast's head, but not in Eve, but because one has found an equal, that is the best of life.[3]

On the day Yeats sat down to write 'Speaking to the Psaltery', Florence Farr had been sitting for hours in front of him speaking out poems by Shelley and himself while plucking the strings of a psaltery, a string instrument, placed across her knees. Her recitation was not in the mode of ordinary speech, nor could it be described as song, Yeats explains:

> Wherever the rhythm was most delicate, and wherever the emotion was most ecstatic, her art was most beautiful, and yet, although she sometimes spoke to a little tune, it was never singing, as we sing to-day, never anything but speech. A singing note, a word chanted as they chant in churches, would have spoiled everything; nor was it reciting, for she spoke to a notation as definite as that of a song, using the instrument, which murmured sweetly and faintly, under the spoken sounds, to give her the changing notes. Another speaker could have repeated all her effects, except those which came from her own beautiful voice, a voice that would have given her fame if the only art that offers the speaking voice its perfect opportunity were as well known among us as it was known in the ancient world.[4]

Before Yeats introduced Florence Farr to his ideas of the 'music' of the human voice, he had only known one other person in Dublin who shared his view on the occult significance of sound and rhythm, namely his friend George Russell (A.E.). One day when he and Russell had been walking the streets of Dublin together, Russell had begun to speak in verse, Yeats later recalled, 'with the confidence of those who have the inner light'(15), undisturbed by people who stopped and looked at them or even crossed to the other side of the street to avoid the odd couple.

Like Yeats, Russell had no knowledge of music. Still, he claimed that he wrote his poems 'to a manner of music' (15). Russell had once asked a classical violinist to make a notation of his intonation when he recited his own poems to him. Afterwards he wanted him to play the notes taken down. The violinist told him, however, that this could not be done since his reading contained quarter-tones and would therefore be 'out of tune' (15). Russell did not accept this explanation. Neither did Yeats. So they decided to visit another acquaintance, one of Yeats's friends who had grown up with the musical tradition of peasant culture in Co. Galway. Here they were met with greater understanding. The friend told them that in Russell's recitations he heard two basic motifs. He compared them with 'very simple Arabic music' (15). This observation spurred Yeats's curiosity since he had long held the Celts to be the 'Orientals' of Europe. He began to conduct his own voice experiments and to make notations of the tones that came to his mind during the process of writing.

It was this kind of transcribed sound that he presented to Florence Farr. He had known her since 1890 when they had met at sessions in the English section of the German occult order *Die Goldene Dämmerung*. The Order of the Golden Dawn was a society whose ideas and ceremonies were to exert an enormous influence on Yeats for the rest of his life. Originally, it had been a learned society for the study of Rosicrucian mysticism. But after its foundation in London in 1889, elements of Cabbalism and esoteric theosophy had been added, and it soon developed into a secret society for people of all sorts but with a common interest in ritual magic, i.e. methods by which to control the energies of the mind through the systematic pursuit of supernatural powers. The order attracted many artists because the rituals performed at its sessions contained many theatrical elements, and the study of magic within the order encouraged adepts to reflect over the correspondences between colours, numbers and symbols.[5]

It was from the time Yeats became a member of the Golden Dawn that the term 'magic' began to enter his vocabulary. A little more than ten years later, in his essay 'Magic' (1901), he summed up the doctrines of his magical beliefs in three points:

I believe in the practice and philosophy of what we have agreed to call magic, in what I must call the evocation of spirits, though I do not know what they are, in the power of creating magical illusions, in the visions of truth in the depths of the mind when the eyes are closed; and I believe in three doctrines, which have, as I think, been handed down from early times and been the foundations of nearly all magical practices. These doctrines are

(1) That the borders of our minds are ever shifting, and that many minds can flow into one another, as it were, and create or reveal a single mind, a single energy.

(2) That the borders of our memories are as shifting, and that our memories are part of one great memory, the memory of Nature herself.

(3) That this great mind and great memory can be evoked by symbols.[6]

Yeats's interest in the evocative power of the symbol makes it impossible to distinguish between Yeats the poet and Yeats the occultist.[7] Yeats believed that poetry, by virtue of he poet's use of symbols, had the same power as magic rituals.

An interest in ritual magic seems to have been exactly what Yeats aimed at with his voice experiments. This explains why he later placed 'Speaking to the Psaltery' immediately before his essay on 'Magic' in *Ideas of Good and Evil*. It also explains why it follows right after his introductory essay 'What Is "Popular Poetry"?'. For in the latter, Yeats takes the origin of poetry back to an ancient age in which people, allegedly, had not distinguished between art, craft and mystery. To the people of that time, sound, rhythm and cadence had opened a direct door to truths of a metaphysical nature:

I learned from the people themselves, before I learned it from any book, that they cannot separate the idea of an art or a craft from the idea of a cult with ancient technicalities and mysteries. They can hardly separate mere learning from witchcraft, and are fond of words and verses that keep half their secret to themselves. Indeed, it is certain that before the counting-house had created a new class and a new art without breeding and without ancestry, and set this art and this class between the hut and the castle, and between the hut and the cloister, the art of the people was as closely mingled with the art of the coteries as was the speech of the people that delighted in *rhythmical animation, in idiom, in images, in words full of far-off suggestion, with the unchanging speech of the poets.* [my italics] (10-11)

It was not solely because Florence Farr possessed the skill to interpret his poems with a sense of their rhythmic, sonorous and semantic qualities that Yeats became so excited by listening to her that day. It was also because he felt that her voice added a 'new quality', namely an inherent, 'uncommunicable genius', to his poems (16, 17).

And, finally, Yeats uses the word music in a sense close to the Protagorean notion of the music of the universe.

It was by virtue of the capacity of rhythm, colour, and other formal qualities to transmit cosmic energies that Yeats's poetics had metaphysical significance. Music was a product of the individual consciousness; but as such it revealed ontological truth. But there were also wide cultural implications, as we shall now see.

If it were true that the 'music' of the human voice conveyed a deeper kind of truth about life than that which could be grasped by reason, then the 'new art' that he was discovering, Yeats writes, would need trained 'speakers' and 'hearers' to be appreciated (18). His point was that the ancients, i.e. people in Antiquity and the Middle Ages, had understood the music of the universe intuitively, but few people in the modern age were capable of grasping its spiritual messages because they believed only in rational and factual truth. But he hoped to be able to open people's ears and predicted that '[t]he relation between formal music and speech will yet become the subject of science, not less than the occasion of artistic discovery' (20). He expressed a hope that one day, after new kinds of spoken poetry and drama had been developed, it would once again be possible for 'poetry and rhythm' to 'come nearer to common life' (19), and he envisioned a time in which this rediscovered ancient art would be fully revived. This, he predicted, would not only mean a revolution for literature and drama but also for the way in which people communicated with each other (20-21).

As we see here, Yeats's personal, poetic and cultural projects were closely connected with each other. They were all a matter of restoring a sense of unity between the individual human mind and the great 'mind' of culture and cosmos. But they were also tied up with his political project, as I will demonstrate before we take the leap up to our own time.

Occult Politics

Yeats's politics might be described as a politics of felt identity. For it was the national identity of the Irish as a feeling for the land that he was concerned with; not conventional politics. It may also be described as a cultural politics, for the purpose of national politics, for Yeats, was to help recuperating an original, authentic and unitary Irish nation.

In this project, poetry and drama could be useful. Yeats was convinced that the new forms of literature he intended to create would be essentially - and, by definition, authentically - Irish. Yet, because this new literature and drama were artistic manifestations of cosmic energies shared by all mankind, it was also of universal significance. His ultimate ambition with a 'Celtic' theatre was to help revitalising and regenerating not only Irish but also European culture as a whole. Through a theatre based on the symbolic language of ancient Irish myth, he imagined that the universal streams of cosmic energy might be led back into a civilisation suffering under the materialism and cultural fragmentation of modernity.

This anti-modernist stance pushed Yeats ever more in the direction of apocalyptic visions. The artistic culmination of this movement was 'The Statues'. In the last stanza of this poem, we are presented with a vision of the 'Irish' rising from the darkness and decadence of the old cosmic cycle in order to lead other peoples into a new age. The authority of the Irish to lead came from their possession of a deep knowledge, a *gnosis*, which goes back to the mystic traditions of the 'Oriental' Europe of Antiquity:

> We Irish, born into that ancient sect
> But thrown upon this filthy modern tide
> And by its formless spawning fury wrecked,
> Climb to our proper dark, that we may trace
> The lineaments of a plummet-measured face.

By the time Yeats wrote this, however, his ideas as to who 'We Irish' actually were had been slightly modified, compared to his ideas of his youth, especially after the post-1922 regime had begun to implement a programme for an Ireland that differed significantly from his own. Although occasionally representing whiggist convictions as a member of the Free State Senate, his experience of majoritarian democracy nourished an elitist outlook and attracted him to Mussolini and, for a short period, General O'Duffy's Blueshirts. Yeats believed naively - and ignorantly - that both represented forces that would eventually restore national unity – the lost balance between individual and nation – and bring an end to the cultural disorder of modern mass society.

The critic Elizabeth Cullingford thinks that it was Yeats's individualism which kept him from embracing fascism fully.[16] Michael North argues, more convincingly, that what attracted him to fascism was that 'it allowed him to indulge both his nationalism and individualism, because, in fact, it served as the last, most extravagant, reconciliation of a conflict present in his thought from the beginning'.[17] Against the background of my own analysis, we may add that the seeds of this elitism were already laid in his youth when he adopted an occult social and cultural philosophy, which, as we shall now see, has parallels in our own age.

Screams of the Angels of Modernity

John Waters wrote *An Intelligent Person's Guide to Modern Ireland* (1997), a harsh criticism of modern Irish life, out of personal concern about the problems of modern society: drug addiction, crime, alcoholism, loss of cultural identity, social and spiritual rootlessness.[18] Taking a deliberately unfashionable, anti-modern stand, he admits that he has a 'soft spot' for an Ireland of the past (58). There may have been many things wrong with the Ireland of the 1950s, he concedes, but 'even for those of us who considered ourselves outsiders, it was still a kinder, gentler, more innocent place than it is now,' quite different from the dysfunctional and 'morally fragmented society that Ireland has become' (69, 79).

For Yeats cultural diversity was a product of modernity; a modernity which he associated with England. In contrast Waters thinks that modernity leads to a culture of sameness and that it originates in North America. Modernity may take various forms, he writes, but in sum it is a world which increasingly resembles 'a version of the USA in every possible way'; a world 'ruled by greed, lust, fear, competition, consumption, instant communication, mass marketing, hype, obsession, celebrity, commodification and – increasingly – cultural homogeneity', where people seek surrogate experiences in art and popular culture in order to disengage from the 'awfulness of modern life'.[19]

But modernity has a special history in Ireland according to Waters. He thinks that present-day social problems in Ireland are a result of a continuous battle in Irish history between 'the people' and successive social and political elites over ownership over land, society and culture (96). First there was the Anglo-Irish land-owning class with its alien English culture. Then came the nationalist elite imposing its own vision of a Gaelic-Catholic Ireland on the people. Last came the liberal, market-fixated urban middle classes, whose political representatives surrendered the country for their own economic advantage by handing out privileges to American companies and by making Ireland join the European Union.

As a result of the liberal elite's political and cultural hegemony, today's Ireland, 80 years after gaining political independence, is incapable of sustaining itself economically and culturally, Waters claims. The lack of popular ownership over Ireland has dire mental and cultural implications because it is precisely the bond between people and land that can prevent a society from breaking down under the impact of modernity. Evidence of modern national *malaise* may be seen everywhere: large sections of the Irish population left destitute, tens of thousands psychologically depressed, widespread drug abuse and an excessive consumption of alcohol – all signs of a deep spiritual crisis in the Irish population (159).

The only thing to hope for in these circumstances, Waters writes, is that people might realise that they rely 'on something above and beyond the resources of the mere individual'. What Ireland needs is a new national 'magic'; a 'spiritual renewal' which may restore cultural self-sufficiency and a sense of community (186-87). The popular obsession with the Celtic Tiger image of Ireland suggests in itself that '[m]odern Ireland has a hankering for something else, that deep down we are still aware of some common channel in which joy and wealth and well-being can be achieved collectively and that individualism is not capable of giving the Irish people what they think they want' (186). The individual must find a spiritual nation in order to repossess his own true Irish identity. For it is loss of individual and collective identity that the Irish suffer from. They yearn for a sense of who they are and where they belong in the modern world.

Waters's notion of true Irish identity is strikingly similar to ideas found in Yeats's writings. It is something to be derived from feeling, vision and an intuitive, subconscious and wordless 'knowledge', and which can only be accessed through magic ritual. This is the hidden agenda of his second book, *Race of Angels: Ireland and the Genesis of U2* (1993). On the surface level, *Race of Angels* is a book about music. But there is a deeper level than mere conventional music to its argument, as we shall now see.

Waters begins his book with a personal narrative of his childhood in a small town, Castlerea in Co. Roscommon, in a lower middle-class family where music was not a natural element of life. His parents did not own a radio until he was seventeen. Music was not anything that was given conscious thought, and this was quite typical for such social layers after the war, Waters wants us to believe. The music played at the local dances did not appeal to young people like himself, and it did not seem to have anything to do with the expression of their own identity. In fact, it was only 'for dancing to, or cheering yourself up, or having a bit of a singsong' (9).

But this did not mean that young people like himself did not listen to music at all. They certainly did. But their music was a non-Irish type, namely the English and American pop and beat music played on Radio Luxemburg. This had implications for their developing sense of themselves. For since they had little sense of themselves as being Irish, they uncritically adopted the images and attitudes conveyed by this music instead of creating their own identities. They tended to become like the music and lyrics they listened to – 'English' or 'American' – forgetting that they were indeed Irish (78).

The schools offered no alternative. Waters holds Irish politicians under the Free State accountable for this failure, since they had never thought of giving Ireland an educational system of its own. Apart from minor revisions (mainly dictated by the ambition to re-Gaelicise the Irish nation), they had just let the 'Murder Machine' grind on, with the socialisation into English class values that this had implied. Consequently, Ireland had remained a mentally colonised society characterised by widespread cultural –

and personal – schizophrenia and a lack of self-confidence and intellectual independence.

However, like Yeats, Waters believes that it is possible to revive Ireland culturally and spiritually by tapping subliminal spiritual resources and energies. And, again like Yeats, his belief is based on personal experiences of the mystery and magic connected of music. He relates how, in the late 1970s, he

> turned on the radio and heard a young London Irish band called The Pogues, playing with accordions and tin whistles, and a singer with the voice of a rootless angel. This might have been the music, had we the confidence to believe in it, [that] we could have made for ourselves, had we not been numbed by the heavy hand of the Murder Machine. It then struck me that what made a culture was not the instruments or the tunes, or the style even, but *the feelings that went into the playing, the source of the inspiration*. (88, my italics)

The 'voice of a rootless angel' is a phrase which refers not only to the singer of the Pogues, but also to a whole generation. To Waters, his own generation consisted of individuals without anchor, colour and roots. They were the children of what Fanon had once called a 'race of angels', i.e. nations who had not only been colonised politically and physically but also mentally. Hence the title of the book, in which Waters attempts to adapt Fanon's analysis to the mental case of modern Ireland by interpreting the history of modern popular music.

The Pogues was a punk band. But what was punk really about? he asks. Punk was only marginally about music. Primarily it was about staging an oppositional identity: 'A reasonable description of punk would be to say that it was an attempt to recreate in the visible, external world the chaos that the external world had enacted inside human beings.'(52-53) Culturally, then, punk was an assault on the modern, market driven world; it was an anti-modern 'virus' meant to kill modernity. In its stead it sought to create a world in which individuals could feel part of a community and, as a consequence, experience existential authenticity and belonging: 'It was an assertion of control over one's own existence, and of connectedness with others of like mind, anywhere, everywhere. It was a way into the world for those who had no other.'(51)

Punk completely changed the course of pop music. It revived the anarchic essence of rock'n'roll. But it was not an aim in itself. It was only a passage into something new. It marked a transition to a kind of music which negated the values of commercial pop and gave young people what they really wanted. After the 'exorcism' of punk, a new music would be created in which the old 'magic' of rock'n'roll seeped through so that the new generation could rediscover for themselves that music might be a source of 'identity' and 'truth'. Such identity and truth, however, could only be grasped intuitively as 'mystery'. The truth was to be found in both 'the thing itself and, deeper down in its core, in the knowledge of its existence, in the thrill of the search and the glimpse of the mystery' (14).

In this central part of Waters's argument, he reveals himself as an anti-modern occultist of 1890s extraction and as a spiritual heir of W. B. Yeats. This impression is born out by his interpretation of the music and lyrics of U2, with the aid of Bono, the master shaman.

What U2 has achieved, we learn, is to create a mysterious meaning which conflicts with the modern world and offers glimpses of a better world to those who know how to unravel the secrets of their tunes. Waters quotes Bono for having said that rock 'n' roll is about 'mystery and mischief', understanding 'mystery' in the light of the American writer Flannery O'Connor. O'Connor once wrote that mystery is a 'great embarrassment' to the modern mind, and she saw the artist as someone who might reveal the 'mystery of our position on earth' (19).

As life in the modern world is often lived on the surface, it is crucial, Bono went on telling Waters, to develop 'rituals' by which deeper truths may be accessed. Such rituals may help modern individuals get 'outside of the concrete – into the abstract', i.e. into forms of existence underneath surface reality (26).

How can this be done? Apparently by rather simple means, such as sounds, for instance. Certain sounds may release hitherto unknown images from the subconscious, we learn, and Waters expounds his claim by relating what he himself experiences when listening to U2's 'A Day Without Me'. In this tune, the band uses an echo device. He explains how the echo always makes him feel as if he were going out of his personal self to merge into a larger, impersonal and universal Self:

> I can play this song a hundred times a day without it losing a shred of its mystery. I don't know what it's 'about'. ... I only know that this song represents a place, described in the reverberating guitar and the climbing bass and the tripping, tumbling drums, a place I need to go once in a while to breathe and cry. ... At first, I think, I heard 'A Day Without Me' as a narcissistic cry for recognition, an indulgent fascination with the absence of the 'I' from the world. As I grow older, the song ages with me, acquiring the maturity of acceptance that comes with realising that none of us, individually, ultimately matters, *but that all of us, together, must. It grows and grows. Or maybe it's me.* (26-27, my italics)

Waters, as it appears from this description, feels that he leaves his own private place behind only to discover that there is a place for 'all of us'; a place where deeper existential purpose and meaning are restored. He gets in touch with his authentic self by becoming part of a mysterious community and fellowship. At this subconscious level individual and collective mind fuse into each other and Waters discovers a true 'Ireland' which appears to be an antidote against modernity and cultural/existential alienation. So this is where Waters's enters his own version of Yeats's occult and holistic 'Celtic Ireland'.

To Waters, the music of U2 represents something genuinely Irish. It expresses the feelings of all those young people who have been cut off from their national roots, yet who have kept on yearning to belong and feel at home in a land of their own. Because it is tapping 'a primitive fund of feeling and knowledge', he thinks, U2's music has the potential to cause an 'Irish cultural reawakening' which will eventually emancipate the young generation from their colonised mindsets and make them discover a new Irish identity:

> [U2] have tapped into the well of expression, of music and language, that runs in all of us. ... They go against the grain of cynicism and pessimism which has characterised Western art and politics and culture through the history of Western imperialism. They have suggested to us, the Irish, ways

> of liberating ourselves from stereotyped ideas of what we are or what it is possible for us to become. They give voice to what it is to be Irish in the modern world. They *are* what it is to be Irish in the modern world. (99, 132-33)

But this new Irishness neither can nor should be articulated rationally. What makes U2's music so Irish is exactly the way in which it has the power to express an experience which is beyond reason and thought; the way in which it expands the imagination 'by means of the senses rather than the intellect, [and] evokes feelings and perceptions which transcend the medium of rock'n'roll' (120). Waters wonders (with the philosopher Richard Kearney) whether earlier attempts to recreate an Irish identity have not failed precisely because people tried to express it in a language which placed 'too much emphasis on facts and not enough on feelings' (143). But in 'U2 language', words are 'codes for the deeper language [of feeling]': 'The gaps between language and reality are filled by the sound of a guitar and a bass drum.' Everyday language has been abused by becoming the instrument of a technocracy. Therefore 'someone must search on our behalf, for those deepest and dearest sounds that might make sense of who we are'. This search will finally take the Irish into their own land, their own 'landscape' (45, 146).

The basic message of Waters's book, then, is that it takes a kind of music therapy for the Irish to understand themselves - both as individuals and as an Irish nation. Identity is not a matter of an individual finding words for feelings - as Seamus Heaney would hold - but depends on his willingness to open himself up to experiences beyond word, fact and thought; indeed to give in to the power of mystery and magic and leave reason behind. It seems, therefore, as if 'Irishness', in Waters's conception, has ultimately been reduced to being a kind of inarticulate primal scream from the throat of a modern nation of 'lost angels'.

One may finally ask if there are any political perspectives and implications of this occult notion of national identity, as there were for Yeats? Yes, I think there are.

Political Shamanism

One of the keys to understanding Waters's politics is his first book, *Jiving at the Crossroads*.[20] But it is a good idea to read it again after having read *Race of Angels*. For the latter book may open one's eyes to the meaning of passages in the former which, at a first reading, may sound rather bland and innocent.

In *Jiving at the Crossroads*, Waters argues that not only culture but also politics is, basically, a matter of feeling and intuition. The only good Irish politicians, it appears, are those who empathise with the interests, values and identity of common Irish folk. The problem with modern liberal politics is, that [e]verything [has been] reduced to the dry, neutral language of ideology and conceptual politics' (83). But politics is 'a matter of faith, not of belief' (38).

Much of the book is autobiographical. It deals with Waters's own experience of growing up in Castlerea. But perhaps more than anything else, it deals with his relationship with his own father.

John's father had a heart which 'lay with the countryside, where he had been born and where his soul, at least, intended to remain' (66). This made him a perfect representative of common Irish people who, from time immemorial, had had a religious and mystical sense of being rooted in the land. In this - rural - land, local politics used to be a given. John's father voted Fine Gael, but, on a certain level, party politics did not matter, and John was socialised into a certain notion of what constituted the Irish nation:

> My father defined my politics in the same way that de Valera had defined the nation's up to his death and beyond. As a child I had accepted my father's word and writ, yet as I grew up I rebelled against him, thought him old-fashioned, backward-looking. In him I had someone to both measure myself against and to rebel against when the time came. Although, so to speak, we were on the other side of the family, I was Dev's political grandson. (56)

But John was not only Dev's spiritual grandson, he was also a child of Whitaker, and he was increasingly to feel squashed between the 'realistic' traditionalist and the illusory liberal politics that each represented, or, as Waters puts it, between the '*reality* of our culture and origins and the misty *mirage* of our imagined futures [my italics]' (58). The new society that evolved in the '60s brought with it a new politics; a politics in which politicians and ordinary people were disconnected. The 'thread of history' was broken and the link lost between politics and the historical values of the Irish nation (61). People were left with an empty rhetoric which tried to summon up 'old, tribal allegiances', but which did not able to fool those who knew better (61).

The modern political rhetoric - that of liberal, urban Ireland - caused young people to be alienated from the countryside in which they had their roots. Instead they gave in to the 'fragile illusion' that they were part of a 'thrusting, modern, forward-looking Ireland' and citizens of the 'Universal City' (66). In Waters's own case, this illusion caused a rift between himself and his father and changed the course of his life. The father wanted him to study agriculture in the Regional Tech in Sligo. Like his friends, John wanted instead to find a job in Dublin or London.

Although he persevered and did end up in Dublin - and London - he never escaped the feeling of being caught between two worlds, between country and city. But then one summer, after having returned from Dublin to drive his ailing father's post van, he began to notice an alien quality in the 'sounds and voices' that he was listening to every day broadcast on national radio from Dublin. These sounds opinions might as well have come 'from another world', he felt (71).

They were the voices of 'Dublin 4', i.e. postal district that is Waters's metaphor for the liberal middle classes. The vision of Ireland that they spoke of suddenly seemed like 'the antithesis of the past' (83), a vision totally lacking the mysterious qualities of de Valera's Ireland.

In the battle for his own soul - and the soul of the Irish nation - Waters was, eventually, to take the side of the 'country' against the soulless city of Dublin and its politics. Most of the rest of *Jiving at the Crossroads*, therefore, is the story of how a prodigal son found his way back to his father and gradually adopted many of his father's values, including the vague, occult notion of the land as the source of communal life and collective identity. This story transpires implicitly through a series of essays in which he barely succeeds in covering up his admiration for charismatic, populist but shady political figures such as Sean Doherty and Charles Haughey. Doherty was first used, later hated and derided and eventually 'defrocked' by 'Dublin 4'. But at his best, he knew how to communicate with and represent his constituents more truthful than any other contemporary Irish politicians.

But it took the journalist John Healy – himself an admirer of Haughey – to bring Waters to awareness. In his heyday, Healy was the champion of the great but anonymous people of Ireland. He was the one journalist at the *Irish Times* with whom Waters's own father had ever been able to identify. He had articulated the 'essence of [his father's] own experience and view of the world' (145), which is summed up as the 'anti-ideology' of 'land', 'tribe', and 'clan'(148). Healy became Waters's spiritual father, and he identified with him to such a degree that, when he was once offered to meet him and write a journalistic profile about his career for *In Dublin* magazine, he was to experience their encounter as a revelation, since there 'was a truth about his life which seemed also to contain the truth of my own' (149).

So what was it about Healy that Waters found so attractive?

> He was, in fact, as we all should aim to be, an *organic part of his own life and times*. ... Healy did not see himself as belonging on the sidelines. *Immersed in the mystery of his own life and times*, he has fashioned a *vision* of what he wanted his country to become. ... I had never met a man, *apart from my father*, who seemed to understand so much. He could tell what would happen in the future of Irish politics because *he understood its past – not just in terms of politics and history, but as experienced in the lives of his fellow Irish people*. (150-51, my italics)

The message of this paragraph is rather disturbing. Primarily for the way in which it turns politics – matters of state – into a popular shamanism predicated upon a notion of Irish nationality which cannot be defined and articulated rationally, but can only be 'known' by those who 'immerse' themselves in and become an 'organic part' of the 'mystery' of their own lives and times. This kind of politics resembles the more extreme versions of cultural nationalism which could be found all over Europe in the first half of the twentieth century, for example in the writings of W. B. Yeats.

Two years before his death in 1939, Yeats wrote:

in blood and ferocity, morbid, *bizarre*, repulsive and very offensive in its adaptation of scriptural phraseology to situations the reverse of sacred'.[7] Though the public debate of the play never quite reached the scale of what followed in the wake of the publication of Wilde's Decadent novel, *The Picture of Dorian Gray* (1891), its history is fraught with controversy and scandal.[8]

Salomé's way to the English stage was much delayed, as the Lord Chamberlain's Examiner of Plays, E. F. S. Pigott, banned it after only three weeks of rehearsals in 1891 - a ban upheld until 1931. The censorship was based on Henry VIII's interdiction against mystery plays, which made it impossible to dramatise biblical elements on stage. Yet, there can be little doubt that the ban was in the service of Victorian public morality. What leaves us puzzled is not that a ban was imposed, but that Wilde would at all submit a play to the Censor, which represents biblical characters engaged in aberrant sexual activities. However, that a ban was perhaps expected after all may explain why Wilde initially wrote the play in French. It was common knowledge that the examiner of plays would often licence works in French that no English play with similar contents could get away with.[9] Because the play could not be licensed for the stage in London, its first stage performance was on 11 February 1896 at the Théâtre de l'Œuvre in Paris - though just for a single showing. The script to the play was published in English on 9 February 1893 with a set of now famous illustrations by Aubrey Beardsley.[10] This edition by publishers Elkin Mathews and John Lane purported to be a translation of the French script, which had been published the year before in French by Libraire de l'Art Indépendant. In the English edition no name of any translator is given on the frontispiece, but Lord Alfred Douglas, Wilde's homosexual lover, was acknowledged in the foreword with the dedication: 'To My Friend Lord Alfred Bruce Douglas the Translator of My Play'. In his autobiography, Douglas not only denied that he was the translator but confused the matter by claiming that Wilde had first written the play in English and then translated it into French.[11] Yet, later examinations of all manuscript versions defy this claim.[12] Wilde had in fact asked Douglas to translate an original French draft of the play into English but was so dissatisfied with the result that he undertook such extensive revisions that the translation in effect became his own. In his prison-letter to Douglas, of which extracts were later published as *De Profundis*, Wilde recalls the difficulty he had with Douglas's translation: '…new scenes occurred, the occasion of them being my pointing out the schoolboy faults of your attempted translation' (*Letters* 431-32).[13] Because the first draft version written in French was possibly submitted to Pierre Louÿs, Marcel Schwob, Stuart Merrill and Adolphe Retté for corrections, there is all the more reason to take Wilde's English version of the play - which he seems to have insisted on drafting entirely by himself - as an 'original' play.[14] Hence, it is this version that will concern us here.

The original source material of the play is the biblical story of the beheading of John the Baptist. These accounts are merely anecdotes found in Mark 6:14-29 and Matthew 14:1-12 (neither place is the name 'Salome' actually mentioned; though her dance features prominently in both). The basic story line may be given in short summary. The Babylonian princess Salomé abandons a banquet given by her stepfather, King Herod. On the terrace outside his castle, she becomes intrigued by the voice of the prophet Iokanaan (Wilde's name for John the Baptist), who is imprisoned in a cistern. She persuades the guard, a 'Young Syrian', to let her see him. Being physically attracted to Iokanaan, she urges him to allow her a kiss from his lips, but this the prophet refuses. The Young Syrian, who has shown infatuated interest in Salomé's beauty, is so disturbed by the Princess's sexual interest in Iokanaan that he stabs himself out of jealousy and despair. When Herod, who is likewise driven by sexual attraction to Salome, insists that she dances for him, she agrees on the condition that he will grant her a wish. After the dance, she asks for Iokanaan to be beheaded. Herod offers her all his wealth and his kingdom in lieu of her demand for the prophet's head, but she is adamant and Iokanaan is killed. Triumphantly holding his decapitated head, Salomé can now finally kiss the prophet. However, this display of sexual perversity becomes too much for Herod, who consequently orders Salomé killed. In the last scene, the Princess is crushed under the shields of Herod's guardsmen.

Salomé: 'The daughter of too many fathers'

As a theme, the beheading of the prophet has fascinated many painters and writers of the Symbolist movement. Of visual representations, we find the famous study by Georges Henry Regnault, a pastel by Lucien Lévy-Dhurmer, two paintings by Gustave Moreau, and one by Pierre Puvis de Chavannes. The figure of Salomé also inspired a well-known painting by Gustav Klimt and drawings by Picasso. Musically, Strauss's *Salomé* (1905), which is based on Wilde's play, is probably the most well-known production of the story, but the two librettists Paul Milliet and Henri Grémont had already in 1881 produced an opera, *Hérodiade*, with music by Massenet. Among the written material, we find Heine's 'Atta Troll' (1841), J. C. Heywood's *Salome, the Daughter of Herodias* (1862),[15] Mallarmé's *Hérodiade* (1866), Banville's 'La Danseuse' (1870) and 'Hérodiade' (1874), and Flaubert's 'Hérodias' (1877), Arthur Symon's 'The Dance of the Daughters of Herodias' (1897), and Hermann Sudermann's *Johannes* (1898).[16]

A thorough reading of the works predating the play will reveal that Wilde draws widely on this Symbolist/Decadent adaptation of the story rather than the biblical anecdotes alone. Wilde's debt was readily recognised at the time. An anonymous reviewer of the *Pall Mall Gazette* (27 February 1893) wrote: '*Salomé* is a mosaic. Mr. Wilde has many masters, and the influence of each master asserts itself in his pages...the reader of *Salomé* seems to stand in the Island of Voices, and to hear around him and about utterances of friends, the whisperings of demigods'. These voices he assigns to Gautier, Maeterlinck, Schwob and, above all, Flaubert and concludes negatively: 'Salomé' is the daughter of too many fathers. She is a victim of heredity'.[17] Wilde's appropriation of these precursor texts relies partly on direct copying of themes and settings and (in a sense that may almost resemble a Bloomian *misreading*) reversals and transformations of narrative lines. The exact relationship between *Salomé* and its precursors would make an interesting study but must be pursued elsewhere.

On the level of stylistics, Wilde's play is no less self-consciously plagiarising a well-established aesthetics. The terse and incantatory repetition of words and sentences has mistakenly been attributed to the author's far from perfect command of the French language. Yet, this is missing the point. Wilde was deliberately framing his verbal style so that the play would be recognised as belonging to a particular *genre*. The way the dialogue is constructed as choppy phrasebook sentences closely resembles the peculiar diction of the *symboliste* playwright Maurice Maeterlinck's first published play *Princesse Maleine* (1889), for which William Heinemann had asked Wilde to write an introduction.[18] In the to date only book-length study on *Salomé*, William Tydeman and Stephen Price have half-salvaged Praz' notion of the play as a 'parody' by suggesting that what may have started out as a Maerterlinckian pastiche gradually came to take on a life of its own, when Wilde realised the dramatic potential of his play.[19]

The musical quality of the many chorus-like repetitions seems to fulfil the idea that Walter Pater, the chief progenitor of the Aesthetic movement in England, expressed in his famous essay on Giorgione from *The Renaissance* (1873, revised 1877 and 1888), that '*All art constantly aspires towards the condition of music*'.[20] Like in many French *symboliste* plays, there is here an aspiration towards a musical method of organising the dramatic composition. The recurrent image-clusters serve the same function as a Wagnerian *leitmotif.* In a passage from *De Profundis*, I shall quote later in another connection, Wilde himself writes of *Salomé* in terms of 'refrains', 'recurring motifs' and 'ballad', commenting that it 'is so like a piece of music'.[21] Stylistically, one of the densest passages of the play is found in Salomé's expression of her sexual attraction to Iokanaan:

> *Salomé*. Iokanaan! I am amorous of thy body! Thy body is white like the lilies of a field that the mower hath never mowed. Thy body is white like the snows that lie on the mountains, like the snows that lie on the mountains of Judæa, and come down into the valleys. The roses in the garden of the Queen of Arabia is not so white as thy body. Neither the roses of the garden of the queen of Arabia, nor the feet of the dawn when they light on the leaves, nor the breast of the moon when she lies on the breast of the sea ... there is nothing in the world so white as thy body. Let me touch thy body. (*CW* 559)

The images used in Salomé's wooing (she will later praise the blackness of his hair and the redness of his mouth) are taken from the much disputed Song of Songs, the clearly erotic Book of Solomon, which somehow found its way into both the Jewish and Christian biblical canon. In fact, almost all of the objects Salomé will draw in for comparison (grapes, snow, lilies, cedar etc.) are to be found here. It is interesting here to note that Paul Fort's Théâtre d'Art (Paris) in late 1891 staged a dramatisation of the Song of Songs by Paul-Napoleon Roinard. This was at a time when Wilde was a resident in the French capital and working on his manuscript for *Salomé*. It is possible that Wilde would have known about this dramatisation in advance, as several of his Parisian associates were involved in the production.[22] In any case, this piece of Hebrew verse was a model example of *synaesthesia*, which had become the hallmark of Baudelairean and Symbolist expression. For, no other book of the Scriptures contains such exceptional mingling of sight, sound and smell. This shows how *Salomé* openly signals its debt to a particular category of literary representation popular at the time and means us to recognise that fact.

Decadent Drama

Salomé is set in the historic reign of the Roman Tetrarch of Galilee and Petrea, Herod Antipas. Wilde's conception of Herod, as the Roman heathen, who has stolen the 'veil of the Sanctuary' from 'the Temple of Jerusalem' (*CW* 566), is entirely within the framework of Decadent self-representation, as the Decadents often associated contemporary culture with the Roman Empire in its decline – caught no more clearly than in Mallarmé's famous dictum: 'I am the Empire in its *Decadence*'.[23] The action of the play takes place during a lavish feast at Herod's court. This is a feast teeming with Decadent dandies, who with their 'painted eyes and painted cheeks, and frizzled hair curled in twisted coils' and 'long nails of jade and russet cloaks' (*CW* 555) belong as much to the aristocratic society balls of *fin-de-siècle* Paris or London as it does to Rome of the first century. The dramatic strategy by which historical settings can be made to reflect modern situations had been theorised by Wilde as early as 1883. In a letter to Mary Anderson, he explains that in *The Duchess of Padua* (1883) the audiences will find modern life transposed to the action of an Italian tragedy: '*the essence of art is to produce the modern idea under an antique form*' (*Letters* 137).

Wilde's drama is finely tuned to catch the spiritual and religious dejection of modernity. The death of God is one of the recurrent scenarios enacted in artistic and philosophical representations as a paradigm for modernity, emblematised in Wagner's *Götterdämmerung*, Nerval's Jesus descending from the sky crying: 'Non, Dieu n'existe pas!', 'Dieu n'est pas, Dieu n'est plus' ('Le Christ aux Oliviers', ll. 8, 14), or in Heidegger's definition of the modern age as an era of 'der entflohenen Götter' (the 'flown gods').[24] The *fin-de-siècle* artist felt intensely what J. Hillis Miller has referred to as the 'disappearance of God', i.e. the inability of the Victorian artist to maintain a belief in an authority that orders the cosmos.[25] In *Salomé*, there is from the very beginning an endless strife about religion unfolding. The Jews, for instance, argue amongst themselves about who and what God is, and whether there are angels, but, significantly, never reach any agreement. We are also told that the Cappadocian has been looking for his lost gods in the mountains, but in vain: 'I called them by their names, and they did not come. I think they are dead' (*CW* 553).

There is also another ways in which the play reflects on a *fin-de-siècle* mentality. What is more fundamental in the conception of Wilde's Salomé than the expression of emancipated feminism or homosexual subtext is the way she summarises the Decadent writers' fascination with death. We observe how Salomé's wooing of Iokanaan is a lust for sterility and artificiality. Salomé is infatuated with Iokanaan's resemblance to images of death: 'How wasted be is? He is like a thin ivory statue. He is like an image of silver. I am sure he is chaste, as the moon is. He is like a moonbeam, like a shaft of silver. His flesh must be very cold, cold as ivory'. We are here reminded of Olive Custance's poem 'The White Statue', which begins 'I love you, silent statue!' and yearns 'To press warm lips against your cold white mouth!' (ll. 1, 8).[26] The unnatural connection between death and pleasure can also be in Baudelaire's eulogy over the beauty of a carcass in 'Une charogne', John Gray's rapture on the suicide of Ophelia 'On a Picture' or

Lionel Johnson's musings on the 'perfect death' in 'Nihilism'.[27] Similarly, in Gabrielle D'Annunzio's novel *The Triumph of Death* (1894), the protagonist claims that 'death attracts me' and finally commits suicide by throwing himself off a hill-top.[28] Death is not so much a last desperate resort as an expression of the Decadent desire to violate and thwart everything that is healthy and natural. Already from the beginning, Salomé's lust after Iokanaan is of the Decadent order, as it may be seen from her macabre praises: 'Thy body is white like the lilies of a field that the mower hath never mowed' and 'Thy mouth ... is like a pomegranate cut in twain with a knife of ivory' (*CW* 559) – revealing the true nature of Salomé's desire.

In fact, Wilde re-invents the biblical story of the beheading of John the Baptist as drama of depravity, unnatural perversion and sexual deviance, as this became a cult for what was termed 'the bad Nineties'. Arthur Symons, the leading Decadent poet writing in English, made this clear by making it his artistic intention to derive pleasure from the poet's 'spiritual and moral perversity'.[29] *Salomé* is a wall-to-wall tapestry of Decadent motifs. The long list of metaphors for degenerate human practices reaches absurd proportions. In addition to Salomé's sexual lust towards all the death-like aspects of Iokanaan's body (a sick *eros* towards a Kristevan *abject*), which in turn will lead to near-cannibalism. There is the Page's homosexual interest in the Young Syrian. There is Herod's fratricide, his incestuous marriage with his brother's wife, and his incestuous lust for his brother's daughter. These are all examples of the destructive energies in man, his vice and perverted sexuality, which is rampantly exhibited in the fiction of Wilde's contemporaries Jean Lorrain, Rachilde, Pierre Louÿs, Joséphin Péladan and A. C. Swinburne. Generally, a fascination with the exploration of the fringes of sexuality meant a renewed interest in the work of Marquis de Sade, which was extensively re-published during the 1880s).[30] As a loosely defined artistic direction, Decadence is a celebration rather than a lamentation of man's social and moral decline. It went beyond a simple revival of the Byronic obsession with 'great, bad man' to become a daring exploration of a decaying civilisation and the human decaying with it. The acceptance of the modern condition was its triumph.

This is perhaps no better illustrated than on front page of an issue of Anatole Baju's magazine *Le Décadent,* where we find the programmatic statement:

Not to recognise the state of Decadence we are in would be the height of insensibility ... religion, customs, justice, everything decays ... Society is disintegrating under the corrosive action of a decaying civilisation ... We will be the stars of an ideal literature ... in a word, we will be the Mahdis screaming and preaching eternally the dogma of elixir, the quintessential word of triumphant *décadisme*.[31]

The critic Matei Calinescu has pointed out that the appearance of the aesthetic-historical category of Decadence is simply the 'culmination' of a wider calling into question the idea of progress, material as well as spiritual.[32] The latter half of the nineteenth century had gradually, but steadily, failed to sustain the mid-century pride in scientific and social progress. To understand Decadence as an artistic movement, we must understand it on this background; the widespread notion that civilisation had entered into a 'crisis'. The Austrian critic Max Nordau led a diatribe against modernity, summarising its whole essence in the title of his book *Degeneration* (*Entartung* 1892 – Eng. trans. 1895). Nordau gave a voice to a general mood, making *degeneration* the pathological term by which the age was discussed. *Degeneration* was seen as a real disease in the population. The notion 'underlying the word *fin-de-siècle*', he writes, 'means a practical emancipation from traditional discipline… unbridled lewdness, the unchaining of the beast in man… the trampling under foot of all barriers which enclose brutal greed of lucre and lust of pleasure … the shameless ascendency [sic] of base impulses and motives'.[33] He would at length connect the unnatural *fin-de-siècle* literary and artistic tendencies and fashions' with the statistical increase in 'crime, madness and suicide' and a host of other pathological diseases of *degeneration* (34-44).

If Wilde would not have read Nordau at the time of composing his play, he was almost certainly familiar with the work of Nordau's friend and teacher, the Italian criminologist Cesare Lombroso (to whom *Degeneration* is dedicated). Lombroso's works had been translated into English and were popular enough for Wilde to refer to them in prison. In his attempt to appeal to the Home Secretary for an attenuated sentence, he cites Lombroso's theory that there is an 'intimate connection between madness and the literary and artistic temperament' (*Letters* 401-05). Especially Lombroso's *The Man of Genius* (which came out as part of the Contemporary Science Series edited by Havelock Ellis in 1891) spells out the connection between art and crime. In an advanced civilisation that allows the education of an over-cerebral elite, certain modes of artistic representation can be seen to reflect a civilisational insanity. In the 'Conclusion' to the book, Lombroso sums up his long psychological observations of insanity in art: 'Between the physiology of the man of genius, therefore, and the pathology of the insane, there are many points of coincidence; there is even continuity'. His enumeration of the symptoms of insanity reads almost like a checklist of Wilde's style in *Salomé*:

> In literature and science, a tendency to puns and plays upon words…an extreme predilection for the rhythm and assonances of verse in prose writing, and even an exaggerated degree of originality may be considered as morbid phenomena. So also is the mania of writing in Biblical form, in detached verses, and with special favourite words, which are underlined, or repeated many times, and a certain graphic symbolism.[34]

This may further go to show how Wilde in *Salomé* – a play occupied with what Lombroso called 'sexual perversion', which he locates in Baudelaire and other writers (316) – deliberately constructed a palimpsest of the mood and tendencies of the age.

Fin de Siècle, Fin de Globe

It is perhaps not surprising that the *fin-de-siècle*, so concerned with the notion of the end, will understand the decline of Western civilisation in eschatological terms (*eschatos,* Greek 'last'). Nordau, wrote that 'In our days there have arisen … vague qualms of a Dusk of Nations, in which all suns and all stars are gradually waning, and mankind with all its institutions and creations is perishing in the midst of a dying world…the horror of world-annihilation has laid hold of men's minds' (3). Eugen Weber has in a recent book treated how the *fin-de-siècle* arts coincided with a flurry of actual apocalyptic prophecies, such as those propounded by Leon Bloy and Cammille Flammerion.[35] Throughout *Salomé*, there is a significant strain of apocalyptic rhetoric that comments directly on its self-conscious pose as a *fin-de-siècle* play. The imprisoned Iokanaan, whom we hear only as a disembodied voice in most of the play, is a dissident speaking against the tyrannical Roman Empire, so absorbed in its own lust and moral depravity. He does so is in a form of prophecy that promises God's Last Judgment on the evils kings on earth:

... the sun shall become black like sackcloth of hair, and the moon shall become like blood, and the stars of the heavens shall fall upon the earth like ripe figs that fall from the fig-tree, and the kings of the earth shall be afraid. (*CW* 566)

The words here fairly accurately follow those of St. John in the Book of Revelation (6:12-15). This is the concluding book of the biblical canon, which, in the mode of symbolic visions, describes how human vice and sin will culminate in the days before the Last Judgment only then to be destroyed and eradicated for all eternity in the Lord's Kingdom. In the play, Iokanaan's prophesy actually comes true – at least in the minds of Herod and Herodias. Towards the end, they look up to the sky:

Herod. ... Ah! Look at the moon! She has become red. She has become red as blood. Ah! the prophet prophesied truly ...

Herodias. Oh., yes, I see it well, and the stars are falling like unripe figs, are they not? And the sun is becoming black like sackcloth of hair, and the kings of the earth are afraid. That at least one can. see. The prophet is justified of his words in that at least, for truly the kings of the earth are afraid... (*CW* 569)

Imagining the total victory that results from the battle between the evil kings of earth and the army of heaven, St. John directs our attention to the loser's faith without flinching:

Then I saw an angel standing in the sun, and with a loud voice he called to all the fowls that fly in the midst of heaven, Come, gather yourselves together unto the supper of the great God, That ye may eat the flesh of kings, the flesh of captains, the flesh of mighty men, the flesh of horses and of them that sit on them, and the flesh of all men, both free and bond, both small and great. (Rev. 19.17-18)

The threat of the biblical birds of death, which will punish sinful kings, is present throughout the play. For instance, when Herod feels 'an icy wind' and despairs: 'wherefore do I hear in the air this beating of wings? Ah! One might fancy a huge black bird that hovers over the terrace, Why can I not see it, this bird? The beat of its wings is terrible. The breath of the wind of its wings is terrible' (*CW* 568).[36] It is out of the fear of Judgment that Herod will finally hide himself at the end of the play. A parallel between the cultivated vice of the Decadent movement and the preponderance of sin that will precede the Last Judgment lies at the core of the play. It is to this aspect, I shall now turn.

Salomé: 'A New Hedonism'

It is Heine's 'Atta Troll', which provides Wilde with the macabre finale in which the prophet's decapitated head is kissed. But Wilde's conception of this scene is entirely different. He makes Salomé and not her mother perform the act. In fact, Wilde is the first in the tradition to shift all initiative and evil action from Herodias to Salomé. And whereas Heine had Herodias kiss the prophet only as an imposed punishment, Wilde's Salomé is moved purely by her own perverted lust. This is unequivocally testified by Salomé's reply to Herod, after he has accused her of acting on her mother's behest: 'I do not heed my mother. It is for my own pleasure that I ask the head of Iokanaan in a silver charger' (*CW* 570).

Despite her centrality in the plot and the fact that her name gives the play its title, Salomé is clearly *not* the tragic character of Wilde's 'Tragedy'. Her death at the end of the play is an event without any tragic content. If we judge her character within the logic of dramatic composition, she evokes terror – never pity. It has gone unnoticed in critical commentaries, how the figure of Salomé's fits into the schema laid out in the Revelation of St. John and followed by Wilde in the play. In the final all-out battle between Good and Evil – the army of God, Christ, and the company of the earthly Saints will be faced with an initial opposition raised by Satan, the Beast and the Great Whore. In St. John, the Great Whore, or 'Babylon the Great, Mother of Harlots and abominations of the earth' is the female figure representing mankind's sinning. It is no coincidence that Wilde's Salomé is a 'Babylonian' princess. The connection is made by Iokanaan in the play: 'Daughter of Babylon! Daughter of Sodom! ... Daughter of adultery', 'Ah! The wanton one! The harlot! Ah! The daughter of Babylon' (*CW* 565).

In seeing Salomé as the biblical 'Whore of Babylon', Wilde was here most certainly influenced by a passage in Karl-Joris Huysmans's *A rebours* (1884) – a work which provided a 'breviary of the Decadence' as Arthur Symons commented. At one point, Huysmans's hyper-Decadent anti-hero, Jean Floressas Des Esseintes, goes into a rapture from looking at one of Moreau's paintings of Salomé. His appraisal of painting turns into a highly sexual vision, in which he sees 'her breasts rise and fall, the nipples hardening ... the lascivious movements of her loins; who saps the morale and breaks the will of a king with the heaving of her breasts, the twitching of her belly, the quivering of her thighs'. The radiant sexuality that Moreau has given Salomé in his modern interpretation of the figure signifies something more than the biblical source material can possibly contain:

> She had become, as it were, the symbolic incarnation of undying Lust the Goddess of immortal Hysteria ... the monstrous Beast, indifferent, irresponsible, insensible, poisoning, like the Helen of ancient myth ... She no longer had her origins in Biblical tradition; she could not even be likened to the living image of Babylon, the royal harlot of Revelations, bedecked like herself with precious stones and purple robes, with paint and perfume, for the Whore of Babylon was not thrust by a fateful power, by an irresistible force, into the alluring iniquities of debauch ... ultimate cause of every sin and every crime ...[37]

As Salomé to Des Esseintes sums up the very nature of vice, so is Wilde's Princess a prism of all of human sin since the beginning of times. This is given a comic turn in the scene where Herod asks Salomé to take a bite of the apple he is holding out for her. Wilde here casts Salome as Eve in the garden of Eden just before she is about to commit the Original Sin:

> *Herod.* ... Salomé come and eat fruits with me. I love to see in a Fruit the mark of thy little teeth. Bite but a little of this fruit that I may eat what is left.
>
> *Salomé*. I am not hungry Tetrarch. (*CW* 562)

But though she here rejects to bite the fruit, this is only false pretence, for after she has had her will and Iokanaan has been beheaded, she will later taste his decapitated head as a sweeter fruit:

> *Salomé*. Ah! Thou wouldst not suffer me to kiss thy mouth, Iokanaan. Well, I will kiss it now. I will bite it with my teeth as one bites a ripe fruit. Yes, I will kiss thy mouth, Iokanaan. (*CW* 573)

The figure of 'Whore of Babylon', varying with the time, place and persuasion of the interpreter, has been called in to identify the Jews, the Ottomans, the Pope, France, Charles I, Cromwell, the Church, the aristocracy, capitalism, the American slaveholders or whatever forces in society that the interpreter wanted to oppose. The figure belongs with the kind of apocalyptic image that Tom Thatcher in a recent article has defined as the 'empty metaphor'.[38] The Revelation of St. John is our most important text, as he writes, which utilises 'metaphors and narratives whose emptiness creates a vacuum' so 'the reader is invited to fill this emptiness with material drawn from the intertexts that in some way express her own heritage or experience' (p. 550). Richard Ellmann was the first to suggest that in Salomé Wilde created an image of Decadent philosophy.[39] Subsequently, other critics have pointed out that *Salomé* impresses us as 'a cipher by which the Nineties may be read' and that, in her constant search for sterility and death, she 'fully represents one aspect of Decadent art'.[40] This allegorical function of the figure seems to be corroborated by one of the illustrations Beardsley made to the printed play. In 'The Toilette of Salome', the Princess is shown sitting in a boudoir anachronistically stocked with such 'bad' French authors as Baudelaire, de Sade and Zola.

The allegorical technique employed by Wilde by which Salomé comes to represent a particular mode of art, was a method Wilde also employed in his Decadent novel *The Picture of Dorian Gray*, published in 1891 – the same year that he composed *Salomé.* That the title character is at once a psychological study of degenerate human nature and the art of the Decadents, who embraced this, is further evidenced by the fact that he encompasses both aspects: existing both as a human and as a picture. Dorian Gray is the Decadent Dandy who derives pleasure from the 'corruption of his own soul' (*CW* 206) and will look on evil 'simply as a mode through which he could realise his conception of the beautiful' (*CW* 236). He is the embodiment of a society that is morally ill, a fact to which he readily admits: 'Culture and corruption...I have known something of both' (*CW* 150). Dorian's function as a sign for the age is pointed out to the reader near the beginning of the book, where he is described as a 'new Hedonism...what our century wants ... its visible symbol' (*CW* 35).

On the allegorical level, *The Picture of Dorian Gray* is an account of the confrontation between a Victorian 'ivory tower' theory of art and a modern literature exploring the depravity of modern man. The lovely Sybil Vane, the actress Dorian courts purely for her *artificiality* as a bad actress, is a figure of the lily-white Victorian illusion of spotless innocence that has now come to pass. Confronted with Dorian, and the Decadence he represents, Sybil cannot survive. Her purity is ruined by 'the stain of an age ... at once sordid and sensual', as Lord Henry Wotton reflects on her suicide (*CW* 165). The fact that Sybil's name connects with Hellenic mythology, and that she is at one point described as a 'Greek head' points us towards the opposition between Greek and modern art that we find in Walter Pater's *The Renaissance*, which has already been quoted. This piece of highly idiosyncratic art history more than any other book dominated the age, albeit more for its programmatic statements on art and its prescriptive approach to its enjoyment than for its value as a historical study. It is for these qualities Wilde in *De Profundis* refers to it as 'that book which has had such a strange influence over my life' (*CW* 917-18).

Many Decadents saw Pater's book as a spiritual beacon lighting the artist at the *fin-de-siècle* to the creation of a wholly 'modern' form of art. In the essay on Leonardo da Vinci, Pater establishes that the unaffected beauty of the Greek art can no longer satisfy contemporary man. For with the Greeks an awareness of profanity and corruption had not yet evolved. Modern art, he prescribes, must find a way of expressing the discovery that evil had become part of human nature. Pater turned to da Vinci as an artist who, despite his placing in the past, had come closest to creating an ideal for what this 'modern' art was to be. According to Pater, in the painting of Mona Lisa, one finds the rightly balanced combination of pure beauty and pure evil. Mona Lisa is identified equally with St. Anne (the mother of Mary) and the vampire, who 'has been dead many times, and learned the secrets of the grave' (189). In Wilde's play, the characters all look to the moon, which functions as a telltale mirror of Salomé in the way that the portrait shows the real nature of Dorian in *The Picture of Dorian Gray*. It is most likely, I will suggest, that Wilde's conception of Salomé reflected in the moon as both 'a virgin', who 'has never defiled herself ... never abandoned herself to men' *and* 'a woman rising from a tomb' (*CW* 555) had its origin in Pater. But this is not where Pater's influence stops. His contemplation on beauty and the danger it poses to its admirers provides a significant backdrop for the action in *Salomé*. Though, as we shall see, Pater was not alone in these speculations.

The Tragedy of Beauty

As one critic has recently commented, *Salomé* is 'a play which is in every sense about the nature and production of the gaze and its effects and consequences'. Throughout, the dangers of the gaze that insatiably seeks for beauty 'is both thematised and theatricalised'.[41] A victim is the Young Syrian, whose gaze is already led astray as he 'much loved to gaze at himself in the river' (*CW* 560), but it is from gazing too long at Salomé's beauty that he will finally commit suicide. His gaze becomes his destiny, having ignored the Page's warning that 'You are always looking at her. You look at her too much, it is dangerous to look at people in such fashion. Something terrible may happen' (*CW* 553). Herod slips in the pool of blood that the Young Syrian's death leaves behind. This he takes as an omen, as the Young Syrian's mistake is also his own. For, more than anyone Herod has surrendered his will to the gaze.

It is to Herod we must look to approach an understanding of the play as 'A Tragedy'. He is the only character in the play, who undergoes any real change. Herod's realisation that he 'has looked to long' at Salomé and yielded to the fatal attraction of her beauty fits into an Aristotelian scheme of *tragedy*. Herod's affliction in realising his 'error of judgement' (*hamartia*) involves the three key-elements of tragic representation. There is the reversal (*peripeteia*) by which Salomé from having dominated all other characters in the play will finally be destroyed. There is recognition (*anagnorisis*) as Herod comes to understand that his infatuation with Salomé's beauty has brought death and terror. This recognition takes the form of an involuntary *imitatio Christi* 'involving pain', 'physical agony' and metaphorical 'wounding' (*pathos*) (see Sophocles, *Poetics* 1.451a). Much like Sophocles' Oedipus, he sees no alternative than to blind himself and flee:

> *Herod*. Come! I will not stay in this place. Surely some terrible thing will befall. ... put out the torches. I will not look at things, I will not suffer things to look at me. Put out the torches! Hide the moon! Hide the stars! Let us hide ourselves in our palace, Herodias. I begin to be afraid. (CW 574).

It is only appropriate that Herod, whose error has been his 'gaze' attempts to extinguish sight.

Significantly, Herod's 'recognition' resembles a religious conversion:

> *Herod*. Pour water on my hand. Give me snow to eat. Loosen my mantle. Quick! quick! Loosen my mantle. Nay, but leave it. It is my garland that hurts me, my garland of roses, The flowers are like fire. They have burned my forehead. (He tears the wreath from his head, and throws it on the table.) Ah! I can breathe now. How red those petals are! They are like stains of blood on the cloth. (CW 568).

Herod feels his wreath of roses become a crown of thorns, whereby Iokanaan's vision of the Coming of Christ finally comes true – as a purgation of evil within Herod himself. These *stigmata* fulfil the biblical promise of eradicating Evil, albeit in a way that is decidedly tragic rather than celebratory. Herod does not become a Christian, but he realises that his worshipping of Salomé's beauty was his error. As in many other conversion stories, from Augustine and onwards, what is truly interesting about the conversion is not as much what the as yet uncertain future may bring, but the convert's *deconversion* from his former beliefs. From a higher state of consciousness the subject is now, for the first time, enabled to reflect on the evil ways of the past.[42] For Herod, it is only after the mesmerised gaze at Salomé is broken that he achieves introspection, addressing Salomé: 'Thy beauty has grievously troubled me, and I have looked at thee over-much. Nay, but I will look at thee no more'. (*CW* 571). As it is revealed in his speech to Herodias, his eyes have been opened to the real nature of the beauty he lustfully has coveted: 'She is monstrous, thy daughter, I tell thee she is monstrous. In truth, what she has done is a great crime. I am sure that it is. A crime against some unknown God' (*CW* 572).

The idea of Beauty as a cruel *femme fatale* that destroys her worshippers was a common metaphor at the time. One example is Baudelaire's reflections on Beauty in *Les Fleurs du Mal* (1857). In 'Hymne à la Beauté', this ideal is addressed as a personified goddess, the 'monstrous scourge' whose 'kisses are a drug', her 'mouth the urn':

> Tu marches sur des morts, Beauté, dont tu te moques;
> De tes bijoux l'Horreur n'est pas le moins charmant,
> Et le Meurtre, parmi tes plus chères breloques,
> Sur ton ventre orgueilleux danse amoureusement.
>
> L'éphémère ébloui vole vers toi, chandelle,
> Crépite, flambe et dit: Bénissons ce flambeau!
> L'amoureux pantelant incliné sur sa belle
> A l'air d'un moribond caressant son tombeau.[43]

[You walk upon the dead, O Beauty, scorning them / Horror is not the least fascinating among your gems. / Murder, one of your dearest trinkets / Dances lustfully on your proud navel. / The dazzled moth wings towards you, its candle. / Cracks and flames, and cries: I bless this torch! /

The quivering lover outstretched on his beloved / Looks like a dying man caressing his own tomb (my translation)]

Wilde's Salomé shares a common metaphorical frame of reference with Baudelaire's Beauty. Baudelaire's moth that is inexorably drawn to its death in the candle-flame and yet still reveres the instrument of its death is basically the same metaphor we find in the story of the Young Syrian, who praises Salomé's beauty as he kills himself for it (see *CW* 559-60). Baudelaire's unresolved questions elsewhere in the poem of whether Beauty derives from Heaven or Hell and whether she is an 'Angel' or a 'Siren' corresponds to the questions asked about Salomé in Wilde's play. Some critics strive to see a development in Salomé, starting out as pubescent and virginal Innocence to become vampire-like Evil at the end of the play. But there is no real development in Salomé's character. We are much closer to Baudelaire's conception of the double-edged nature of Beauty. Her seemingly serene purity is deceptive as her path is strewn with the corpses of the worshippers she has destroyed. What we see in the figure of Salomé is a gradual unveiling of the inherent Evil in Beauty.

In his notebook, Gustave Moreau wrote that he saw the Salomé he painted as an 'emblem of sensuality, of unhealthy curiosity, and of that terrible fate reserved for searchers after a nameless ideal'.[44] This brings to the centre of attention the theme of the Decadent aesthete, who in the search after beauty is destroyed. Wilde's Herod may be read as a representation of the artist searcher constantly directing his gaze after ephemeral Beauty that cannot possibly mix with mortal life. For, as Wilde himself commented on Salomé, 'her beauty has nothing of this world about it'.[45] The theme is regurgitated by William Butler Yeats in *A Full Moon in March* (1935), which is best seen as 'reading' Wilde's drama, summarised into the condensed form of the Japanese *Noh* play. Yeats not only has the moon as a central symbol but also features a cruel virgin Queen, who demands the beheading of a Swineherd. Displacing the character functions slightly, it is the Swineherd, who seeks the Queen's beauty. Helen Hennessy Vendler has seen this as 'the meeting of Muse and poet', the Swineherd being the symbol of human 'mire and blood', which is destroyed in the attempt to reach super-human Beauty. In the same vein, Harold Bloom, has seen it as 'a final fable of the moon-like Muse and the self-sacrificing poet'.[46]

That the cult of Beauty could be dangerous to those who made this pursuit a philosophy of life is suggestively told through the exclusions and revisions Walter Pater made in the re-published versions of *The Renaissance*. The original 'Conclusion' of 1873 to the book became infamous as the English Decadents adopted it as their manifesto. Pater here propounds the idea that the purpose of existence is 'to rouse, to startle it [the human spirit] to a life of constant and eager observation'. It is in the very 'moment' of sensual enjoyment of observations that one really lives: 'Not the fruit of experience, but experience itself, is the end'. Pater's philosophy is consequently a sensualist Epicureanism: 'To burn always with this hard, gemlike flame, to maintain this ecstasy, is success in life'. The unceasing search after sensation becomes a remedy for the decay that marks modern civilisation, for 'While all melts under our feet, we may well grasp at any exquisite passion, or any contribution to knowledge that seems by a lifted horizon to set the spirit free for a moment, or any stirring of the senses, strange dyes, strange colours, and curious odours, or the work of the artist's hands, or the face one's friend'. Not to fall into the abyss of the dreariness of modern life, 'our only chance', Pater writes, 'lies in expanding that interval, in getting as many pulsations as possible into the given time … Of such wisdom, the poetic passion, the desire of beauty, the love of art for its own sake, has most'.[47]

In the second edition of the book (1877), Pater felt compelled to omit the notorious 'Conclusion', though the reason for the exclusion remained unexplained. Yet, when it was restored in the third edition of 1888, it had been altered. This alteration is explained in a footnote: 'This brief "Conclusion" was omitted in the second edition of this book, as I conceived that it might possibly mislead some of those young men into whose hands it might fall'.[48] In so far that Herod is a representation of the Aesthete-cum-Decadent in possession of typical Decadent objects of art, such as 'beautiful, white peacocks' with 'their beaks gilded with gold' and feet 'stained with purple' (we may here recall Des Esseintes's gilded tortoise) and a long list of precious stones (*CW* 571-72), it is possible to view both him and certainly Dorian Gray as evolving out of Pater's hypothetical men of the age he imagined could be led astray by his philosophy of 'sensationalism'.

Recently, Vicki Mahaffey has noted that a pervasive theme found in Wilde is the dangerous 'slippage between the personal and the textual'. This is illustrated in *The Picture of Dorian Gray*, which documents the horror of 'interchanging life and art through the medium of Dorian's portrait. The same, she notes, is later dramatised from the humorous side in *The Importance of Being Earnest* seen in 'the confusion of written and human characters ... when Miss Prism mistakes a novel for a baby'.[49] If we look at the first reviews of *The Picture of Dorian Gray*, they generally condemned the book for treating immoral subjects. This, however, was met with resistance by Wilde. In a letter to the editor of *St. James's Gazette*, Wilde explicitly pointed to the 'terrible moral' of the book:

> And the moral is this: all excess, as well as all renunciation brings its own punishment. The painter Basil Hallward, worshipping beauty far too much, as most painters do, dies by the hand of one in whose soul he has created a monstrous and absurd vanity. Dorian Gray, having led a life of mere sensation and pleasure, tries to kill conscience, and at that moment kills himself. Lord Henry Wotton seeks to be merely the spectator of life. He finds that those who reject the battle are more deeply wounded than those who take part in it. (*Letters* 259)

In a second letter to the *Gazette*, Wilde wrote: 'It is proper that limitation should be placed on action. It is not proper that limitations should be placed on art' (*Letters* 261).[50] A statement that may be seen to echo Pater's warning against his own philosophy of 'sensationalism'. Pater himself, who reviewed the book in the *Bookman* (November 1891), was apparently well aware of the lesson Wilde was trying to put across, calling Dorian 'a quite unsuccessful experiment in Epicurianism in life as a fine art'.[51] *Salomé*, where so much of the dialogue is concerned with the 'looking too much', is, in much the same way, a cautionary tale of seeking Beauty.

Like at the end of in *The Picture of Dorian Gray*, where the eponymous protagonist tries to destroy the painting that has so driven his life to Decadent perversion, Herod's only escape is a destruction of the beauty that has clouded his judgement. With much pain he orders the soldiers to crush Salomé under their shields - destroying the very object he desired. But if Herod is punished for his excessive gaze, then Iokanaan is punished for his renunciation of gazing. The devoutness of his faith is a total rejection of all temptation: 'I do not wish to look at thee. I will not look at thee, thou art accursed, Salomé thou art accursed' (*CW* 560). It is this fact that Salomé will lament at the very end of the play: 'Ah ! Ah ! wherefore didst thou not look at me, Iokanaan? If thou hadst looked at me thou hadst loved me' (*CW* 574).

Fin-de-Fin: The End of Decadence

Wilde's narrative of Herod's journey into and final rejection of Decadence may in fact share more than a little resemblance to Wilde's own biography, for as Richard Ellmann has suggested, 'Beardsley divined the autobiographical element' of this character. That Herod may be Wilde's personal confession is based on the fact that the illustrator in 'one of his drawings gave the Tetrarch the author's face'.[52] At several points in his letters, Wilde would explain the connection between personal experience and his art. In his confession of 'having lived for pleasure', Wilde writes in *De Profundis*:

> I did it to the full ... There was no pleasure I did not experience. I threw the pearl of my soul into a cup o wine. I went down the primrose path to the sound of flutes. I lived on honeycomb. But to have continued the same life would have been wrong. Because it would have been limiting. I had to pass on ... Of course all this is foreshadowed and prefigured in my art ... a great deal of it is hidden away in the note of Doom that like a purple thread run through the gold cloth of *Dorian Gray* ... it is one of the refrains whose recurring motifs make *Salome* so like a piece of music and bind it together as a ballad... (*CW* 922)

Another letter written from Reading Gaol to Douglas (2 June 1897) yields a similar insight:

If I were asked of myself as a dramatist, I would say that my unique position was that I had taken the Drama, the most objective form known to art, and made it as personal a mode of expression as the Lyric or the Sonnet, while enriching the characterisation of the stage, and enlarging – at any rate in the case of *Salome* – its artistic horizon. (*Letters* 589)

Yet, one should not overestimate the importance of such statements. Wilde was capable of finding inspiration in real life and then, adding a good measure of poetic licence, making it a generalisation about the human condition. This practice is not least suggested by the fictionalisation of his acquaintance John Gray into his Decadent protagonist Dorian Gray.[53]

Wilde's protracted journey into a life of pleasure and his final arrival at a station from which he would reject his former preoccupations is eerily reflected in the lives of almost all the prominent Decadent writers in England. They all came to retract from their dalliances with Decadence. For many the rejection of Decadence was intimately connected with a conversion to Catholicism. This was the case for Lionel Johnson, Ernest Dowson, Aubrey Beardsley, Frederick Rolfe (also known as Baron Corvo), John Francis Bloxam, Katherine Bradley and Edith Cooper (who wrote under the pseudonym Michael Field), Renée Vivien, and others. As Ellis Hanson has recently documented, 'No other literary movement can claim so many converts to Rome'.[54] Wilde himself constantly flirted with Catholicism. His first poetry is distinctly Catholic and he would eventually, on his deathbed, find consolation in the Catholic faith, which he for a time in his life had abandoned. Even in the writings of a poet like John Gray, who had already converted to Catholicism as early as 1890, there is a marked conversion to be seen between his Decadent masterpiece *Silverpoints* (1893) and the later devotional verse of *Spiritual Poems* (1896). An exception, however, was Symons, who chose Methodism as a religion after being cured of his insanity.

In France, Huysmans followed a similar pattern with a final conversion to Catholicism, which included taking up life as a lay monk at the Benedictine Abbey of Ligugé. In a preface written twenty years after the first publication of *A rebours*, he would confess that composing the novel had been his salvation. For, not unlike Herod in Wilde's drama, from his explorations of ultimate

Decadent perversion in *A rebours* and the occult and satanic *Là bas* (1891), the seeds of hope had been sown: 'It was through the glimpse of supernatural evil that I first obtained insight into the supernatural of good. The one derived from the other'.[55] Huysmans's necessary exploration into Evil to arrive at a new mode of being on the other side finds a striking parallel in Nietzsche, where it is worked into a philosophical reflection on modern man. In one of his last works *The Case of Wagner* (1888), he writes: 'Nothing has preoccupied me more profoundly than the problem of Decadence – I had reasons. "Good and evil" is merely a variation of that problem'.[56] Nietzsche, who had been a friend and an admirer of the German composer, writes in from a stage of clear-sightedness that 'Wagner belongs only to my diseases'. He admits in the preface to his book that 'I am just as much a child of my age as Wagner – i.e., I am a Decadent. The only difference is that I recognised the fact, that I struggled against it. The philosopher in me struggled against it' (xxix-xxx). The term 'Decadent' offered Nietzsche a synthesis of what his whole philosophical project set out to reject: the decline, sickness, hostility to life and other related concepts that are constitutive of the modern spirit. *The Case of Wagner* is an attack on the composer (who Baudelaire in his *L'art romantique* of 1869 had praised in ecstatic terms) founded on a very personal experience:

> When in this essay I assert the proposition that Wagner is harmful, I wish no less to assert for whom he is nevertheless indispensable – for the philosopher. Others may be able to get along without Wagner; but the philosopher is not free to do without Wagner. He has to be the bad conscience of his time: for that he needs to understand it best ... I understand perfectly when a musician says today: 'I hate Wagner, but I can no longer endure any other music'. But I'd also understand the philosopher who would declare: 'Wagner sums up modernity. There is no way out one must first become a Wagnerian'. (155-56)[57]

Nietzsche confesses to know the value of truth from having embraced a 'harmful' attraction and, therefore, cannot fail to recognise the value of that attraction. To emerge unscathed after having lived and finally denied the attraction is a key-element in Nietzsche's championing of Life over Death. This, then, is the definitive judgement Nietzsche passed on Decadence: it is the ashes of all human value from which a new, rejuvenated culture may rise. By facing the ultimate depravity of human nature, Decadence becomes (to use Richard Rorty's term) 'therapeutic' thinking. Good requires a passage through negativity. We may here recall the comments Wilde made on the 'moral' of *The Picture of Dorian Gray* to *St. James's Gazette*: it is impossible to stand outside 'the battle', the deepest wound is afflicted on he who tries to be just 'to be merely the spectator of life'.

Though there were parodic forgery of Decadence in circulation at the time - as for instance Gabriel Vicaire and Henri Beauclair's *Les Déliquescences, poèmes décadents d'Adoré Floupette* (1885) - the self-critical moral delivered in works we now see as centrally placed in the Decadent canon should not be overlooked. To mention only the perhaps most famous example, Huysmans gives an enticing account of how des Esseintes succeeds to elevate his life into art, seductively living and breathing sublime beauty. Yet, as a consequence, his body of flesh and blood gradually deteriorates from the unnatural things he asks of it.[58] Like *A rebours*, *Salomé* is a tragedy wrapped in the attire of dark satire. It shows the pursuit of a Decadent life as abortive and finally wrong. Comparing Herod with the autobiographical reflections in *De Profundis* and 'The Ballad of Reading Gaol', it would not be entirely wrong to describe much of Wilde's writing as Faustian, for it often deals with how souls are sold to sin and the tragedy in trying to repurchase the mistaken bargain.

Notes

1. For the psychoanalytical approach, see for instance Alan Bird, *The Plays of Oscar Wilde* (London: Vision, 1977) 54-91. For *Salomé* as a homosexual drama, see Edmund Bergler, 'Salomé, the Turning Point in the Life of Oscar Wilde', *Psychoanalytic Review* 43.1 (1956): 97-103; Kate Millett, *Sexual Politics* (Garden City, NY: Doubleday, 1970) 152-56; Regenia Gagnier, *Idylls of the Marketplace: Oscar Wilde and the Victorian Public* (Stanford: Stanford UP, 1986) 163-69; Jonathan Dollimore, *Sexual Dissidence: Augustine to Wilde, Freud to Foucault* (Oxford: Clarendon, 1991) 64-73; Alan Sinfield, *The Wilde Century: Effeminacy, Oscar Wilde and the Queer Moment* (London: Cassell, 1994), esp. 84-108.

2. Millett 152; San Juan, *The Art of Oscar Wilde* (Princeton: Princeton UP, 1967) 121-22; Gagnier 169.
3. Elaine Showalter, *Sexual Anarchy: Gender and Anarchy at the Fin de Siècle* (London: Bloomsbury, 1991) 144-68; Sally Ledger, *The New Woman: Fiction and Feminism at the Fin-de-Siècle* (Manchester: Manchester UP, 1997); Jane Marcus, '*Salome*: The Jewish Princes was a New Woman' in *Bulletin of the New York Library* 78 (1974-75): 95-112. More generally on the 'New Woman', see Linda Dowling, 'The Decadent and the New Woman in the 1890s', *Nineteenth Century Fiction* 33 (1979): 434-53; and Bram Dijkstra, *Idols of Perversity: Fantasies of Feminine Evil in Fin-de-Siècle Culture* (New York: Oxford UP, 1987).
4. Barbara Charlesworth Gelpi, *Dark Passages: The Decadent Consciousness in Victorian Literature* (Madison: U of Wisconsin P, 1965) 65; Philippe Jullian, *Oscar Wilde,* trans. Violet Wyndham (London: Constable, 1969) 247.
5. M. H. Abrams, *A* Glossary *of Literary Terms*, 7th ed. (Fort Worth: Harcourt Brace, 1999) 55.
6. Mario Praz, *The Romantic Agony,* trans. Angus Davidson (Oxford: Oxford UP, 1933) 298.
7. Rpt. in Karl Beckson, *Oscar Wilde: The Critical Heritage* (New York: Barnes and Noble, 1970) 133.
8. For a history of responses to the production of *Salomé* on the English stage, see William Tydeman and Stephen Price, *Wilde:* Salomé (Cambridge: Cambridge UP, 1996) 78-112. For the debate over *The Picture of Dorian Gray,* see Stuart Mason, *Oscar Wilde, Art and Morality: A Record of Discussion Which Followed the Publication of* Dorian Gray (London: Palmer, 1912).
9. For a discussion of Wilde's problem of licensing the play, see Kerry Powell, *The Theatre of the 1890s* (Cambridge: Cambridge UP, 1990) 33-54.
10. On the illustrations to the printed edition of the play, see Elliot L. Gilbert, 'Tumult of Images: Wilde, Beardsley, and *Salomé*', *Victorian Studies,* 26 (1993): 133-59
11. *The Autobiography of Lord Alfred Douglas* (1929) rpt. (Freeport, NY: Books for Libraries, 1970) 160 n.
12. For further information on the history of the manuscript, see Joseph Donohue, 'Dance, Death and Desire in *Salomé*', *The Cambridge Companion to Oscar Wilde,* ed. Peter Raby (Cambridge: Cambridge UP, 1997) 120-22; Norman Kohl, *Oscar Wilde: The Works of a Non-Conformist Rebel* (Cambridge: Cambridge UP, 1989) 176-80; and Peter Raby, *Oscar Wilde,* British and Irish Authors (Cambridge: Cambridge UP, 1988) 102.
13. All references to Wilde's letters are to *The Letters of Oscar Wilde,* ed. Rupert Hart-Davis (London: Hart Davis, 1962) and will be cited in parentheses in the text. When referring to *Salomé* in his writing, Wilde often omits the final accent. I have followed Hart-Davies's editorial decision to leave it out, when I quote from the letters.
14. On the corrections of the French text, see Wilde's letter to Edmond Bailly (*Letters* 324-25).

15. The poem was first published anonymously, then republished as *Herodias: A Dramatic Poem* under the authors name in 1867. It was known to Wilde, who reviewed it in *Pall Mall Gazette*, 15 February 1888.
16. For the many treatments of the Salome figure, see Sylvia C. Ellis in *The Plays of W. B. Yeats: Yeats and the Dancer* (Basingstoke: Macmillan, 1995) 1-85, and Christa Satzinger, *The French Influences on Oscar Wilde's* The Picture of Dorian Gray *and* Salome (Lewiston: Edwin Mellen, 1994) 235-89.
17. Rpt. in Beckson 135-36.
18. For verbal and visual parallels between *Princesse Maleine* and *Salomé*, see Raby, *Oscar Wilde* 105.
19. See Tydeman and Price, *Wilde* 14.
20. Walter Pater, *The Renaissance: Studies in Art and Poetry* [text of 1893] (London: Macmillan, 1911) 135. The idea of poetry as music ultimately harks back to Mallarmé's writings on Schopenhauer.
21. Oscar Wilde, *Complete Works*, intro. Vyvyan Holland (London: Collins, 1966) 922. All references to Oscar Wilde's literary works are to this edition which will henceforth be cited as *CW* in the main text.
22. Before the Théâtre d'Art, which staged *symboliste* orientated plays, became defunct, productions of both *Princesse Maleine* and *Salomé* were considered. See Tydeman and Price, *Wilde* 6. Generally, on Wilde's stay in France during 1891 and his acquaintances there, see Satzinger 60-86.
23. On the Decadents and their comparisons with the declining Roman Empire, see the introduction in Bonner Mitchell, *Les manifestes littéraires de la belle époque 1888-1914: Anthologie critique* (Paris: Seghers, 1966) 13.
24. Gerard de Nerval, *Selected Writings* (London: Penguin, 1999) 369; Martin Heidegger, *Hölderlin und das Wesen der Dichtung* (Munich: Langen-Müller, 1937) 13.
25. J. Hillis Miller, *The Disappearance of* God: Five Nineteenth-Century Writers (Cambridge, MA: Belknap P of Harvard UP, 1975).
26. Olive Custance, *Opals* (London: John Lane, 1897) 67.
27. Charles Baudelaire, *Oeuvres Complètes*, ed. Claude Pichois (Paris: Gallimard, 1974) 31-32; John Gray, *Silverpoints* (Oxford: Woodstock, 1994) 21; *The Complete Poems of Lionel Johnson*, ed. Ian Fletcher, (London: Unicorn, 1953) 205-06.
28. Gabrielle D'Annunzio, *The Triumph of Death,* trans. Georgina Harding (Sawtry: Dedalus, 1990) 66.
29. Arthur Symons, 'The Decadent Movement in Literature', *Harper's Monthly Magazine* 87 (1893): 858-67.
30. For Wilde's own references to Sade in his work, see Christopher S. Nasaar, 'Wilde's *The Picture of Dorian Gray* and *Salomé*', *The Explicator* 57.1 (1998): 33-35.
31. Rpt. in Mitchell 20. My translation.
32. Matei Calinescu, *Five Faces of Modernity: Modernism, Avant-Garde, Decadence, Kitsch, Postmodernism* (Durham, NC: Duke UP, 1987) 157.
33. Max Nordau, *Degeneration* [Translated from the Second Edition of the German Work] (London, William Heinemann, 1895) 5.

Part Three
1890s/1990s

American Specters:
Two Versions of Ghostliness in American *fin-de-siècle* Culture

Ib Johansen

In his introduction to an early twentieth-century edition of Charles Brockden Brown's *Wieland; or the Transformation: An American Tale* (1798) Fred Lewis Pattee comments on the particular characteristics of the American Gothic and on the narrative strategy adopted by Brockden Brown in order to forward his literary objective(s): 'To secure his Gothic effects *in a new land bare of castles and utterly free from ghosts* called for materials startlingly unusual and yet materials, in the opinion of his readers, not impossible'.[1] In this perspective the ghost story appears to be a genre utterly foreign to the American mentality itself, insofar as the climate of opinion of the public and the ideological outlook of the intellectual élite in America after the War of Independence were rather based on a radical will to demystify and demythologize the ontological premises of any such type of 'credulity', i.e. the belief in the existence of ghosts, spirits, and demons in the 'real' world. Nevertheless, it is an indisputable fact that the ghost story *has* played an important role in American literature from the very beginning; important writers like Irving, Hawthorne, Poe, Henry James, Charlotte Perkins Gilman, Ambrose Bierce, Jack London, and in the twentieth century, H. P. Lovecraft, Stephen King, Paul Auster, Toni Morrison, William S. Burroughs, Alison Lurie, and others, have all of them contributed to the development of the genre on American ground.

In recent years, i.e. in the late 1980s and the 1990s, there have been a remarkable number of books/studies focusing on *the notion of spectrality* itself, and in this context it is interesting to notice that

Fins de Siècle/New Beginnings, ed. Ib Johansen, *The Dolphin* 31, pp. 127-59.

ISBN 87 7288 382 0; ISSN 0106 4487.

the ghost is no longer simply a purely *literary* phenomenon (or a popular superstition): it has likewise invaded the field of philosophy and poststructuralist theory on a grand scale, and at the same time it is obvious that this interest in spectres and phantoms is related to the particular cultural and political climate of the new *fin de siècle*, to what Francis Fukuyama has termed *the end of history*, i.e. to the apparent triumph of liberalism and a new 'world order' since 1989, comprising the end of the Cold War and the breakdown of the communist régimes behind the Iron Curtain.[2] Studies such as Jacques Derrida's *Specters of Marx* (1993, 1994), Jean-Michel Rabaté's *The Ghosts of Modernity* (1993, 1996), and Aris Fioretos's *En bok om fantomer* (*A Book on Phantoms*, 1996) all of them contribute to establishing an extraordinary and pervasive atmosphere of *ghostliness* within the whole cultural sphere of the said (twentieth-century) *fin-de-siècle* and *fin-de-millennium* world. Derrida focuses on Marx's obsession with ghosts, spectres, and spirits – and in this context also on the demise of Marxism as a militant, theoretically aggressive and dominant force in post-communist Europe[3] – whereas Rabaté's approach to 'a spectral modernity'[4] 'aims at combining psychoanalytical and philosophical concepts in order to reread the history of modernity'.[5] Finally, Aris Fioretos's *En bok om fantomer* draws attention to the way(s) in which the (post)modern media world is constantly invaded by spectral presences of various kinds; as a matter of fact, already in Avital Ronell's remarkable *The Telephone Book. Technology, Schizophrenia, Electric Speech* (1989) the telephone is (among other things) classified as 'a ... double and phantom of an organ (like Woman, reduced to the phantom of a missing organ)',[6] and the phone is furthermore posited 'as a missing mouth, displaced genital, a mother's deaf ear or any number of M.I.A.-organs such as the partial object-ear transmitting and suturing the themes of *Blue Velvet*'.[7] Whereas Ronell adopts the language of psychoanalysis in the passages quoted above, we are also reminded of Deleuze and Guattari's *desiring machines* in their *Anti-Oedipus* (1972), for here technology (represented by the telephone) is explicitly eroticized – or to put it the other way round: the body itself is envisaged in terms of a 'weird' technological apparatus.[8] Whether the approach to spectrality is thus Derridean, Lacanian (Rabaté), or Deleuzian (Ronell), the centrality of the concept itself is obvious.

References to the ways in which our culture is (literally) *haunted* by spectres and *revenants* abound in the 1890s as well as in the 1990s, i.e. it looks as if *fin-de-siècle* culture *per se* favours the emergence of all these phantasms, these fleeting and spectral apparitions, on the philosophical/literary/artistic scene. The late Victorian decadent poet Ernest Dowson offers a gloomy vision of the decline and fall of everything human in his poem 'Dregs' (published in *Decorations* in 1899), and here the ghost metaphor is used explicitly to underscore the *vanitas* motif:

> Ghosts go along with us until the end;
> This was a mistress, this, perhaps, a friend.
> With pale, indifferent eyes, we sit and wait
> For the dropt curtain and the closing gate:
> This is the end of all the songs man sings'.[9]

Of course, ghost stories do not by definition belong to any particular period, but the point that should be stressed in our context is that *the sense of an ending*, characteristic of *fin-de-siècle* culture as such, offers a particularly convenient and congenial setting for this type of narrative. At the end of a century, when the (radically) new is already within reach and within sight, the shadows of the past tend to deepen, and it becomes increasingly difficult to come to terms with and *overcome* all these spectral presences.

The precursor text behind a great many modern and post-modern ghost narratives – and likewise behind the above-mentioned recent attempts to come to theoretical terms with the ghosts of modernity (cf. e.g. Derrida, Rabaté, and Fioretos) – is Shakespeare's *Hamlet*, a tragedy that is incidentally also linked up with an early *fin-de-siècle* context, at least if we can trust its modern editor, Harold Jenkins, who argues in his introduction to the Arden edition of the drama: 'A date between the middle of 1599 and the end of 1601 appears ... beyond dispute'.[10] Thus *Hamlet* belongs, in a historical perspective, both to the old and the new century, and the motto of the play could, in this respect, very well be Hermann Broch's famous *noch nicht, und doch schon*.[11] Of course, such an uneasy consciousness with regard to the notion of temporality itself is precisely what is foregrounded in Hamlet's famous couplet after the first encounter with the Ghost: 'The time is out of joint. O cursed spite, / That ever I was born to set it right'.[12] The Prince of Denmark is *both* a representative of Renaissance scepticism (in the manner of Montaigne) *and* a member of the aristocratic caste in a feudal/late feudal society, dominated by another code of behaviour and by another set of (traditional) values and beliefs, i.e. he is hovering between a modern and a premodern world. And the Todorovian structural 'hesitation' vis-à-vis the natural and the supernatural sphere, characteristic of fantastic literature, is already anticipated in Shakespeare's tragedy, where the protagonist is unable to verify the true nature of the ghost; actually, this is why Hamlet uses the stratagem of the play-within-the-play, i.e. in order to test the conscience of the King (Claudius):

> If his occulted guilt
> Do not itself unkennel in one speech,
> It is a damned ghost that we have seen,
> And my imaginations are as foul
> As Vulcan's stithy.[13]

The thing is that

> The spirit I have seen
> May be a devil, and the devil hath power
> T'assume a pleasing shape, yea, and perhaps,
> Out of my weakness and my melancholy,
> As he is very potent with such spirits,
> Abuses me to damn me'.[14]

Even if the protagonist here uses a demonological phraseology, it is obvious that he accentuates the psychological dimension of the temptation scene he sketches in the passage quoted above (cf. the reference to 'my weakness and my melancholy'). This reminds us of Irène Bessière's emphasis on the narrative role of the compact with the devil, thematized so often in early fantastic literature:

> Le contrat diabolique devient thème littéraire lorsqu'on admet qu'il puisse être faux ou illusoire, et que le verdict de sa fausseté appartienne à la fois à l'autorité ecclésiastique et au jugement de l'homme privé.

[The diabolical contract becomes a literary theme, when it is admitted that it can be false or illusory, and furthermore when it is presupposed that the right to assert its falseness belongs simultaneously to the ecclesiastical authorities and to the judgement of the private individual.][15]

According to Harold Bloom, *Hamlet* belongs, together with the playwright from Stratford-on-Avon, to the very centre of the canon,[16] and thus it is no wonder that this tragedy tends to overshadow/dominate not only the philosophical reflections on spectrality of Karl Marx (and Friedrich Engels), in *The German Ideology* (1845-46) and elsewhere, but also the very interpretive project of Derrida in *Specters of Marx*. Actually, one of the points emphasized in Shakespeare's *Hamlet* is that the ethical demand of the ghost is never going to loosen its grip on you: whether you address it as a scholar (Horatio) or as an obedient son (Hamlet), the ghost is going to pursue you to the end of the world, above ground or below ground, and in the meantime it is never going to open its visor (thus it can watch you without being watched itself, which is of course close to Foucault's notion of *panopticism*).[17] Derrida emphasizes the fact that a ghost always begins by *coming back*, i.e. its appearance is, in Freudian terms, based on a compulsion to repeat : 'a specter is always a *revenant*. One cannot control its comings and goings because it *begins by coming back*'.[18] If it is always already there, however, it cannot be *exorcized*. But Marxism teaches us (among other things) *to speak to the spectre* ('Herein lies perhaps, among so many others, an indelible lesson of Marxism').[19] Reading Marx in the light of Shakespeare's *Hamlet* – emphasizing what this play has to tell us about ghosts and ghostliness – offers the philosopher (Derrida) a unique opportunity to highlight the premodern heritage/philosophical premises of the project of Enlightenment, exemplified in this case by the way(s) in which Marx echoes Shakespeare when administering his intellectual *coup de grâce* to his Hegelian and post-Hegelian precursors; what we envisage here is a radical will to *exorcize* all the ghosts of the past (cf., e.g., the many passages in *The German Ideology* where Max Stirner's 'impure history of phantoms'[20] is foregrounded and satirized) – and the inescapable *failure* of the said project on the part of Marx. For the moderns are *also* addressed by the ghost: 'If he loves justice at least, the "scholar" of the future, the "intellectual" of tomorrow should learn it and from the ghost ... they are always *there*, specters, even if they do not exist, even if they are no longer, even if they are not yet'.[21] But this is precisely a lesson the governess in Henry James's *The Turn of the Screw* has *not* learned, and this is why she is unable to come to terms with the (imaginary?) Beyond, however hard she tries to do so – and why no final act of exorcism has been possible (cf. the ending of the narrative).[22] Inasmuch as the governess appears to be extremely unwilling to learn 'from the ghost[s]' (Derrida), the latter is/are bound to return over and over again – the question is, in this context, whether its/their dangerous impact on the living can ever be eliminated. Anyway, trying to put these self-same ghosts behind bars in a narrative that encapsulates/frames them may, in the long run, turn out to be both a self-destructive and a self-defeating enterprise; however many narrative screens the author puts between his readers and the said dangerous 'kernel', i.e. the ghosts (cf. the triple system of narrators in *The Turn of the Screw*),[23] there is no way of preventing the latter from invading/infiltrating the public space from which they have been excluded; thus the 'hushed little circle' of listeners presented to us in the frame-narrative (*TS* 4) prefigures, precisely by listening to the story/stories, the reception of the whole narrative, i.e. Henry James's *The Turn of the Screw*, by the general public; and in this context it is obvious that the effect aimed at by the self-same narrative is, in the last resort, *silence* (cf. the reference in the frame-narrative to 'our *hushed* little circle', i.e. a circle of listeners *overawed* by what they hear). But I shall return to this problematic later.

According to Jacques Derrida, 'the figure of the ghost is not just one figure among others. It is perhaps the hidden figure of all figures. For this reason it would perhaps no longer figure as one tropological weapon among others. There would be no meta-rhetoric of the ghost.'[24] The privileged position of ghosts in Marxian thought – the topic of Derrida's *Specters of Marx* – must be supplemented, however, with the equally decisive role of the self-same ghosts in *Freudian* discourse (and according to Derrida, spectrality is a common denominator within both the Marxian/Marxist and the Freudian/psychoanalytic hermeneutical/philosophical model). Of course, in this connection the key-text is

Freud's essay 'Das Unheimliche' (1919), and Derrida points out that to Freud being haunted by ghosts constitutes no less than what is 'perhaps the strongest' example of uncanniness, or, in a Derridean perspective, more than just an *example* of this phenomenon, for 'what if it were the Thing itself, the cause of the very thing one is seeking and that makes one seek? The cause of the knowledge and the search, the motive of history or of the *epistemē* [sic]? If it is from there that it drew its exemplary force?'[25] Thus the ghost becomes literally the *personnage régnant* in Derrida's spectacular rereading of the two master-thinkers of the Victorian age (Marx and Freud).[26] In *Hamlet* we noticed that the appearance of the ghost was associated with the melancholy disposition of the Prince of Denmark (see above), and in Derrida's study the process of mourning (or the work of mourning, the *Trauerarbeit*) plays a similar role, for it is precisely when this process has somehow gone sour that the spectre(s) enter(s) the scene (cf. the subtitle of Derrida's *Specters of Marx: The State of the Debt, the Work of Mourning, and the New International*). According to Derrida, 'Marx lived more than others ... in the frequentation of specters ... Where I [i.e. Derrida] was tempted to name thereby the persistence of a present past, *the return of the dead which the worldwide work of mourning cannot get rid of*, whose return it runs away from ... Marx, for his part, announces and calls for a presence to come...'[27] For in *The Communist Manifesto* (1848) it is precisely in an invocation addressed to the *future* that the famous ghost is summoned: 'A specter is haunting Europe – the specter of communism...'. It is within this general context that the ghost narrative/story as a (sub)genre is related to fantastic literature, and here, once more, Derrida offers a pertinent comment on the political dimensions/implications of the fantastic in a Marxian/Marxist perspective, for according to Marx the revolution itself (in Derrida's words) must be placed '*within a fantastics as general as it is irreducible*',[28] and 'the spirit of the revolution is *fantastic and anachronistic through and through*'.[29] In this connection it is apparent that the reality principle itself has become contaminated by the fantastic mode, or by what Nicolas Abraham has called 'the phantom effect'.[30]

Even if it is Jean-Michel Rabaté's project in *The Ghosts of Modernity* to relate the masters of nineteenth- and twentieth-century *modernism* to their ghosts, he, too, like Derrida, in the end – in the final chapter, 'The "Moderns" and Their Ghosts' – turns to Marx and Freud in order to put his reflections on the moderns, from Mallarmé to Barthes, in perspective, and to Rabaté Marx's polemical attack on Stirner offers a case in point:

> Everything has become spectral in this haunted modernity: Stirner's only response lies in a concentration, a severe reduction to the 'ego' – that is, to a transcendental egoism that will resist with all its strength the constraints of abstract ideas ... [but] What seems at stake in [Marx and Engels's] struggle for the reduction of ghosts is the staunch Marxist refusal to conceive of an idea without determination, an 'I' that only positions itself as 'ego' or the 'unique' in order to refute any positioning and hence disappear...[31]

However, the true protagonist of Rabaté's study is no doubt Samuel Beckett, for

> Beckett's historical perception of our moment as that of the 'ghost' would tend to assert that our present postmodernity is spectral. This can be understood in two senses, either that history is haunted by a specter that resists any rational reduction, or any modernity or postmodernity will be in themselves 'spectral', endlessly generating ghosts ready to haunt an unwitting future, sweeping beneath a stream of virtual images everything that will be conceived of as rationality.[32]

We notice in this quotation that the distinction between modernity and postmodernity is deliberately *blurred*, and furthermore that what is under attack is Western rationality (or the project of Enlightenment) itself. This establishes yet another link to the sphere of the fantastic!

Aris Fioretos's reflection on phantoms and spectrality in *En bok om fantomer*, like Derrida's *Specters of Marx*, takes as its point of departure Shakespeare's *Hamlet*, and in this case what the opening scene of the tragedy provokes in the reader is essentially a moment of supreme doubt (or Todorovian hesitation) vis-à-vis the inexplicable and weird appearance: '"Am I seeing things properly?" I may wonder ... Like a wide-open book the gesture [i.e. the Ghost *spreading its arms*] has given us access to the unexplored...'[33] But the main object of Fioretos's research – the film on which he offers a series of lyrical reflections in his study and to which he returns over and over again – is Carl Th. Dreyer's *Vampyr, ou l'étrange aventure de David Gray* (1932), focusing in particular on the strange camera angles (e.g. viewing the external world from the point-of-view of a corpse [!]), the somewhat eccentric sound-track, and the general proliferation/multiplication of the self/selves in the movie. In this context it is also interesting to notice that according to Fioretos, phantoms haunt the modern media world to such an extent that they can be found everywhere, functioning as a kind of white noise within the communication systems: '...They constituted waste products, side-effects, inexplicable relics and remainders belonging to communication as such, and they were only generated if distance, and thereby the possibility of interruption, was established...'[34]

The above-mentioned examples (cf. the references to Derrida, Rabaté, Fioretos, *et al.*) should suffice to demonstrate the extraordinary interest in spectres and spectrality characteristic of the new *fin de siècle*. What I shall focus on in my paper are *two* narrative texts (ghost stories) belonging to the 1890s and the 1990s respectively. From the 1890s my textual example will be Henry James's *The Turn of the Screw* (1898), and at the end of the twentieth century I shall concentrate on William S. Burroughs's *Ghost of Chance* (1993). Thus the ghost narratives in question bridge not only the gap between two different *fins-de siècle*, but also the literary no man's land between early *modernism* and a belated version of *post*modernist fiction

Another Turn of the Screw

According to T. J. Lustig, in his study *Henry James and the Ghostly* (1994), ghosts and the spectral played an important role in Henry James's fiction:

> At a very general level a great deal of James's fiction is ghostly in its enigmatic impalpability, its vague precision, its subtle allusiveness, its hovering uncertainty, its fascination with anxiety and awe, wonder and dread. Many of the catalytic moments in James's fiction are profoundly eerie and many of James's characters possess an almost psychic sensitivity

to shades: shades of meaning, certainly, but also shades in their sense as ghosts...'[35]

Henry James's own disparaging remarks about his excursions into this genre (the ghost-story) should not deceive us:

'It is also true that James repeatedly deprecated his ghost-stories as pot-boilers. Yet there was meaning and method, as well as a certain amount of disingenuousness in this modesty. James's ghostly fiction raised distinctly uncomfortable questions about the nature of his literary project, suggested a more one-sided indebtedness to the sensational and to romantic disconnection that [than?] he would have liked openly to admit...'[36]

Furthermore, the question of *framing* is explicitly raised in Lustig's study and associated with the notion of the ghostly, insofar as the said critic sums up his reading of *The Turn of the Screw* in the following manner: 'One of the finer insights in "The Turn of the Screw" is the relation that James establishes between the governess and the ghosts: both haunt the margins and are intimately associated with categorial anxieties. In spite of herself, the governess acts as a medium of exchange, crossing borders and enabling borders to be crossed.' The ghostly takes over, as it were, and thereby the natural/empirical world is put under erasure: 'As a ghost seer and as the narrator of ghostly experiences, she herself becomes an apparitional figure...'[37]

If we take a look at the way the narrative is transmitted to its readers, we also notice how spectrality takes over and *invades* more and more space outside the original setting of the ghost story (Bly): the governess sends 'the pages in question [to Douglas] before she dies' (*TS* 2), and Douglas 'committed the manuscript' to the first (anonymous) narrator of *The Turn of the Screw* 'before his death – when it was in sight' (*TS* 4). Thus *the death of the addresser* (as well as that of the *mediator*[?]) appears to be a *conditio sine qua non* of the very communicative act by means of which the narrative in question reaches its addressees (its readers). The birth of the text presupposes *the death of the author,* as it were (*pace* Roland Barthes).[38] In this manner the second and the third narrator (Douglas and the governess) are literally *turned into ghosts* (cf. also Lustig's comments on the governess-as-apparition, cf. note 42); in the last resort they only 'exist' – as spectral presences – within the confines of the text. But even the first narrator – and the 'hushed little circle' of listeners to whom Douglas reads the governess's account (*TS* 4) – are somehow contaminated by the same spectrality as the other characters (Douglas, the governess, the 'ghosts' of Bly). The very *house* where the reading takes place (during the Christmas season) is characterized, at the beginning of the frame-narrative, as exactly similar to a haunted house mentioned in *another* ghost-story which 'had held us, round the fire, sufficiently *breathless*' (*TS* 1, my italics); the said story (which is only summarized very briefly in the frame-narrative) took place 'in just such an old house as had gathered us for the occasion' (*TS* 1). Thus both the setting of the frame-narrative and the fact that the 'hushed little circle' is, as it were, *reduced to silence* by the very impact of the scary narrative(s) point in the same direction: the *breathlessness* of the listeners (cf. above) suggests a certain degree of *lifelessness* (or a trance-like state of mind) on their part – they appear to have left this world behind and entered a totally different, 'enchanted' space (the 'haunted' space of the ghost story whose plot is just sketched at the beginning of the frame-narrative and, proleptically, the equally haunted space of the governess's narrative). As far as the first narrator is concerned, we also notice that his very anonymity makes him a very *shadowy* figure (we are presented with next to no data with regard to his character or his personal life, so that he becomes a mere cipher, so to speak). Thus the spectral takes over on a number of narrative levels, and even if this spectrality is *metaphorical* in some of the places where it manifests itself, it nevertheless tends to *hegemonize* the story in its entirety, to dominate the fictional universe as such(!).[39]

The Turn of the Screw can be read as a/the supreme example of the *pure fantastic* (PF). Actually, according to Christine Brooke-Rose,

> The complexity and subtlety of the pure fantastic [such as we come across it in James's novella] lies in its absolute ambiguity, so that instead of one diffuse *fabula* [story] we have two clear, simple, but mutually exclusive fabulas, and consequently a superficially transparent, non-replete (economical) *sjužet* [discourse], which is in fact dense and utterly baffling.

That is why pure fantastic texts are usually short, relatively: it would be impossible to keep it up over a trilogy.[40]

The two *fabulas* focus on: (1) the hallucinations of a (possibly) sexually frustrated governess, seeing things that are (as a matter of fact) only figments of her imagination, and (2) the supernatural experiences of a courageous young woman, willing to take up the struggle against the Powers of Evil, represented by the ghosts. Of course, these two *fabulas* can never be reconciled to each other or embedded in the 'same' narrative!

In connection with *The Turn of the Screw* it is also worth-while bearing in mind the Todorovian category of the *marvellous*. Todorov notices on this literary category: 'In the case of the marvelous, supernatural elements provoke no particular reaction in either the characters or in the implicit reader. It is not an attitude toward the events described which characterizes the marvelous, but the nature of these events'.[41] And furthermore, 'We generally link the genre of the marvelous to that of the fairy tale. But as a matter of fact, the fairy tale is only one of the varieties of the marvelous, and the supernatural events in fairy tales provoke no surprise...'[42] Even if *The Turn of the Screw* must, in general terms, be characterized as a fantastic text, it is nevertheless on the other hand true that some of the formal and thematic elements of its plot point in the direction of the fairy-tale. Bly is, to begin with, i.e. before the governess has come across its ghostly (and ghastly) inhabitants, portrayed as 'a castle of romance inhabited by a rosy sprite [i.e. Flora], such a place as would somehow, for diversion of the young idea, *take all colour out of story-books and fairy-tales*. Wasn't it just a story-book over which I had fallen a-doze and a-dream?' (*TS* 10, my italics). We are, at this point, within the sphere of the pure marvellous, and the seductive power of this sphere is explicitly foregrounded: Flora (the child, here characterized as 'my little conductress') is portrayed as a kind of psychopomp, when she shows her governess the whole place, 'step by step and room by room and secret by secret' (*TS* 9). Of course, this fairy-tale world is later represented as a sham, as something that is simply *imposed* upon the naïve and inexperienced narrator, and when the governess is convinced of the corrupting 'influence' of her otherworldly opponents (Peter Quint and Miss Jessel), she is *disenchanted* in a thorough-going manner: 'Oh yes, we may sit here and look at them, and they may show off to us there to their fill; but even *while they pretend to be lost in their fairy-tale they're steeped in their vision of the dead restored to them...*' (*TS* 48, my italics). We notice in this connection, however, that the governess's disillusionment or disenchantment is still positioned within the confines of a transcendental realm, i.e. the Otherworld of ghostly visitants and presences(!).

The enchanted castle has become a haunted country house. Like the prototypical heroine of a fairy-tale the governess has to undergo numerous trials and tribulations before she can reach her goal (and marry the prince on the white horse); she has to be put to the test and prove her *worth* in this connection. Of course, this archetypal fairy-tale plot is undermined in various ways in *The Turn of the Screw* – it is submitted to ironic turns and reversals. But the governess herself still basically interprets her own situation in these or similar terms: she refers to 'my monstrous *ordeal*' (*TS* 80, my italics), and at the end of the said chapter (Chapter XXII) her relationship with Miles is ('whimsically') read as a euphoric fairy-tale ending, where the heroine is finally able to marry her true love: 'We continued silent while the maid was with us – as silent, it whimsically occurred to me, as *some young couple who, on their wedding-journey, at the inn, feel shy in the presence of the waiter*' (*TS* 81, my italics). It is a consummation devoutly to be wished, but we know from Mary Shelley's *Frankenstein* (1818) that the monster is still lurking in the shadows – and we remember the said creature's sinister promise: 'remember, I shall be with you on your wedding-night'. Peter Quint (the spectre) is biding his time in the wings...

However this may be, *The Turn of the Screw* is permeated by a profound *sense of wonder* (an emotion provoked by the presence of what Todorov terms *the marvellous*, i.e. when this marvellous appears *out of context*, as it were). In this connection we must bear in mind that such a sense of wonder is what characterizes the responses of travellers, settlers and pioneers from Columbus and onwards in their first encounter with the (so-called) New World. According to Stephen Greenblatt, 'Columbus's voyage initiated a century of intense wonder. European culture experienced something like the 'startle reflex' one can observe in infants: eyes widened, arms outstretched, breathing stilled, the whole body momentarily convulsed'.[43] We still come across this sense of wonder in an American context long after the fifteenth and sixteenth centuries, and we notice in this connection that the marvels of the New World are ambiguously invested: somehow the divine and the demonic threaten to merge when it comes to assessing the precise tenor/semantic value of this complex. In *The Turn of the Screw* we come across a number of instances where such a response is thematized (even if the setting is, formally speaking, British and not American). The circle of friends belonging to the narrative community of the frame-narrative are overawed by the very impact of the stories they are listening to ('The story had held us, round the fire, sufficiently *breathless*', and 'our *hushed* little circle' takes in the astounding *forcefulness* of the governess's account of her experiences at Bly, cf. *TS* 1 and p. 4, my italics). In this context we remember the 'startle reflex' of the infant evoked by Greenblatt, where 'breathing' is 'stilled' (!). But wonder operates on many other levels as well – usually associated with (what Cotton Mather had called) *the wonders of the invisible world*.[44] The circle of listeners in the frame-narrative reflect on 'our mild *wonders* of the previous night' (*TS* 4, my italics). In the story proper (the governess's account) the 'hush' of this circle becomes 'that *hush* in which something gathers and crouches' (my italics), and when the change comes it is 'like the spring of a beast' (*TS* 15), bringing to mind, incidentally, Henry James's famous story 'The Beast in the Jungle' (1901, 1903, 1909).[45] Immediately after her first encounter with Peter Quint, i.e. at a time when she is overwhelmed by 'a *wonder* that in a few seconds became more intense', *TS* 17, my italics), this sense of wonder is reinterpreted in positive terms when she reflects on her pupils (Miles and Flora) as 'a *marvel* for a governess' (*TS* 19, my italics). Later Mrs. Grose, after having mentioned Peter Quint's death, refers to 'the *wonder* of it' that he should come back from the dead (such as it is asserted by the governess who proclaims that she has actually *seen* the person in question, cf. *TS* 24, my italics), and in Chapter VII the governess herself 'looks *prodigious* things', when she proclaims her firm conviction that the children *know* about the un-dead (p. 31, my italics). There are quite a few other examples where the prominent position of this sense of wonder in the scheme of things is made obvious.[46] Finally, what the governess postulates is the boy's *inability* to communicate with the evil Beyond any longer is also transformed into a marvellous happening: 'What was *prodigious* was that at last, by my success, his [i.e. Miles'] sense was sealed and his communication stopped...' (*TS* 85, my italics). Thus even *absence* or *lack* (or ontological *loss*) can be recuperated for the category in question (the wonderful or the marvellous)! As a matter of fact, this indicates precisely how *powerful* this concept is in American culture.

Silences and blanks are important *textual effects* in *The Turn of the Screw*. T. J. Lustig has written extensively on the blanks of the narrative: 'Considered in its entirety, "The Turn of the Screw" systematically blanks out beginnings and endings. This overall strategy is replicated on a reduced scale in many of its parts...' (Lustig).[47] As far as the politics and poetics of *silence* in the novella is concerned, we might bear in mind Barbara Johnson's interesting (unpublished) paper 'Muteness Envy' (n.d.), where she comments on the symbolic position of *woman-as-muta-persona* in Western culture (and within the Western canon): 'There is, of course, nothing new in saying that, in Western poetry [*pace* Keats, Mallarmé, and the French Parnassian poets], women are often idealized, objectified, and silent. Feminist criticism has been pointing this out for at least thirty years. But why is female muteness a repository of aesthetic value? And what does that muteness signify?'[48] By and large the answer(s) to these questions can be related to Lacanian theory – and to Lacan's reflections on sexual difference: 'Interesting enough, the silence of women seems to be a *sine qua non* of sexual difference for Jacques Lacan, too, in his translation of Freud's story of anatomical destiny into a story of discursive destiny' (focusing on women's alleged *lack* of linguistic/discursive competence).[49]

As far as the female voice is concerned, speech and non-knowledge are intimately linked up with each other in Western philosophy – and Western metaphysics – from Plato to Lacan. Hélène Cixous makes an ironic comment on this notion of womanhood in her article 'Castration or Decapitation?' (1976, in English 1981):

> Old Lacan takes up the slogan 'What does she want' when he says, 'A woman cannot speak her pleasure'. Most interesting! It's all there, a woman *cannot*, is unable, hasn't the power. Not to mention 'speaking': it's exactly this that she's forever deprived of. Unable to speak of pleasure = no pleasure, no desire: power, desire, speaking, pleasure, none of these is for woman.[50]

Of course, what Cixous here alludes to is obviously Lacan's famous comment on female sexuality, where his postulate is 'that the woman knows nothing of this *jouissance*', even if we (in the majestic plural) have been 'begging them on our knees to try to tell us about it, well, not a word! We have never managed to get anything out of them'.[51]

The silences of *The Turn of the Screw* are clearly related to this problematic, i.e. to the inability of the subject/characters to articulate its/their response to sexuality as such (*in casu* to the sexual 'secrets' of Bly): Douglas 'had had his reasons for a long *silence*' (*TS* 2, my italics), and we also remember 'our *hushed* little circle' of listeners, to whom Douglas reads the governess's narrative (*TS* 4, my italics). During the said narrator's first encounter with Peter Quint this silence takes on cosmological proportions/dimensions, and 'I can hear again, as I write, the intense *hush* in which the sounds of evening dropped' (*TS* 16, my italics). Furthermore, when the governess sees Miss Jessel for the first time, something similar happens, for at this point 'all spontaneous sounds from [Flora] had dropped...' (*TS* 30); in the middle of this intense silence the little girl apparently re-enacts (in symbolic terms) *the primal scene* (what she has witnessed between Peter Quint and Miss Jessel, or what she has even experienced herself, if we presuppose that she herself has been exposed to sexual abuse [?]):[52] 'She had picked up a small flat piece of wood which happened to have in it a little hole that had evidently suggested to her the idea of sticking in another fragment that might figure as a mast and make the thing a boat. This second morsel, as I watched her, she was very markedly and intently attempting to tighten in its place...' (*TS* 30). In this case the very silence of the setting (cf.

above) obviously appears to screen – or to point in the direction of – *a sexual secret* (!). But the silence in question has actually been initiated by the governess herself even *before* her 'vile predecessor' (cf. *TS* 59) turns up: playing a game with her pupil Flora, '[the governess] forget[s] what [she] was on the present occasion; I [i.e. the governess] only remember that I was something very important *and very quiet* and that Flora was playing very hard. We were on the edge of the lake, and, as we had lately begun geography, the lake was the Sea of Azof' (*TS* 29, my italics). Whatever she says to the contrary, the governess herself is drawn into this aura of silence, surrounding a sexual 'secret' that is continually eluded, and nevertheless at the same time continually *hinted at*.

According to Michel Foucault, the injunction to speak continually about our sexual lives [characteristic of Western civilization as such] – or the *putting-into-discourse* of sexuality itself – is related to the confessional practices of our culture (and to confession as an *institution*, codified and sanctified by the Roman Catholic Church):

> Since the Middle Ages at least, Western societies have established the confession as one of the main rituals we rely on for the production of truth ... The truthful confession was inscribed at the heart of the procedures of individualization by power ...[and t]he confession has spread its effects far and wide ... One confesses – or is forced to confess. When it is not spontaneous or dictated by some internal imperative, the confession is wrung from a person by violence or threat...[53]

This is precisely what happens in *The Turn of the Screw*, for here Miles is literally *urged* to confess by the governess, i.e. to speak up and declare openly what he has witnessed (or been initiated into) by his depraved mentor (Peter Quint) or (possibly) by the governess's 'vile predecessor' (cf. above). This is stated quite explicitly by the governess in one of her discussions with Mrs. Grose, where the (meta)logic of confession is put-into-discourse: 'I'll get it out of him. He'll meet me. He'll confess. If he confesses he's saved...' (*TS* 78-79). What we notice of course is that when the secret *is* finally wrung from Miles, i.e. when he is compelled to pronounce the names of the pair of (un)dead, viz. Peter Quint and Miss Jessel, this 'confession' does not 'save' him, but on the contrary *it kills him* (the final tableau of the narrative): 'They are in my ears still, his [i.e.

Miles'] supreme surrender of the name and his tribute to my devotion...' (*TS* 88). However, immediately after this name has been wrung from him – and when it turns out that he cannot *see* the bearer of the name, but only 'the quiet day' (envisaging, as it were, or translating into visual terms, the enforced *silence* of the scene) – 'he uttered the cry of a creature hurled over an abyss' (*TS* 88); and when the governess catches him in his fall, she realizes that 'We were alone with the quiet day [absorbed by the same silence as Peter Quint had disappeared into earlier on, cf. above], and his little heart, dispossessed, had stopped' (*TS* 88). The rest is silence – the final *textual effect* of a spooky past, a past we have not been able to come to terms with.

The blanks and silences introduce a hermeneutical dilemma which might be termed a *double bind* (cf. Jeremy Hawthorn's use of this term in his analysis of *The Turn of the Screw*).[54] According to Shlomith Rimmon in her reading of Henry James in *The Concept of Ambiguity – the Example of James* (1977), 'The reader is ... made aware of an *informational* gap at the core of the narrative' (insofar as the governess is our only source of information with regard to finding out what *really* took place at Bly).[55] The communication gaps or *Leerstellen* of the text are essentially impossible to tackle on the basis of regular interpretive procedures – they rather constitute a *black hole* (or a memory gap) into which all relevant information *in casu* tends to disappear. At the end of the narrative, in the very last paragraph, this 'informational gap' (Shlomith Rimmon) surfaces on the *thematic* level, insofar as the disappearance of the ghosts here takes on a *traumatic*, heart-rending poignancy (cf. my discussion of this passage above): 'With the stroke of the loss I was so proud of [i.e. Miles's inability to 'see' Peter Quint] he [i.e. Miles] uttered the cry of a creature hurled over an abyss, and the grasp with which I recovered him might have been that of catching him in his fall...' (*TS* 88). However, even if the governess *does* catch Miles in his fall, she soon begins 'to feel what it truly was that I held' (*TS* 88). For 'We were alone with the quiet day, and his little heart, dispossessed, had stopped' (*TS* 88).

This death scene hints at a classic *Gothic* scenario, inasmuch as 'the cry of a creature hurled over an abyss' reminds us of the final tableau of Matthew Gregory Lewis's *The Monk. A Romance* (1796), where the protagonist (Ambrosio) is dropped from an immense height by the Devil: 'Headlong fell the Monk through the airy waste; The sharp point of a rock received him; and He rolled from precipice to precipice, till bruised and mangled He rested on the river's banks...'[56] After several days' slow torture, after having been scorched by the sun and devoured by insects and other animals, Ambrosio finally expires within this sterile setting, and the waves carry away with them 'the Corse of the despairing Monk'.[57] Of course, James's account of Miles's death uses much less drastic and sensational devices to convey the horror of these agonizing moments to the reader, but even this low-key rendering of the classic/archetypal scene manages to make the reader '*think* the evil, [to] make him think it for himself', thus saving the author from 'weak specifications' ('The New York Preface', *TS* 123 [James's italics]). And the archetypal 'abyss' – the gap into which Miles disappears, leaving the governess with nothing but 'the quiet day' (an *empty transcendence*) – still resonates with these intertextual echoes from the Gothic past.[58]

The metaphysical framework of the whole setting likewise recalls the Fall of the Disobedient Angels, immortalized in Milton's *Paradise Lost*. In that case, Miles is an *ephebic* version of the rebel angel, imitating in a more earth-bound, but still ethereal manner 'the deep fall / Of those too high aspiring, who rebelld / With Satan...'[59] Of course, there are many other references to the Gothic tradition (e.g. to Ann Radcliffe's *The Mysteries of Udolpho*, 1794, and to Charlotte Brontë's *Jane Eyre*, 1847, cf. *TS* 17, where the governess asks herself: 'Was there a "secret" at Bly – a mystery of Udolpho or an insane, unmentionable relative kept in unsuspected confinement [an obvious allusion to Bertha Mason in *Jane Eyre*]?').

Anyway, these literary echoes – or these spectres from the past – continue to haunt James's narrative – just as Peter Quint and Miss Jessel continue to haunt the governess's pages, leaving the reader in the lurch as to whether what we are reading about is simply the outcome of the narrator's 'mere infernal imagination' (*TS* 50) or whether she is after all a reliable witness (there are many indications that she is *not*). Anyway, it is interesting to notice that the *muteness* of the spectres is, on one occasion, denied by the governess, even if the reader has been told a *different* story immediately before (cf. my earlier reference to Barbara Johnson's concept of 'muteness envy', a concept that is relevant here insofar as the governess is apparently profoundly disturbed by the silence of the ghosts, preferring in this case to provide them, *in casu* Miss Jessel, with the linguistic competence the latter actually lacks) – the question is of course whether there is *ever*, on *any* occasion, anything else to see (or to hear) during these strange encounters than 'the quiet day' (cf. *TS* 88). The open-ended final scene leaves too many questions unanswered, too many riddles unsolved – from this profound (spectral) silence after the last curtain-call *nothing* can be retrieved.

A Poetics of Endangered and Lost Species: William S. Burroughs's *Ghost of Chance* (1991)

Under the auspices of postmodernism a ghost narrative can be can be *carnivalized* (cf., e.g., Angela Carter's story 'The Ghost Ships', published posthumously in her *American Ghosts and Old World Wonders*, 1993).[60] Another option is presented to us in William S. Burroughs's novella *Ghost of Chance* (1991), where an adventure story is combined with a scathing critique of the very premises of Western culture, its excessive, but ultimately self-defeating obsession with *control* as well as the global ecological disasters that Burroughs envisages as the ultimate outcome of this manic behaviour on the part of those in power (represented in *Ghost of Chance* as a kind of cosmic death-drive). Thus the ghost narrative is turned into an ecological fable. Whereas Angela Carter in her aforementioned story lets the pre*modern* world 'haunt' its latter-day descendants (the Christmas customs of Merry Old England are hard to eradicate), the time perspective is much longer in Burroughs's novella, for here it is the pre*historic* world that returns to eighteenth-century Madagascar as a 'stone temple [that] is the entrance to the biological Garden of Lost Chances'.[61]

The protagonist of *Ghost of Chance*, the French pirate Mission, comes across the said stone temple as he is moving inland, observing the rich animal life of the island (Madagascar) and exploring the forest until he reaches a 'clearing' (comparable, as a matter of fact, to a Heideggerian *Lichtung*, where a veritable epiphany takes place).[62]

The stone structure he comes across may remind us of the South American temple in Steven Spielberg's first Indiana Jones film, *Raiders of the Lost Ark* (1981), but the presentation of the site in question is much more slow-paced - and much less melodramatic - than it happens to be the case in this Hollywood movie (actually, Burroughs's novella can, in this respect, be read as a *parodic* re-writing of such an adventure film):

Before him stood an ancient stone structure, overgrown with creepers and green with moss. He stepped through an archway, stone slabs under his feet. A large snake, of a glistening bright green, glided down the steps leading to an underground room. Cautiously he descended. At the far end of the room an arch opened to admit the afternoon light, and he could see the stone walls and ceiling.

In the corner of the second room was an animal that looked like a small gorilla or a chimpanzee. This surprised him, since he had been told that there were no true monkeys on the island ... He also saw a large pig creature of a light pink color, lolling on its side against the wall to his right.

Then, directly in front of him, he saw an animal that looked at first like a small deer. The animal came to his outstretched hand, and he saw that it had no horns...

Slowly the animal raised one paw and touched his face, stirring memories of the ancient betrayal [i.e. man's betrayal of the animal kingdom]. Tears streaming down his face, he stroked the animal's head. He knew he must be back to the settlement before dark. There is always something a man must do in time. For the deer ghost there was no time.[63]

The ancient stone structure in Burroughs's novella is a far cry from the age-old architectural monstrosities we come across so often in Gothic or horror fiction. We might compare this site to H. P. Lovecraft's description of a 'crypt' where nameless ceremonies have been carried out in the remote past in 'The Rats in the Walls' (1923): 'Norrys and I, by the light of lanterns, tried to interpret the odd and nearly effaced designs on certain irregularly rectangular blocks of stone generally held to be altars, but could make nothing of them'.[64] In Lovecraft's writings dread is the predominant feeling provoked by these ruinous relics, belonging to bygone aeons (cf. similar architectural fantasies in 'The Outsider', 1921, and 'The Call of Cthulhu', 1926). But in Burroughs's *Ghost of Chance* tenderness prevails, and the relationship between the main character

Henry James's ghosts were, at least in a certain sense, *marginal*,[84] Burroughs's postmodern ghosts are much more difficult to pinpoint, for they are everywhere and nowhere - on the outskirts and at the very *centre* of our empirical world. As a matter of fact, these postmodern ghosts *have shortened the distance* between ourselves and the Otherworld and they *have* (to some extent at least) *overcome this distance*. Now they are here in our very midst, and it is more urgent than ever that we should learn how to communicate with them - that we should listen to what they have to tell us. For they definitely have *a story to tell us*.

Notes

1. Charles Brockden Brown, *Wieland or The Transformation, Together with Memoirs of Carwin the Biloquist: A Fragment*, ed. Fred Lewis Pattee (New York: Harcourt, Brace & World, 1926) xxviii (my italics).
2. Cf. Francis Fukuyama, 'The End of History?', *The National Interest* (Summer 1989) and *The End of History and the Last Man* (London: Hamish Hamilton, 1992) *passim*.
3. Cf. Jacques Derrida: *Specters of Marx: The State of the Debt, the Work of Mourning, and the New International*, trans. Peggy Kamuf (New York: Routledge, 1993) (first published in French in 1993) *passim*. Of course, the most famous thematization of spectrality in Marx's *oeuvre* is presented to us in the famous opening lines of *The Communist Manifesto* (1848): 'A specter is haunting Europe - the specter of communism' (Karl Marx and Friedrich Engels, *Essential Works of Marxism*, ed. Arthur P. Mendel [New York: Bantam, 1961] 13).
4. Jean-Michel Rabaté, *The Ghosts of Modernity* (Gainesville: UP of Florida, 1996) ix.
5. Rabaté ix.
6. Cf. Avital Ronell, *The Telephone Book: Technology, Schizophrenia, Electric Speech* (Lincoln: U of Nebraska P, 1989) 107.
7. Ronell 107.
8. Cf. Ronnell 112: 'In a streaming way, the lines of inquiry are opened with the aid of a hidden telephone, linking up systems of auditory hallucination to the very concept of voice, which often overlays the voice speaking from different topoi of the self (for example, in terms of high-psychoanalysis, the hookup to the superego and other regions of aphonic calls).' This is, incidentally, the very moot point in Henry James's *The Turn of the Screw* (1898): does the ghost (in the plural) have a *voice*? Or is the governess simply hearing voices (like a true schizophrenic)?
9. *The Poetical Works of Ernest Dowson*, ed. Desmond Flower, 3rd ed. (London: Cassell 1967) 113.

10. William Shakespeare, *Hamlet*, ed. Harold Jenkins, The Arden Shakespeare (London: Methuen, 1982) 1. (It must be admitted, however, that Jenkins favours the year 1601 as the most probable year of composition, see 1 ff.)
11. Cf. Herman Broch: *Der Tod des Vergil* (Zürich: Rhein-Verlag, 1958) 66, where the following conversation between Virgil and the Boy takes place, focusing (among other things) on the (self-) alienating effects of the *name* within a linguistic community: ('"You are Virgil" / "I once was; perhaps I shall become so once more" / "Not yet, and nevertheless already", it came from the lips of the Boy'; my translation).
12. *Hamlet* 1.5.196-97
13. *Hamlet* 3.2.80-84. Cf. also the reference to Todorov's theoretical terminology in note 77.
14. *Hamlet* 2.2.594-99.
15. Irène Bessière, *Le récit fantastique: la poétique de l'incertain* (Paris: Larousse, 1974) 78 (my translation).
16. Cf. Harold Bloom, *The Western Canon: The Books and School of the Ages* (Basingstoke: Macmillan, 1994) 46-75 (cf., on *Hamlet*, 38: 'Shakespeare and *Hamlet*, central author and universal drama, compel us to remember not only what happens in *Hamlet*, but more crucially what happens in literature that makes it memorable and thus prolongs the life of the author').
17. On panopticism, cf. Michel Foucault, *Discipline and Punish. The Birth of the Prison*, trans. Alan Sheridan (New York: Vintage, 1979) 195-228.
18. Derrida 11 (Derrida's italics).
19. Derrida 11.
20. Cf. Derrida 120.
21. Derrida 176 (Derrida's italics).
22. Henry James, *The Turn of the Screw*, ed. Robert Kimbrough (New York: Norton, 1966) (hereafter cited as *TS*) 88; when the governess triumphantly points out 'the beast' (Peter Quint) to Miles (her pupil), as someone who 'has lost you forever', her addressee is unable to see anything at all (he is confronting an *existential blank*): 'But he [i.e. Miles] had already jerked straight round, stared, glared again, and seen but the quiet day. With the stroke of the loss I was so proud of he uttered the cry of a creature hurled over an abyss, and the grasp with which I recovered him might have been that of catching him in his fall. I caught him, yes, I held him – it may be imagined with what passion; but at the end of a minute I began to feel what it truly was that I held. We were alone with the quiet day, and his little heart, dispossessed, had stopped'. The *empty transcendence* of this epiphanic moment thus literally kills its subject (the boy) – or maybe the governess's hand is behind that stroke?
23. On framing (and the system of narrators) in *The Turn of the Screw* cf. Shoshana Felman, 'Turning the Screw of Interpretation', *Literature and Psychoanalysis: The Question of Reading: Otherwise*, ed. Shoshana Felman (Baltimore: Johns Hopkins UP, 1982) 121.
24. Derrida. 120.
25. Derrida 173 (Derrida's italics).

26. Cf. Derrida 174: '[our own great problematic constellation of haunting] has no certain border, but it blinks and sparkles behind the proper names of Marx, Freud, and Heidegger: Heidegger who misjudged Freud who misjudged Marx. This is no doubt not aleatory. Marx has not yet been received. The subtitle of this address could thus have been: "Marx – *das Unheimliche*"' (Derrida's italics).
27. Derrida 101 (my italics).
28. Derrida 112 (Derrida's italics).
29. Derrida 112 (Derrida's italics).
30. Cf. on this problematic Nicolas Abraham and Maria Torok, *The Shell and the Kernel: Renewals of Psychoanalysis*, ed. and trans. Nicholas T. Rand (Chicago & London: U of Chicago P, 1994) 1: 176: 'Extending the idea of the phantom, it is reasonable to maintain that the "phantom effect" progressively fades during its transmission from one generation to the next and that, finally, it disappears...'. The question is, of course, whether the wholesale *Entzauberung* usually associated with the project of Enlightenment is really capable of making *all* ghosts 'disappear'.
31. Rabaté 223, 225.
32. Rabaté 230.
33. Fioretos 13 (my translation) ('"Ser jag rätt?" undrar jag kanske ... Likt en uppslagen bok har gesten öppnat det outforskade').
34. Fioretos 106 (my translation) ('De utgjorde slaggprodukter, biverkningar, oförklarliga lämningar eller rester i kommunikationen, och alstrades bara om avstånd, och därmed möjligheten av avbrott, förelåg').
35. J. T. Lustig, *Henry James and the Ghostly* (Cambridge: Cambridge UP, 1994) 2.
36. Lustig 3.
37. Lustig 190.
38. I have modified a famous passage in an essay by Roland Barthes slightly. Cf. Roland Barthes, 'The Death of the Author' (1968), *Modern Criticism and Theory: A Reader*, ed. David Lodge (London: Longman, 1988) 172: '...we know that to give writing its future, it is necessary to overthrow the myth [i.e. of the writer as the only person in literature]: the birth of the reader must be at the cost of the death of the Author'. Cf. also 170: 'For [the modern scriptor] ... the hand cut off from any voice, borne by a pure gesture of inscription (and not of expression), traces a field without origin – or which, at least, has no other origin than language itself, language which ceaselessly calls into question all origins'. See also Roland Barthes, *Image–Music–Text*, trans. Stephen Heath (Glasgow: Fontana-Collins, 1977), where the English version of this essay appeared for the first time, 148 and 146.
39. It has also been argued that *language itself* takes on a ghostly quality in *The Turn of the Screw*. Cf. Darrel Mansell, 'The Ghost of Language in *The Turn of the Screw*', *Modern Language Quarterly* 46 (1985): 48-63. Cf. ibid. 63: 'All communication at Bly flags. At the Sea of Azof the governess enters into the children's game by playing "something ... very quiet" (chap. 6). Scenes occur in an "intense hush" (chap. 3), a "still hour" (chap. 6), the "quiet day" of the last sentence. Flora's interrupted *O*'s turn into the "nothing" Miles finds in

the governess's unposted letter (chap. 24)'. Mansell likewise focuses on an element of deictic uncertainty in the text, insofar as quite a few of the personal pronouns are presented to the reader in such a manner that the precise referent(s) cannot be positively identified (cf. *ibid.*, pp. 58-60, Mansell's italics). Cf. likewise, on the spectral character of language itself, Shoshana Felman, 'Henry James: Madness and the Risks of Practice (Turning the Screw of Interpretation)', *Writing and Madness (Literature/Philosophy/Psychoanalysis)*, trans. Martha Noel Evans and the author with the assistance of Brian Massumi (Ithaca, NY: Cornell UP, 1985) 195, where Felman operates with the equation: '*to see ghosts = to see letters*' (Felman's italics; as a matter of fact, she refers to the passage in *The Turn of the Screw*, where the governess declares about her first encounter with Peter Quint (the ghost), placed as he is at the top of the tower: 'So I saw him as I see the letters I form on this page', *TS* 17). According to Shoshana Felman, 'This remark, which creates a relation between the letters and the ghosts through the intermediary verb "to see", seems to posit an equivalence between two activities, both of which present themselves as a mode of seeing' (ibid. 195). All this suggests (according to Felman) 'that the ghosts are in fact contained in the letters, that their manifestations have to do with *writing*' (ibid. 195, Felman's italics).

40. Christine Brooke-Rose, *A Rhetoric of the Unreal: Studies in Narrative and Structure, Especially of the Fantastic* (Cambridge: Cambridge UP, 1981) 229.
41. Cf. Tzvetan Todorov, *The Fantastic. A Structural Approach to a Literary Genre*, trans. Richard Howard (Cleveland: P of Case Western Reserve U, 1973) 43.
42. Todorov 43.
43. Stephen Greenblatt, *Marvelous Possessions: The Wonder of the New World* (Chicago: U of Chicago P, 1991) 14.
44. Cotton Mather's treatise *The Wonders of the Invisible World* (1692) is reprinted in Cotton Mather, *On Witchcraft: Being the Wonders of the Invisible World* (New York: Bell Publishing Company, n.d.).
45. At the end of 'The Beast in the Jungle' the main character realizes what has been missing in his life all along, i.e. a passionate commitment to – love for – another person than himself, and when he realizes this, 'He saw the Jungle of his life and saw the lurking Beast; then, while he looked, perceived it, as by a stir of the air, rise, huge and hideous, for the leap that was to settle him. His eyes darkened – it was close; and, instinctively turning, in his hallucination, to avoid it, he flung himself, face down, on the tomb' (1903). Quoted from Henry James, *Fifteen Short Stories*, ed. Morton Dauwen Zabel (New York: Bantam, 1961) 435.
46. Apart from the places already mentioned, the word 'wonder' – including its derivatives or synonyms – makes its appearance on *TS* 21, 22, 34, 35, 39, 41, 65, 69 and 85.
47. Lustig 121. Cf. also Henry James's own comment on *The Turn of the Screw* in 'The New York Preface' (1908): '...my values are positively all blanks save so far as an excited horror, a promoted pity, a created expertness ... proceed to

read into them more or less fantastic figures...' (*TS* 123). Lustig refers to this passage in his reading of James's 'blanks' in *The Turn of the Screw* (15-16).

48. Barbara Johnson, 'Muteness Envy' (unpublished paper, n.d.) 5.
49. Johnson, 'Muteness Envy' 5.
50. Hélène Cixous: 'Castration or Decapitation?', *Signs* 7.1 (1981): 45 (Cixous's italics).
51. Cf. *Jacques Lacan and the école freudienne: Feminine Sexuality*. Edited by Juliet Mitchell and Jacqueline Rose. Translated by Jacqueline Rose (Basingstoke: Macmillan, 1985) 146.
52. According to Lustig (referring to a number of critics focusing on the sexual or would-be sexual elements of the novella), 'Sexual spectacle, outrage, illegitimacy; homosexual seduction of children by adults; heterosexual seduction of children by adults, of adults by children, of superiors by inferiors and inferiors by superiors: if all these speculations have equal value, the sexual life of the residents at Bly, past and present, has been clearly and busily transgressive...' (159).
53. Michel Foucault, *The History of Sexuality*, vol. 1: *An Introduction*, trans. Robert Hurley (New York: Vintage, 1980) 18.
54. Jeremy Hawthorn, *Cunning Passages: New Historicism, Cultural Materialism and Marxism in the Contemporary Literary Debate* (London: Arnold, 1996) 206. Cf. also on double bind Gregory Bateson: 'Towards a Theory of Schizophrenia', *Steps to an Ecology of Mind. Collected Essays in Anthropology, Psychiatry, Evolution and Epistemology* (1972; London: Paladin-Granada, 1973) 173.
55. Shlomith Rimmon: *The Concept of Ambiguity – the Example of James* (Chicago: U of Chicago P, 1977) 127 (my italics). There are many references to Rimmon's influential reading of *The Turn of the Screw* in later criticism, e.g. in both Christine Brooke-Rose's and Jeremy Hawthorn's discussions of the novella (see above). According to Jeremy Hawthorn, 'It seems to me that the case for the ambiguity of *The Turn of the Screw* (as defined by Rimmon) is unassailable...' (216).
56. Matthew Lewis, *The Monk*, ed. Howard Anderson (Oxford: Oxford UP, 1980) 441-42.
57. Lewis 442.
58. According to Camille Paglia, '[t]he governess whose psychic space is invaded by eye-potent spectres [i.e. Peter Quint and Miss Jessel] is the oppressed turned oppressor, hovering in a Gothic [Blakean] cloud over her charges. She imposes a Manichean duality on the children, who are torn between heaven and hell' (*Sexual Personae: Art and Decadence from Nefertiti to Emily Dickinson* [1990; London: Penguin, 1992] 613). Furthermore, according to Paglia, 'the governess is a Decadent artist, joining moral and aesthetic extremes, evil with beauty, a Beardsleyesque black and white...', i.e. James's *fin-de-siècle* sensibility is explicitly foregrounded(!).
59. John Milton, *The Complete Poems*, ed. B. A. Wright (London: Dent, 1980) 276 (6. 898-900).

60. In 'The Ghost Ships. A Christmas Story' (published posthumously in *American Ghosts and Old World Wonders*) Angela Carter establishes a *link* between the 'ghost ships of Christmas past' (belonging to Merry Old England) and the allegedly *demythologized condition américaine* of the Puritan colonies of New England. See Angela Carter, *American Ghosts and New World Wonders* (1993; London, Vintage, 1994) 91.
61. William S. Burroughs, *Ghost of Chance* (1991; London: Serpent's Tail, 1995) 17.
62. Burroughs 3: 'He moved through giant ferns and creepers in green shade without need of his cutlass, and stopped on the edge of a clearing...' According to Heidegger in 'The End of Philosophy and the Task of Thinking', '[t]he forest clearing [or opening] is experienced in contrast to dense forest, called *Dickung* in our older language ... To open something means to make it light, free and open, e.g., to make the forest free of trees at one place ... The clearing is the open space for everything that becomes present and absent' (Martin Heidegger, *Basic Writings*, ed. David Farrell Krell [New York: Harper and Row, 1977] 384).
63. Burroughs 4-5.
64. *The H. P. Lovecraft Omnibus*, 3: *The Haunter of the Dark and Other Tales*, intro. August Derleth (London: Grafton, 1985) 32. The spectral rats of this tale by Lovecraft clearly *negativize animality as such*! Cf. also Michel Foucault, *Madness and Civilization*, trans. Richard Howard (New York: Pantheon, 1965) 77, on the problematic relationship between man and beast in Western culture: 'From the start, Western culture has not considered it evident that animals belong to the plenitude of nature, in its wisdom and its order: this idea was a late one and long remained on the surface of culture; perhaps it has not yet penetrated very deeply into the subterranean regions of the imagination. In fact, on close examination, it becomes evident that the animal belongs rather to an anti-nature, to a negativity that threatens order and by its frenzy endangers the positive wisdom of nature. The work of Lautréamont bears witness to this...'. Of course, this is precisely the way of thinking that Burroughs puts to the test in *Ghost of Chance*, where the disastrous consequences of such an attitude or ideology are amply demonstrated.
65. Neil Cornwell, *The Literary Fantastic: From Gothic to Postmodernism* (New York: Harvester, 1990) 147.
66. Burroughs 12.
67. Burroughs 28.
68. Fredric Jameson, *The Geopolitical Aesthetic: Cinema and Space in the World System* (1992; Bloomington: Indiana UP, 1995) 3. The idea of conspiracy still looms large in fiction and film in the 1990s. Cf. on this issue Christian Monggaard Christensen, 'Hemmeligheder' ('Secrets'), *Information* (Denmark) 15-16 Nov. 1997: 8.
69. Burroughs 29.

70. Cf. Todorov 25: 'The fantastic is that hesitation experienced by a person who knows only the laws of nature, confronting an apparently supernatural event'.
71. Burroughs 36, 35.
72. Burroughs 36.
73. Burroughs 38 ff., 44 ff., 54.
74. Cf. Burroughs 38, where there is a reference to 'the area of extinct diseases' (ironically enough, this area *also* belongs to 'the zoological and botanical garden of extinct species. The Garden of Lost Chances. The sad streets of Lost Chance...'). When this garden is closed down (and the entrance blocked, thanks to the destructive behaviour of a human agent, in this case acting on behalf of the ever-vigilant 'Board'), it is bound to return sooner or later (the return of the repressed) -and its new shape is bound to be much more *terrifying* than it was to begin with (the extinct species return as 'extinct diseases'). As a matter of fact, in postmodernist fiction there are quite a few other examples of such an obsessive emphasis on endangered and/or extinct species: e.g. Thomas Pynchon, *Gravity's Rainbow* (1973; New York: Bantam, 1974) 125-30 (on the dodo), and T. Coraghessan Boyle, 'The Extinction Tales', *The Descent of Man* (New York: Penguin, 1979) 99-107.
75. Burroughs 51.
76. Burroughs 49.
77. Linda Hutcheon, *A Poetics of Postmodernism: History, Theory, Fiction* (New York: Routledge, 1988) 5.
78. On 'noble bandits' see E. J. Hobsbawm, *Bandits* (Harmondsworth: Penguin, 1972), in particular 41-57.
79. Captain Charles Johnson, *A General History of the Robberies and Murders of the Most Notorious Pirates*, ed. Arthur L. Hayward (1926; London: Routledge, 1955) 358.
80. Burroughs 57.
81. Johnson, *General History* 370.
82. Johnson, *General History* 371.
83. As far as Burroughs and postmodernism are concerned there is, of course, David Lodge's exemplary reading of an extract from *The Naked Lunch* (1959) in the context of *his* (Lodge's) definition of postmodernism in *The Modes of Modern Writing: Metaphor, Metonymy, and the Typology of Modern Literature* (London: Arnold, 1977) 35-38. On Burroughs and postmodernism cf. also Brian McHale, *Postmodernist Fiction* (New York: Methuen, 1987) *passim*. Another issue that I might have taken up (but which I have chosen not to pursue further in the present context) is Burroughs's complex relationship with *science fiction*. What Darko Suvin writes about H. G. Wells's 'first and most significant SF cycle' could, in equal measure, be applied to Burroughs's futuristic phantasmagorias in a novella like *Ghost of Chance* (where Burroughs, with great precision and skill, evokes a hallucinatory reality as well as a *psychedelic imaginary* that are bound to 'haunt' his readers and *give them pause*). According to Suvin, the said H. G. Wells SF cycle 'is based on the vision of a horrible novum as the evolutionary sociobiological prospect

for mankind' (Darko Suvin, *Metamorphoses of Science Fiction: On the Poetics and History of a Literary Genre* [New Haven: Yale UP, 1979] 208). Burroughs's excessive and subversive use of biological tropes in a text like *Ghost of Chance* points in a similar direction, i.e. it likewise calls forth the idea of a 'horrible novum', insofar as our genes are susceptible to being attacked by all the 'extinct diseases' let loose upon the world as soon as the entrance to the ancient and forgotten 'stone structure' is inadvertently exposed to an unprepared (global) community. On the structural link between postmodernism and the *spectral* cf. also Hugh J. Silverman, 'Det postmoderne genfærd' ('The Postmodern Ghost'), interview with Hugh J. Silverman (interviewer: Louise Stigsgaard), *Weekendavisen: Bøger* 15-21 Jan. 1999: 11; according to Silverman, 'The postmodern haunts ["spøger i"] the modern, marking it with its reflection on difference. The differences evoked by the postmodern cannot be erased from the modern, because they are grounded in a pre-modern era...' (my translation) ('Det postmoderne spøger i det moderne, som det markerer med sin forskelstænkning. Forskellene, som det postmoderne fremmaner, kan ikke udraderes af det moderne, fordi de hidrører fra en præ-moderne tid...'). This topic was likewise taken up in Silverman's guest lecture at the Centre for Cultural Research, Århus, Denmark, on 8 January 1999: 'The Return of the Postmodern: the Power of Ghosts'.

84. Cf. the governess's comment on the marginal position of the ghosts in *TS* 49: 'They 're seen only across, as it were, and beyond - in strange places and on high places, the top of towers, the roof of houses, the outside of windows, the further edge of pools; but there's a deep design, on either side, to shorten the distance and overcome the obstacle...'.

Part Four
Approaching 2000 in Literature

The Apocalyptic Predicament: Timothy Findley's Predetermined Novel

Norman Ravvin

While they are among our most influential archetypal narratives, apocalyptic texts demand unusually careful interpretation, since the cultural context they rise out of is a complex mix of Hebraic and early Christian sources. The apocalyptics of *The New Testament*, on which so many of our literary apocalypses are based, represent the birth-narratives of a new faith, and signal a cultural revolution that transformed the late Jewish prophetic texts and narratives of historical suffering into a new dissident credo. Elaine Pagels, a specialist in Gnostic and early Christian texts, has altered the scholarly focus on apocalyptic narratives by highlighting what she asserts are their most salient, as well as their most dangerous, characteristic. Pagels argues that apocalyptic writing developed as sectarian conflicts reached their height in biblical Israel, during the second century BCE.[1] Dissident Jews, including the now-extinct Essenes and the followers of Jesus, denounced members of the Jewish establishment as 'apostates,' accusing them of 'having been seduced by the power of evil [which they] called many names: Satan, Belial, Mastema, Prince of Darkness'[2]. Apocalyptic writing, Pagels concludes, is almost always – as with much sectarian literature – a genre reliant on demonization. Apocalyptic narrative, through its reliance on the twin themes of war between good and evil and the threat of satanic power, favours religious and social revolution, as well as a deep-set yearning for the end of an epoch of perceived decadence and the appearance of a new world cleansed of pollution.

Apocalyptic texts are an excellent prism through which to examine the true status of what is often referred to as the 'Judeo-

Fins de Siècle/New Beginnings, ed. Ib Johansen, *The Dolphin* 31, pp. 163-76.

ISBN 87 7288 382 0; ISSN 0106 4487.

Christian tradition'. By recognizing the manner in which the apocalyptic imagination straddles Christian and Jewish cultural territory, we can ask a number of questions about the ideals that underwrite the guiding narratives of the West: In what way are apocalyptic narratives part of a shared cultural corpus? Can such narratives be read in the same way by Jewish readers as they can by non-Jews? In what way do such narratives exist to distinguish an 'old' dispensation from a 'new' one? And, finally, in what way do they, like the great tragedies, demand a brutal sacrifice? Are we far, when we talk of apocalypse, from the queries that resound in Sophocles' *Oedipus the King*: 'What is the rite of purification? How shall it be done?' the King asks; 'By banishing a man,' Creon replies, 'or expiation of blood by blood ... '.[3]

The last year of the twentieth century capped a period in which apocalyptics, conjured by the turn of the millennium, were a constant in public discussions. But such temporal hallmarks are not alone in stoking a fascination with apocalyptic scenarios. In his 1971 volume *In Bluebeard's Castle: Some Notes Towards the Re-definition of Culture*, George Steiner reminds us of an earlier case of apocalyptic fervour, bound to historic events rather than a century's passing. A deep ennui, Steiner argues, and a sense of cultural decay, haunted the decades following the end of the Napoleonic era:

> It is precisely from the 1830s onward that one can observe the emergence of a characteristic 'counter-dream' – the vision of the city laid waste, the fantasies of Scythian and Vandal invasion, the mongol steeds slaking their thirst in the fountains of the Tuileries gardens. An odd school of painting develops: pictures of London, Paris or Berlin seen as colossal ruins, famous landmarks burnt, eviscerated or located in a weird emptiness among charred stumps and dead water .... Exactly a hundred years later these apocalyptic collages and imaginary drawings of the end of Pompeii, were to be our photographs of Warsaw and Dresden. It needs no psychoanalysis to suggest how strong a part of wish-fulfillment there was in these nineteenth-century intimations.[4]

Steiner reminds us that the popularity of such 'apocalyptic collages' is perennial, not just at end-times like our own, but as a commonly accepted context within which to find meaning in human life, and to characterize the direction in which it is heading, even if that direction leads to an abyss. It is a commonplace to say that detective stories are popular because of the excitement of not knowing how they'll end; but a contrary urge is at work in apocalyptic narratives, since we generally do know how they will come out – in a wasteland world, like the one Steiner sketches for us – yet this knowledge tempts us all the same.

Though it is discomforting to think it, I wonder if the ongoing popularity of apocalyptics – against a background of relative disinterest in other forms of biblical literature – represents an unconscious willingness to entertain narratives whose origin and stereotypic themes address the cultural gap between Christian and Jew. In the structures and motifs of apocalyptic writings, as well as in the historical circumstances of their dissemination, lurks the shadow of the original break between 'old' dispensation and 'new.' An understanding of the way Jewish and Christian elements clash in the apocalyptic tradition is made particularly elusive by the fact that in post-biblical literature, little dialogue has existed between the two traditions. By the time the apocalyptic strain entered the English literary tradition, to be passed down to contemporary authors, writers equipped to recognize the stakes of the cultural war they were reinscribing proved remarkably few. The work of John Milton, informed by his knowledge of Hebrew and his Protestant dislike of things Popish, offers a kind of link, a form of accommodation between Judaic and Christian values. And there is Herman Melville's great book, *Moby-Dick*, so famously ignored in its own time, which manages to embrace a cultural view that bridges the gap between 'old' testament and 'new'. The novel is introduced by a compendium of 'Extracts' beginning with Genesis – 'And God created great whales' – moving on through Job, Jonah, Isaiah, a pair of passages from *Paradise Lost*, before rounding things out with a 'Whale Song'.[5] But it is not in the choice of epigrams alone that Melville signals his sympathy for Hebraic and Christian narratives alike; In Ahab's monomania, his compulsion to follow the whale to his own destruction, and the ethical conundrums this compulsion raises, Melville dramatizes a confrontation between Protestant America and ideas inherited from the Hebraic world. To a nineteenth-century audience monomania suggested a crazed enthusiasm,[6] and Ahab is

Melville's archetypal monomaniac, a man whose failed pursuit of the white whale leads, at the novel's end, to the destruction of the Pequod – a catastrophic erasure of the whaleman's seagoing world:

> For an instant, the tranced boat's crew stood still; then turned. 'The ship? Great God, where is the ship?' Soon they through dim, bewildering mediums saw her sidelong fading phantom, as in the gaseous Fata Morgana; only the uppermost masts out of water; while fixed by infatuation, or fidelity, or fate, to their once lofty perches, the pagan harpooneers still maintained their sinking lookouts on the sea. And now, concentric circles seized the lone boat itself, and all its crew, and each floating oar, and every lance-pole, and spinning, animate and inanimate, all round and round in one vortex, carried the smallest chip of the Pequod out of sight.[7]

And what is left at the end of this catastrophe, overseen by its transfixed pagan onlookers? An epiphany of a sort, a recollection of the God-made world as it appeared in its earliest and purest form: 'Now small fowls flew screaming over the yet yawning gulf; a sullen white surf beat against its steep sides; then all collapsed, and the great shroud of the sea rolled on as it rolled five thousand years ago.'[8] In this vision, Melville brings to the milieu of a Nantucket whaler an end that is impregnated with a memory of the world as it is first seen in the Hebrew Bible, wherein the holy spirit crouches like an animal above the darkened waters.

All of these concerns – apocalypse, demonization, the possibility of a truly shared 'Judeo-Christian tradition' – provide us with a provocative context within which to discuss the role of apocalyptic narratives in *Not Wanted on the Voyage*, an extremely well-regarded Canadian novel by Timothy Findley. Findley is best known for his novel of the First World War, *The Wars*, but in other novels, as well as in short stories and journalistic memoir, his work is ever-present in Canada. Like Margaret Atwood, he is among a small minority of the country's contemporary writers who are highly regarded by readers, university professors, and critics. *Not Wanted on the Voyage* appeared in 1984, a year made ominous by George Orwell's great dystopia, but a time by no means as fascinated with millennial narratives as our own has been. The novel's critical importance was acknowledged by its receipt of a Governor General's Award, and its popularity led to a stage adaptation that ran, somewhat unsuccessfully, in Toronto and other Canadian cities. Its canonical status is confirmed by the regularity with which it appears on university reading lists.

The novel's genre, which could broadly be termed fantasy, can also be characterized as a postmodern rewrite of a master narrative. In this, *Not Wanted on the Voyage* is reminiscent of Jeanette Winterson's *Sexing the Cherry* and Julian Barnes's *A History of the World in 10½ Chapters*. Like Barnes, Findley chooses the story of Noah and his ark for re- and supposedly deconstruction. The novel's chapters are headed by well-known verses from Genesis. 'And Noah went in, and his sons, and his wife,' one of the first of these reads, 'and his sons' wives with him into the ark, because of the waters of the flood.' To this, Findley's narrator responds, 'Everyone knows it wasn't like that... . It wasn't an excursion. It was the end of the world.'[9]

Findley's arch, contrarian approach to the flood story stands in opposition to Melville's open-handed method of choosing his introductory epigrams from Genesis, Job and Jonah. And I will argue that a monomania of sorts takes hold of the key character of Findley's novel, while, more unpleasantly, taking hold of the novelist himself. This word – monomania – likely does not resonate with many contemporary readers. It is far less familiar than a host of Freudian terms for obsessive behaviour. But Findley's novel forces us to consider that monomania is no extinct Victorian oddment. In the ostensibly postmodern *Not Wanted on the Voyage*, with its metafictional play with the biblical text, there is what might be called a monomaniacal attention to things Hebraic, an attention which calls, however covertly, for a purging, an expiation, as Creon puts it, of 'blood by blood.' Like the traditional apocalyptic text, Findley's book yearns for a cleansing of one cosmological order to make room for another. The stakes, then, are high in the case of Findley's novel, because of its popularity, its canonical critical status, and the ease with which its treatment of apocalyptic narratives immerses its readers in the context of culture war.

Findley's narrative begins just before the flood, as a phantasmagoric divinity called Yaweh – an old man in a beaten-up carriage, reminiscent of Marcello Mastroianni's decrepit Casanova in Scola's *La Nuit de Varennes* – sends a message to Noah. The letter brought by a 'ruby dove' makes it clear that Noah's upcoming 'visitor could be one Being. The pink and ruby dove at their feet was plain as an autograph written in the dust – one of the ten thousand names of God. Sometime within the next forty-eight hours, Yaweh Himself would descend from His carriage right on this very spot.'[10]

Noah is Findley's paradigmatic 'Old Testament' man. He exhibits an obsession with blood sacrifice – constantly retreating to the 'family altar' (a Roman domestic accoutrement that Findley inserts in a biblical context).[11] For Findley's Noah, the rigorous attendance to sacrificial ritual is characteristic and central to his code of belief, a monomaniacal form of behaviour that supplants any deeper kind of spiritual expression. Before leading his family on board the ark, Doctor Noyes – as Noah is often called in the novel – undertakes an orgy of sacrifice of the family's beloved menagerie, which cannot be taken aboard. The long passage describing this appears twice in the novel, first as a prologue, and then again as a kind of chorus that is repeated when Mrs Noyes confronts the fire set by her husband:

> Nothing she saw that moved had feet or legs – but only arms and necks and heads – and everything was floating – heaving up through the waves of smoke like beasts who broke the surface of a drowning-pool ... . [E]very time she opened her mouth it was filled with ashes. And the wind – whether fanning the flames or created by the flames – made a noise of its own that was hollowed out of the fire and it seemed to be tangible.
>
> ... Suddenly she was on the ground beneath the smoke and the palms of her hands had been scorched – and what had scorched them was a burning piece of flesh and, looking up, she recognized at last the shapes of what it was that was moving all around her. It was sheep and cattle and goats and dogs ...
>
> ... She fathomed what it was that was happening here – and the panic this caused turned her legs to stone and her mind to paste and she was frozen before a single piece of knowledge: *all that is happening here is deliberate and the meaning of this fire is the sacrifice of hundreds.*[12]

There is even the momentary threat of human sacrifice, as Mrs Noyes wonders 'was he going to kill her too? For Yaweh?'[13] Noah's wife finds him surveying this conflagration at 'the top of [a hill where he] had raised himself as far as possible above the holocaust below.' There he stands, Findley tells us, by 'the family altar,' looking almost like a parody of a biblical prophet, in 'his soiled white robe and his tangled beard and his mane of white hair, thrown back.'[14]

The biblical Noah does not, of course, practice wanton sacrifice. He is, in some ways, an odd choice to represent the 'old' dispensation, not being a Hebrew or, in modern parlance, a Jew. The Bible's development of Noah's lineage suggests that his offspring father the Canaanites, the Phoenicians, the Egyptians, as well as the Persians and Syrians. Noah is one of our first everymen, a representative man, chosen to survive the flood not for his faith nor for his willingness to submit to tribal rites of initiation, as does Abraham in the near-sacrifice of Isaac. Rather, Noah is unique because he is 'righteous and whole-hearted'; he 'walks with God' in only the metaphoric sense.[15] Legend surrounding the biblical story has it that he was the first vintner, and in a midrashic legend about life on his ark, much is made about the fact that Noah provided for his animals, both in terms of their environment and their food, exactly what they were accustomed to in their natural habitat. He was, in effect, one of the first organic farmers and conscious environmentalists.

But Findley's Noah is another kind of man: a fanatical disciple, he sets the precepts of animal sacrifice above all other concerns because they represent '*law*... . The only principles that matter here,' he tells his wife, who challenges her husband's harshness, 'are the principles of ritual and tradition.'[16] And these things are bound up, for Noah, in what he calls

> the old styles of worship: the fathers and the elders, the rabbis and the learned doctors - such as himself - each with his appointed place and function... .
>
> And the altars, the cloths and the basins - all the altars carved of the finest, hardest wood and the cloths embroidered - each with its family symbol - each with its monogram - all the great families vying for the finest cloth and the finest embroidery - all the women sewing by lamplight

– and the smell of linseed thread and the cotton weave of the cloth... . Well – this latest pilgrimage of Yaweh with all His retinue ... surely the Fear of God would put the women in their place again. And the young would bow before the Wrath once more, as he had done – as all the young had done in Noah's youth.[17]

Findley takes his demonization of Noah further, as this maker of sacrificial holocausts is also said to be a believer in racial purity. In this he reveals himself as a charlatan, mixing mock-science and a perverse idealism in ways reminiscent of Aylmer in Nathaniel Hawthorne's 'The Birthmark'. In a long set piece, Mrs Noyes describes Noah's hatred of what he calls 'ape-children', and how this has lead him to apply a kind of euthanizing zeal, reminiscent of Nazi brutality, to his own family.

'... years ago, the Doctor and I had a whole other family. Lots and lots of children – ten of them, in fact. But all of them died. There was a plague ... and that killed six of them.

'... the other four children died for other reasons: accidents, fevers, animals. It took a very long while for Doctor Noyes and me to recover from all those deaths.

'... in time, we began again ... A whole new family. Shem was the first of these children – and, for a while, the only one to live. We had ... two or three more who died. Then Ham. And then ...

'When Japeth was born ... Japeth had a twin ... His name was Adam.... We killed him.'[18]

In contrast with Doctor Noyes's fanatical world of literal-minded attendance to law and archaic ritual, Findley presents two very different cosmological possibilities – spirit worlds existing parallel with Noah's in which the creative imagination and spiritual yearning are in comfortable harmony. One of these is a world of creatures that inhabit the margins of Noah's world – animals, demons, fairies, and dragons that Findley concocts from a mixture of cultural sources including children's tales, pagan myth, Arthurian legend, and New Age archetypes. In Noah's world these figures represent childish innocence and naiveté, along with the fecundity and transformative powers of nature. More important than all this, however, is a somewhat ambiguous body of Christian story and motif, which the narrative places in direct competition –

in all out war by the end of the novel – with Noah's code of conduct and cosmology. The possibility of a post-Noahite, or, better, a post-Hebraic world, is heralded by the appearance of Lucy, Findley's most ingenious fictional creation in *Not Wanted on the Voyage*. A fallen angel who takes the disguise of a drag queen, Lucy hides herself among Noah's family by marrying one of his sons. She is a potent figure of rebellion, a paradigmatic character representing the possibility of a 'new' dispensation. Unlike Milton's Lucifer, she is a rebel against divine authority whose scheming is presented as right rebellion, as a rejection of an authority that should be superseded. The reader is introduced to the terms of her struggle with Yaweh in a scene where Lucy is recognized, near Noah's encampment, by her ex-compatriot the Archangel Michael:

> There was near silence then. Only insects; only frogs. In the trees, the Faeries and the lemurs slept.
>
> 'Wouldn't it be wonderful,' Lucy said, presently; 'if you and I could weep?'
>
> 'If you and I could weep,' said Michael; 'I doubt you'd weep for Him. For yourself, perhaps, with your damned and damnable pride – thinking you were His equal ...'
>
> 'I never thought that. Not ever. All I ever thought and all I ever said was ...'
>
> '*Why*? All you ever said was *why?* Why this and why that and why everything. How dare you ...
>
> 'Michael. *Don't*. I can't be bothered. You're a bore ...
>
> Up Noah's Hill, there was a cock crowing – even in spite of the dark – and, for the first time, the brothers realized how very late it was. And early.
>
> 'I should have known,' said Lucy. 'I still get a twinge, just before dawn. But since my star has fallen – I forget what time it is.'[19]

Here Findley tips his hand and cues us to his novel's implied subject – a time both late and early, of course, is a time of endings and beginnings, a time when a thing depleted is replaced by something vital and new.

In the Hebrew Bible a figure called the *shatan*, a word that can be translated literally as the shadow, appears as a kind of tempter, a tester of men like Job. The *shatan* can wreak havoc with men's lives, but he is resolutely an advocate of God's party. Findley's

Lucy – granting her camp accoutrements – stands within the Christian tradition of Satanic figures. Her self-knowledge and crafty heroism remind us of Milton's Satan, and like Lucifer of traditional legend, this Lucy is connected with Venus, the morning star, as well as with a pride that is both beautiful and daunting. But there is more that links Findley's Lucy with traditional Christian iconography. Mrs Noyes has trouble accepting her as a terrestrial being, as she struggles to imagine Lucy as a proper match for her son Ham:

> The trouble was – the Lucy in her mind was a better match than the Lucy she saw ... in the flesh. Given the romance of daydreams, Lucy's figure – as it toyed with Mrs Noyes's imagination – was glamorous, soft and feminine. Pliable ... But once she appeared in all her seven-foot glory, crossing the lawn or sitting with her knees apart on the fence ... the image changed so radically – how could a mother not go worrying?[20]

Like Jesus, Lucy's femininity suggest a meekness and kindness, while she is also awe-inspiring, a startling vision, more easily seen in the abstract, in the mind's eye, than as a thing made flesh.

There are a number of subtle, yet suggestive ways that Findley's novel reinscribes the triumph of the new dispensation over the old. In plain narrative terms, we find an all out battle at the novel's conclusion, which ends with Lucy's party – supported by Noah's wife and some of her family – ascendant as the flood waters recede, the promise of a new world assured. Noah, interestingly, is not banished or wholly beaten. He lingers, a bit like the Jew of medieval imagination, fossil-like, imprisoned in his cabin with his defunct altar, an unrepentant tyrant who will not abandon his selfish hopes of cultural dictatorship even after he is rendered powerless.

With Yaweh's death at the end of Findley's fable, Lucy is seen to represent the hope of a new world, along with a new way of imagining human life. In a suitably millennial vein she tells her followers, insurrectionists all against the code of Noah:

> 'where I was born, the trees were always in the sun. And I left that place because it was intolerant of rain. Now, we are here in a place where there are no trees and there is only rain. And I intend to leave this place – because it is intolerant of light. Somewhere – there must be somewhere

where darkness and light are reconciled. So I am starting a rumour, here and now, of yet another world.'[21]

Lucy's rumour, or, in plainer words, her gospel, proclaims Noah's vanquishment, and the millennial import of her vision is confirmed as Mrs Noyes looks out over the ark's railing and sees

below her ... all the world: its valleys, hills and woods as she had never dreamed they could be seen. Not even birds could have seen the world as she saw it now – with all its movement still and all its features perfectly limned and shadowless: all its trees – each one – leaning up through the green depths – and the furthest reaches of all the hills untouched by clouds or mist or distance – everything equal – valleys and mountains drowned in the same viridian deep....[22]

It is Lucy who presides over this new world cleansed of the corruption of Noah and Yaweh's rule. She appears before her followers for the last time as a transformed vision of succour, subtly evocative of Jesus:

At first it had not been clear this woman was Lucy. Only her great height was reminiscent of her other incarnations. Now her hair was neither black nor red – but honey-coloured – and neither rolled and set in piles on top of her head, nor close-cropped and wavy. This hair was long and straight and it hung down her back as far as her shoulder blades. The face – this time – was neither round nor angular, but wide and flat, with extraordinary eyes of an almost golden colour: animal eyes, fierce and tender. The eyes of a prophet whose words, like an animal's warning cries, would be ignored.[23]

Part of the motivation of Findley's postmodern fable then, is to replace one iconic figure – that of the grizzled altar worshipper, in his 'soiled white robe and his tangled beard and his mane of white hair'[24] – with a 'fierce' young 'prophet' bearing another cosmological vision; Lucy is a 'new presence' whose good news is not yet fully understood.[25]

One critic has traced some of the more vigorous rewriting of the Noah story in *Not Wanted on the Voyage* to examples Findley could have found in the Wakefield Mystery Plays. There, Michael Foley argues, we find Noah's wife depicted as a rebel, a drunkard, a 'querulous stock character of medieval farce.... The ancient notion of a subversive or rebellious Mrs. Noah, absent from

Genesis, is present in most of the English mystery plays of Noah, especially the Wakefield.'[26] We can't be sure if Findley's rambunctious, tippling Mrs Noyes, who ends up battling her brutal husband, is modeled on medieval sources, but the novel has other aspects that are medieval in their implications as well as in their apocalyptic overtones. Noah's viciousness and literal-mindedness, his compulsion to enact dead ritual, and his skill as a kind of evil alchemist remind us of popular stereotypes of the Jew in medieval Europe. Noah even appears dressed to entertain Yaweh in a 'tall, pointed hat,' the guise required of Jews in medieval Venice and Rome.[27] In a daydream of the rituals once demanded by Yaweh that are no longer adhered to, Findley's Noah yearns for something uncannily reminiscent of the behaviour ascribed to Jews as part of the blood libel. Remembering past sacrificial ceremonies, Noah rhapsodizes about how

> each of the rabbis ... lean[ed] forward with his basin, leaning forward wielding the sacred cloth – the first blood always caught in the golden cup....
>
> And finally, each of the fathers, each of the elders, each of the rabbis, each of the learned doctors drank from the golden chalice the first blood of the firstborn lamb on the first day of Festival.[28]

In Timothy Findley's rewriting of the flood story, all knowledge, much less sympathy, is drained of his revision of an archetypal narrative. Unlike Melville's Ahab, whose monomania confronts and is informed by a world where Hebrew and Christian values intermingle, Findley's imaginative world strives to purge itself of all things Jewish, much as the apocalyptic books of *The New Testament* were written to dramatize an ongoing cosmological battle between these two cultural forces. The power of those two-thousand-year old narratives can be seen in the fact that Timothy Findley may have been largely unaware that they predetermined his novel's outcome.

Notes

1. Elaine Pagels, 'The Social History of Satan, the "Intimate Enemy": A Preliminary Sketch', *Harvard Theological Review* 84.2 (1991): 115.
2. Pagels 108.
3. Sophocles, *Three Greek Tragedies in Translation*, trans. D. Grene, qtd in Philip Roth, *The Human Stain* (New York: Houghton Mifflin, 2000) i. I've chosen this citation of the famous dialogue because Roth's novel addresses many of the issues raised in my discussion of Findley's novel. Where Findley seems unconscious of issues connected with cultural scapegoating and the power of certain archetypal narratives to drive human behaviour, Roth treats such issues directly and compellingly. Of the dangerous ability of fiction to direct reality he writes: 'A story that makes no sense, that is implausible, and yet nobody – certainly not publicly – raises the simplest questions.... [W]ithout seriously questioning the story, they repeat it.... The pathogens were out there. In the ether. In the universal hard drive, everlasting and undeletable, the sign of the viciousness of the human creature' (289-91).
4. George Steiner, *In Bluebeard's Castle: Some Notes Toward the Re-definition of Culture* (London: Faber, 1971) 23-24.
5. Herman Melville, *Moby-Dick or The Whale*, ed. H. Hayford et al, *The Writings of Herman Melville*, vol. 6 (Evanston: Northwestern UP, 1988) xviii-xxviii.
6. 'Monomania,' *The Oxford English Dictionary*, 1989 ed. The *Dictionary* offers the following definition: 'A form of insanity in which the patient is irrational on one subject only.'
7. Melville 572.
8. Melville 572.
9. Timothy Findley, *Not Wanted on the Voyage* (Toronto: Penguin, 1985) 3.
10. Findley 9.
11. Findley 126. This positioning of blood sacrifice as characteristic of pre-Christian culture is reminiscent of a contemporary evangelical tendency to recognize an essential 'Jewishness' in the sacrificial acts called for in Leviticus. The existence of Jews after Jesus has been viewed as an anachronism after Jesus's claim that in him the law was fulfilled, and commandments, such as those calling for animal sacrifice, could hereafter be abrogated. A typical New Testament presentation of this idea is 2 Corinthians 3.6 – 'For the written code kills, but the Spirit gives life.' With the destruction of the temple all sacrifice did in fact end, while the remembrance of such acts in liturgy replaced the responsibility to actually carry them out.
12. Findley 124.
13. Findley 125.
14. Findley 126.
15. *The Soncino Chumash: The Five Books of Moses* (London: Soncino, 1971), Gen. 6.9.
16. Findley 13.
17. Findley 47-48.

18. Findley 162-65.
19. Findley 108.
20. Findley 73.
21. Findley 284.
22. Findley 342.
23. Findley 344.
24. Findley 126.
25. Findley 45-46. One important Canadian critic – Diana Brydon – has noted the conservative Christian overtones of Findley's novel, though she does so without raising the context of apocalyptic writings. Brydon suggests that the novel's 'open contesting of apparent biblical truths' has not been objected to by Christian readers because 'Findley's critique of certain elements of the Old Testament story ... can be assimilated very easily into the standard Christian belief system, which sees the New Testament story of Christ's message of love correcting and superseding the Old Testament....' Though Brydon recognizes how the novel might be seen to advocate for 'true Christian values', she still refers to the flood story as a 'Judeo-Christian story'. In this context, the term 'Judeo-Christian' is employed without any suggestion of what ground is being shared by the two traditions. (Diana Brydon, *Timothy Findley* [New York: Twayne, 1998] 78-82.)
26. Michael Foley, 'Noah's Wife's Rebellion: Timothy Findley's Use of the Mystery Plays of Noah in *Not Wanted on the Voyage*', *Essays on Canadian Writing* 44 (1991): 181.
27. Findley 93.
28. Findley 49.

Feminist Aesthetics at the Threshold of the New Millennium: The Questioning of 'Feminine Essentialism' from Emily Dickinson to Julia Kristeva

Sylvia Mikkelsen

Emily Dickinson has been central to Anglo-American feminist criticism in all stages of its development. As this field expanded, practically transforming itself in every decade, so did the feminist conceptions of Dickinson. In the 1970s and early 1980s Dickinson was seen as the epitome of the nineteenth-century woman poet's predicament in an oppressive patriarchal society and in a male-dominated literary tradition. This critical paradigm projected onto the poet and her life a formula-like pattern of psychological progression, that is, from a state of initial passivity and victimisation, through a usually painful transition, to a state which is almost invariably defined in positive terms as a *poetic female selfhood.*[1]

In the 1980s and early 1990s, with the poststructuralist 'death of the author', there was a shift to linguistic approaches to Dickinson's work. Her disjunctive and idiosyncratic style appealed to the Anglo-American advocates of *l'écriture féminine*, whereas another trend of feminist poststructuralists, adopting psychoanalysis in their critical methodology, and frequently combining it with deconstruction, explored the so-called Dickinsonian double-vision. Dickinson's 'hysterical' discourse, they argued, adopts the masculinity of the gaze in self-representations in an attempt to subvert the authority of phallogocentrism.[2]

Finally, in the 1990s with gay and lesbian studies gaining critical terrain, Dickinson's lesbian identity was explored, in

Fins de Siècle/New Beginnings, ed. Ib Johansen, *The Dolphin* 31, pp. 177-90.

ISBN 87 7288 382 0; ISSN 0106 4487.

particular her close relationship to her sister-in-law, Susan Gilbert Dickinson.[3]

In sum, the first phase of feminist criticism based its studies on the assumption that there exists an essential feminine identity as well as an essential feminine aesthetic consciousness, which, however, nineteenth-century women poets were obliged to sacrifice on the altar of the dominant masculine aesthetic. The second wave argued for an exclusively feminine language, while the third is now arguing for an exclusively lesbian identity (actually this is not a new perspective - it can be traced back to the 1950s), but it can now be properly embedded in a theoretical discourse labelled Queer Theory.[4] Dickinson's work, in other words, can be seen to have lent itself to whatever readings are most central to a particular approach or trend, feminist or otherwise. Indeed, Dickinson's poetry has, more often than not, been discussed with the express purpose of substantiating feminist paradigms. However, her actual work, as I shall argue, by virtue of its self-conscious sophistication and complexity, questions the critical practice of imposing on it readily available stereotypes of gender or discourse.

Assumptions about an exclusively feminine identity and an exclusively female language have been questioned by Julia Kristeva in *New Maladies of the Soul*. Although Anglo-American feminist critics have enthusiastically adopted her more feminist ideas and views, she herself remains sceptical of a universalist theory of female creativity. Although impressed by the number of women engaged in literary production, she nonetheless questions the quality of many of these works. She seems to question, for instance, the essentialist concept of *l'écriture féminine*:

> Thanks to the stamp of feminism, do we not sell many books whose naïve whining or commercialized romanticism would normally be scoffed at? Do female writers not make phantasmatic attacks against Language and the Sign, which are accused of being the ultimate mainstays of male chauvinist power, in the name of a body deprived of meaning and whose truth would only be 'gestural' or 'musical?'[5]

In a recent work, *Le féminin et le sacré*, co-authored with Catherine Clément, Kristeva engages in an informal, epistolary dialogue with Clément in which they both attempt to define the feminine as it is now, at the end of this millennium.[6] It is a grand quest, across cultures and religions, for some kind of feminine essence, a sacred topos located at the interstices of mind and body, identity and gender, creativity and sexuality. However, in the course of their correspondence, they gradually find out that this quest raises more questions than it provides answers. For instance, when discussing Chinese women in terms of their 'unified sensibility' - a sensibility so different to the sensibilities of the women of the Judeo-Christian civilization - Kristeva poses the final crucial question as to whether there could possibly exist a definition of the feminine that could encompass all womanhood across racial, religious and cultural borders: 'Peut-on entrevoir une synthèse de ces mondes si divers? Un nouveau syncrétisme? Nous n'en sommes pas là. Il nous reste à nous émerveiller devant les différences. (Could one expect a synthesis of these different worlds? A new syncretism? It is a long way off. We can only marvel at their diversity. [My translation.]) And, as an after thought, she concludes: 'Et si c'était cela, le cœur du sacré? Ici et maintenant, les diversités' ('And what if that was *it*, the crux of "the sacred", the here and the now, in all its varieties?') (274-75).

Already in her earlier study, *New Maladies of the Soul*, Kristeva saw (or, as she says, perhaps 'imagined' seeing) a new generation of feminists or, rather, a feminine sensibility, emerging in Europe. 'The time may have come', she suggests, 'to celebrate the *multiplicity* of female perspectives and preoccupations [ ] in a more accurate, honest and less self-serving way' (206). This new feminine consciousness, according to Kristeva, could be accounted for as the direct result of a state of general feminist saturation and concomitant desexualization in a Europe which has seen it all. The fight for the ideal of equality from May 1968 strove to obliterate the 'difference' between men and women. The ensuing fight was then, paradoxically, waged under the banner of Universal Woman. This mythical matriarchal society, or counter-culture, imagined to be harmonious, permissive and blissful turned out be anything but that. It scapegoated everything that was other. That brand of feminism, according to Kristeva, was nothing other than a sort of reverse sexism which did not shrink from violence to meet its

articulate her sophisticated bisexual imagination, an imagination that anticipates, as I have argued, Kristeva's blueprint for an aesthetic which interiorizes the tension of conflicting sexual and cultural identities. 'My Wars', Dickinson had confessed, 'are Laid away in Books' (J1549).

This psychic space of unresolved quasi-sexual tensions between Dickinson's artist-self and femininity resembles the psycho-drama which fuelled the creative imagination of the French writer, Marguerite Duras (1914-96). Paradoxically, or perhaps precisely because of her chaotic (modern) background, the liberated and emancipated Duras was not as adept as her nineteenth-century literary ancestress in confining the Kristevan violence 'in equilibrium' to the realm of the imagination. In her case, as in the case of Sylvia Plath - another member of that family of women poets who, for better or for worst, drew on their psycho-bisexual tensions for creative inspiration - there was a tragic spill-over in real life.

Duras, a child of, in her own words, 'white trash' from Indochina, grew up, after her father's untimely death, in sordid poverty and sexual debauchery, her mother encouraging her to peddle her young body for money and jewellery, while her brother abused her physically for doing so. Later, through alcoholism, sexual promiscuity and self-abasement, she derived a perverse pleasure in becoming her own abject muse. As she writes: 'Être à soi-même son propre objet de folie et ne pas en devenir fou, ça pourrait être ça le malheur merveilleux' ('To be one's own object of madness without becoming mad, this is perhaps sublime misfortune' [my translation]).[12] Duras's sadomasochistic drive, using her own debased body as muse enabled her, however, to create a poetic identity - the Duras myth:

> J'écris pour me déplacer de moi au livre [...]. Pour me massacrer, me gâcher, m'abîmer dans la parturition du livre. Me vulgariser. Me coucher dans la rue. Ca réussit. À mesure que j'écris, j'existe moins. (I write in order to transpose myself from me to the book. To abuse, spoil and tear myself to pieces in birthing my book. To debase myself. To lie down in the gutter. It helps. The more I write, the less I exist. [My translation.]) (368)

As a Parisian intellectual in the 1950s and 1960s, Duras's work was willy-nilly embedded in a feminist discourse. It was simply *de rigueur* in those days and in that environment. Her work has fascinated both French and Anglo-American feminist critics, but most feminist approaches often ignore biographical facts such as Duras's extreme views on her own sex and how she irrationally either idolized or bitterly hated women. Significantly, she never attempted to sanitize her female (self)representations in her novels. On the contrary, as a critic puts it, 'the list of mental aberrations ascribed to her characters is quite staggering: narcissism, fetishism, voyeurism, nymphomania, sadism, masochism, sexism…and more'.[13] Indeed, not even Dickinson escapes Duras's sadistic pen, witness one of Duras's last novels, *Emily L.*[14] On the one level, the story is written with none other but Emily Dickinson in mind. She imaginatively takes hold of the illustrious New England virgin and drags her, with Gallic relish, through the mud. Duras, who apparently knew Dickinson's work, must have been aware of a certain family resemblance between them. She undoubtedly admired and perhaps envied a poetic sensibility like Dickinson's which could, with its nimble pen, express in a few verse lines the anguish of an existential void without first having had to put her own female body through the harsh experience of real life (the way Duras had done throughout her lifetime). In other words, Duras was filled with 'anxiety of influence'.

Emily L. is the story of a wealthy, middle-aged couple from the Isle of Wight, England, who anchor their yacht, year after year, in a marina at Quillebeuf, a harbour in Normandy. The narrator, who has been observing them through the years, comments on the way they predictably order, in the same favourite bar, the same favourite drinks: dark pilsners for him and double scotches for her. The eponymous heroine, outwardly showing no signs of wealth in her worn-out shoes, broken fingernails and thin, hennaed hair, hardly ever speaks. She only sits there, looking dejectedly at the floor. The reason for her mental and physical decrepitude, we are told, is that she had lost a baby girl at birth and tried to get over the tragedy by writing poems, which she consistently throws out one by one, finding them uninteresting. Her husband, too, could not make sense of these poems and thought she wasted her time writing them. One day, however, she finally succeeds in writing a poem she is satisfied with, and hides it in a drawer in her bedroom. The husband finds it, reads it, understands it even less than the others, but somehow gets jealous because this particular poem had been hidden from him. He burns it. Emily will be spending all her time from now on obsessively looking for this poem until her husband finally decides that the best thing for them to do would be to leave home and roam the seas. For Emily, the bottle will henceforth replace the pen. Nonetheless, she will always be thinking of the purloined poem, a poem that, according to the narrator, she had reworked so many times, attempting to capture in words the oppression one feels on certain winter afternoons:

> ...certains après-midi d'hiver les rais de soleil qui s'infiltraient dans les nefs des cathédrales oppressaient de même que les retombées sonores des grandes orgues. Dans les régions claires de l'écriture elle disait que les blessures que nous faisaient ces mêmes épées de soleil nous étaient infligées par le ciel. Qu'elles ne laissaient ni trace ni cicatrice visible, ni dans la chair de notre corps ni dans nos pensées. Qu'elles ne nous blessaient ni ne nous soulageaient. Que c'était autre chose. Que c'était ailleurs. Ailleurs et loin de là où on aurait pu croire. Que ces blessures n'annonçaient rien, ne confirmaient rien qui aurait pu faire l'objet d'un enseignement, d'une provocation au sein du règne de Dieu. Non, il s'agissait de la perception de la dernière différence: celle, interne, au centre des significations. (...on certain winter afternoons, the rays of the sun infiltrating through cathedral naves oppress in a similar way as the drawn-out resonance of church organs. In the clean parts of the handwriting, she says that the wounds inflicted upon us by these very same blade-like rays come from the sky. They leave no visible scars, either on our bodies or our minds. They neither cause pain, nor offer relief. It is something else. It is from somewhere else. A place far beyond one's expectations. Those wounds announce nothing, neither do they confirm, instruct, or are sent down from the Kingdom of Heaven as a sign of provocation. No, it is a sense of awareness of the ultimate difference which lies hidden at the very heart of meaning itself. [My translation.]) (84-85)

This is evidently an appropriation of Dickinson's poem J258:

> There's a certain Slant of light
> Winter Afternoons –
> That oppresses, like the Heft

Of Cathedral Tunes –

Heavenly Hurt, it gives us –
We can find no scar,
But internal difference,
Where the Meanings, are – [15]

Laure Adler, who knew Duras personally, claims in her recent biography *Marguerite Duras* that Duras identified with her character Emily L., calling her 'sister', a genius, and the woman she loves most in this world, this old, frail alcoholic in her worn-out shoes (549). The novel *Emily L.* can be seen, then, in terms of an intertextual, if rather ambivalent, homage to Emily Dickinson, in which Duras appropriates Dickinson's poem and maps it onto an abject modern 'sister'. The surname of the character is just a capital 'L.' which is a pun on the French pronoun *elle* (she). Bearing in mind Duras's notorious alcoholism and her *goût de la boue*, there is no doubt a perverse logic of identification here. Emily L.'s predicament in the novel is, I would argue, symptomatic of Duras's ambivalence towards her own female identity. This ambivalence can be seen in terms of a dialectic between Duras's aggressively 'masculine' writer-self and its antithesis, her own abject femininity. In her portrait of Emily L., Duras perversely imagines a modern Dickinson succumbing to the trials of marriage, childbirth, adulterous passions and a tyrannical husband. By appropriating Dickinson's genius, which Duras obsessively belabours with her awkward French paraphrasing, she reveals a rival consciousness which is articulated in an imaginative attempt to pull Dickinson down from her artistic pedestal by demythologizing her *feminine* mystique. In other words, by humanizing, indeed sub-humanizing Dickinson, *the woman*, Duras recreates her in her own image.

In her study of melancholia and depression, *Black Sun*, Kristeva discusses some of Duras's novels, characterizing them as products of an aesthetic of awkwardness which 'makes up a world of unsettling, infectious ill-being', providing no relief or catharsis to its readers.[16] Yet, in an earlier study, *Powers of Horror*, Kristeva theorizes on the necessity of the fledgling subject to debase and reject the maternal body in order to free itself and find its own subjectivity, a thing female subjects have difficulty in doing as they also identify, as women, with the maternal body.[17] Seen in this light, Duras's literary matricide could be put down to some sort of therapeutic writerly *jouissance*. However, there is obviously a limit to how much violence 'in equilibrium' even a Kristeva is ready to put up with as *readerly jouissance*!

On the question of what constitutes readerly *jouissance* there are at least two major positions. According to Norman N. Holland ('Unity Identity Text Self', 1975), we project onto the texts our own subjectivity, in other words we tend to replicate ourselves. We avoid or shun the alien or strange experiences in order to safeguard our own identity.[18] Thomas C. Caramagno, in his book on Virginia Woolf, *The Flight of the Mind: Virginia Woolf's Art and Manic-Depressive Illness* questions Holland's theory. Instead, he aligns himself with Georges Poulet's idea that 'when one reads any text, one's own identity is set aside and the text constitutes a new subjectivity within oneself'. In short, Caramagno argues that literature

> helps us to experience previously undiscovered parts of ourselves, parts which can feel and empathize and understand alien experiences; if we tolerate the insecurity and chaos attending incongruence and if we resist defensive strategies, then we may re-form the self by consciously integrating what had been unrecognized. Once we are 'occupied' by the thoughts of the author, we draw new subject-object boundaries, discovering or re-forming our habitual self by taking in what had been the 'not-self' [...]. What is essential in literature [...] is the ability to open oneself up to experiences, reactions, emotions, and ideas that do not slavishly reinforce our defensive, narrow, entrenched strategies for coping with self-world transactions.[19]

At least, one may hope for the new millennium that the future 'sisters' of Emily Dickinson, Marguerite Duras and Sylvia Plath will also appeal to the reader's hermeneutical and existential openness to new or alien experiences and ideas, including psychosexual transactions and constructions beyond the stereotypes of feminine or feminist essentialism.

Notes

1. In their much-quoted essay 'A Woman-White: Emily Dickinson's Yarn of Pearl', Gilbert and Gubar see Dickinson as a poor child who, notwithstanding her entrapment in her father's house, manages to develop into an 'inventive poet [who] enacted and eventually resolved both her anxieties about her art and her anger at female subordination' (Sandra Gilbert and Susan Gubar, *Madwoman in the Attic: The Woman Writer and the Nineteenth-Century Literary Imagination* [New Haven: Yale UP, 1979] 583). Paula Bennett in *My Life a Loaded Gun: Female Creativity and Feminist Poetics* (Boston: Beacon, 1986), sees a similar pattern of maturation in Dickinson's work.
2. Mary Loeffelholz, in *Dickinson and the Boundaries of Feminist Theory* (Urbana: U of Illinois P, 1991), argues in this poststructuralist vein. For example, Dickinson's poem J41 'I robbed the Woods' is seen by Loeffelholz as suggesting that 'a woman appropriating nature is at most a petty shoplifter' and that Dickinson is thus 'playfully deflating' male romantics and their quests into nature by parodying 'one of middle-class women's few legitimate spheres of public "speech" ' (20-21).
3. A recent publication of Dickinson's intimate letters to her sister-in-law, Susan Gilbert Dickinson, supports Dickinson's lesbian identity (*Open Me Carefully*, ed. Ellen Louise Hart and Martha Nell Smith [Ashfield, MA: Paris, 1998]).
4. Rebecca Patterson argued for Dickinson's lesbian identity in *The Riddle of Emily Dickinson* (Boston: Houghton Mifflin, 1951).
5. Julia Kristeva, *New Maladies of the Soul*, trans. Ross Guberman (New York: Columbia UP, 1995) 220. Subsequent references to this work appear in parentheses in the main text.
6. Catherine Clément and Julia Kristeva, *Le féminin et le sacré* (Paris: Stock, 1998). Subsequent references to this work appear in parentheses in the main text.
7. *Letters of Emily Dickinson*, ed. Mabel Loomis Todd (London: Gollancz, 1951) 42.
8. *Letters of Emily Dickinson*, ed. Thomas H. Johnson and Theodora Ward, 3 vols. (Cambridge, MA: Harvard UP, 1958) 1: 209-10.
9. Gilbert and Gubar 597.
10. Bennett 52.
11. The poems quoted are from *The Complete Poems of Emily Dickinson*, ed. Thomas H. Johnson (Boston: Little Brown, 1955).
12. Laure Adler, *Marguerite Duras* (Paris: Gallimard, 1998) 50.
13. *Critical Essays on Marguerite Duras*, ed. Bettina L. Knapp (New York: Prentice Hall, 1998) 1.
14. Marguerite Duras, *Emily L.* (Paris: Minuit, 1987).
15. The last two stanzas of poem J258 are paraphrased by Duras as follows: 'Il était dit, ou presque dit, que cette différence interne était atteinte par le désespoir souverain dont elle était en quelque sorte le sceau. Le poème se

In the Meantime: Nation in New Labour's Millennium Countdown

Cheralyn Mealor

Amidst the growing popular buzz in the Western hemisphere surrounding the approach of year 2000, discussions of the millennium have been somewhat predictably focused on issues such as apocalypticism, dating and calendrics, millenarian movements (religious and secular), messianism and various other forms of millennialism, both contemporary and historical.[1] Such discussions have also been popularised in an increasing number of timely publications on the millennium.[2] Within this body of work, however, there has been no attempt to problematise the modern conceptualisation of time which necessarily informs the planned global celebrations for the millennium, and which is intrinsic to the idea of nation. Focusing on this conception of time, it will be the aim of this short paper to locate the discourses around the celebration of year 2000 in Britain within postcolonial discussions of the nation and the limits of multiculturalism.

Despite the immanent arrival of the next millennium, the most conspicuous form of millenarian angst in Britain to date does not concern worries about the end of time itself, but whether New Labour's controversial Millennium Dome, currently under construction in Greenwich, will be completed (and on budget) before the big day arrives.[3] Such focus on the staging of a British national exhibition has, in fact, transposed the inception of the millennium into an event more of national than of religious or even historical importance. The planned celebrations for year 2000 have consistently been attached by proponents of the Dome to other events of national importance; the millennium, we are frequently re-

Fins de Siècle/New Beginnings, ed. Ib Johansen, *The Dolphin* 31, pp. 193-214.

ISBN 87 7288 382 0; ISSN 0106 4487.

minded, is not only a significant date for the Christian calendar, and for secular imaginings, but also marks the anniversaries of the Union Jack, the Great Exhibition, and the Festival of Britain.[4] But it is primarily the popular conception that the new millennium begins in Britain that provides the symbolic foundation for the Dome's construction at Greenwich and what amounts to the nationalisation of year 2000.

This is most evident in the appropriation of the millennium in New Labour rhetoric, which has consistently attempted to rouse national pride in order to promote its One Nation vision of New Britain. Although the Millennium Dome project was originally conceived during the previous Conservative government, it has since been so incorporated into the projection of New Labour ideology, that the public response to the Dome, when it opens, will be seen to measure the success and popularity of the New Labour government itself. Whilst the primary rationale for the Dome has been the promotion of a new, more favourable image of Britain abroad, like all national expositions, the Dome must also be understood as an ideological construct; in this case, concerned just as much with selling New Labour's vision of a new Britain to the general public, as with the furthering of foreign investment in British industries. At the initial unveiling of some of the Dome's proposed contents, Tony Blair proclaimed that it was imperative for Britain to 'seize the moment' of the new millennium:

> Picture the scene. The clock strikes midnight on 31 December 1999. The eyes of the world turn to a spot where the new millennium begins – the Meridian line at Greenwich. This is Britain's opportunity to greet the world with a celebration that is so bold, so beautiful, so inspiring that it embodies at once the spirit of confidence and adventure in Britain and the spirit of the future of the world.[5]

Thus Blair foresees, at the beginning of the new millennium, the British people united in a celebration of their nation: 'we will say to ourselves with pride: this is our Dome, Britain's Dome. And believe me, it will be the envy of the world.'[6]

GMT, or, the Naturalisation of Time

The origin of the new millennium is, of course, located at the Royal Greenwich Observatory, hailed in popular and tourist literature as the 'centre of space and time', the 'centre of the world',[7] and 'the place where days begin and end'.[8] As the home of the Prime Meridian of longitude and time, the Observatory is the fixed centre from which time and space, and accordingly the inception of the new millennium, is measured. The building of the Millennium Dome on the prime meridian will enhance the long-standing privileged position that Greenwich has enjoyed in the English imaginary, largely due to its maritime and royal associations. The Dome joins other major tourist attractions, such as the National Maritime Museum, the Royal Naval College, the Cutty Sark (originally exhibited as part of the 1951 Festival of Britain) and, of course, the Observatory, which today houses a permanent exhibition on 'the story of time', which charts the technological innovations in timekeeping and navigational techniques that led to Greenwich's positioning at the centre of time and space. However, because the history of mechanical timekeeping is inextricably bound up with the development of navigation, the story of time is also the story of colonial expansion and conquest, and it is in this context that the Old Royal Observatory, proclaimed to be 'the oldest scientific institution in Great Britain', must be understood.[9]

The so-called 'discovery' of longitude and the fixing of the Prime Meridian at Greenwich is conventionally (and also officially) presented as an exemplar of the achievements of science and co-operation between nations and peoples. The Preface to Derek Howse's book on the Observatory, for example, reads as follows: 'its triumphs have been achieved through knowledge, reason and co-operation, rather than conflict. If Greenwich Time survives to mark the dawn of the year 3000, we hope that its unifying message will continue to show the intervening centuries an example of what peaceful scientific endeavour can achieve for the common good.'[10] This type of rhetoric, which draws on the Enlightenment belief in scientific and material progress, is somewhat naively sustained by the view that the naturalisation of zero-longitude at Greenwich was a triumph of global democracy. On the jacket of this book, for instance, it is stated that 'by the drawing of an imaginary line around the earth, the world was united in its perception of time'.

It was at the 1884 International Meridian Conference in Washington when the Greenwich Meridian was voted by representatives of those nations present as the prime meridian of time and longitude. But the idea that this was agreed on democratically by the world community is misleading. Apart from the fact that only proportionally few nations of the world were represented at this conference, the recommendations finally put forward do not reflect unanimity. Whilst the standardisation of world time was becoming an issue of practical necessity, the global adoption of the Greenwich meridian did not come into effect without a great deal of contention (particularly from the side of the French), and was finally only realised through international pressure (particularly from the side of the U.S.). The definition of a prime meridian predictably raised the issue of neutrality,[11] but the fact that the Greenwich meridian was already that most widely used (largely due to the vast reach of the British Empire), and that the United States had adopted Greenwich time, only one year prior to this conference, for the standardisation of its time zone system, meant that it was the most convenient.[12]

However, the adoption of the Greenwich meridian by individual nations was a long process, and some countries did not conform until well into the latter half of the twentieth century. In France, GMT was adopted as legal time in 1911, but only after attempts to persuade the English to switch to the metric system, and until its substitution by Coordinated Universal Time (UTC) in 1978, it was always expressed as 'Paris Mean Time, retarded by 9 minutes, 21 seconds.' Such disputes still continue today: New Zealand refuses to recognise the new millennium as beginning in Greenwich, that is at 00h 00m 00s Universal Time on 31st December, insisting instead that '*their* new century will definitely begin 12 hours earlier (or thirteen because of Daylight Saving Time).'[13] Such controversies only serve to demonstrate the importance of time and space in nationalist ideology. To set one's watch to one's own nation, so to speak, is also to position it at the centre of the map, of time and space, and not in some distant, peripheral time zone.

The rhetoric of scientific progress and of its benefits to all mankind, frequently attached to the Observatory, invariably converges with British nationalist assertions. The English watchmaker, John Harrison, for example, is often portrayed as a national hero, as the 'lone genius' who won the European race to determine longitude.[14] Popular histories of Greenwich locate the town not only at the centre of time and space, but also position it firmly within the national imagination, reviewing it as the historic site of royal births, of Lord Nelson's funeral, the home of Chaucer, C. Day Lewis, and a favourite haunt of, amongst others, Wilkie Collins and Charles Dickens.[15] Greenwich is also presented as the 'birthplace of classical architecture in England',[16] with its monumental buildings by Inigo Jones, Wren, Hawksmoor and Vanbrugh – and the Millennium Dome is seen as a fitting addition to this great architectural tradition. Accounts of maritime Greenwich are quite predictably awash in romantic nationalism,[17] and the town is also typically heralded, due to the Royal Observatory, as a place of science and erudition. Often, descriptions of the Observatory itself take on romantic national proportions. Here, for example, is Dava Sobel's account of tourists gathering at the Observatory to watch the time ball:

> [A]t 12:55 P.M., a slightly battered red ball climbs halfway up the mast to the weather vane. It hovers there for three minutes, by way of warning. Then it ascends to its summit and waits another two minutes. Mobs of school groups and self-conscious adults find themselves craning their necks, staring at this target, which resembles nothing so much as an antiquated diving bell.
>
> This more frequent, oddly anachronistic event has a genteel feel. How lovely the red metal looks against the blue October sky, where a stout west wind drives puffs of clouds over the twin observation towers. Even the youngest children are quiet, expectant.[18]

Such national sentiments are, of course, intimately connected to the notion that Greenwich itself, despite its modest appearance, represents Britain, as it once was imagined, at the pinnacle of civilisation and progress. Whilst popular histories of time-keeping and Greenwich recount how navigation was improved by the scientific advances being made at the Observatory, and how this must have saved the lives of many sailors, Greenwich's association with the slave trade and imperial expansion is invariably omitted or forgotten.[19] Moreover, the fact that the Observatory, which naturalised the tradition of imperial cartography, is a famous landmark in the history of Eurocentrism and global totalisation is also overlooked.

The institution of a single temporal frame and definition of the Prime Meridian at Greenwich divided the globe into two hemispheres, East and West; a division of great significance for the tradition of Orientalism, of the West and the rest. The naturalisation of time at Greenwich, and its codification as the 'centre of space and time', bestowed on the Observatory what can be described as its normalising panoptic function. The tradition of mapping not only of spatial, but also temporal others that can be traced back to the Mercator projection map of the world was thus naturalised in a South East London suburb: as José Rabasa points out, Mercator himself perceived History as the 'eye of the World' (*oculus mundi*).[20] Based on an objective, functional perspectivism, Renaissance maps continued a tradition inherited from Ptolemy, and offered a graphic representation of the world that at once accounted for its creation and confirmed mankind's place in the cosmos. In Mercator's *Atlas*, the division of the globe by meridians into the Old World and the New shows how the Other was mapped into this totalising system not only spatially, but was also assimilated into the universalising single narrative of European history. David Harvey's explanation of the spatial inscription of the Other is equally applicable to the question of temporality: 'the problem with Enlightenment thought was not that it had *no* conception of "the other" but that it perceived "the other" as necessarily having (and sometimes "keeping to") a specific *place* in a spatial order that was ethnocentrically conceived to have homogeneous and absolute qualities'.[21] In the same way that the Other was mapped into homogeneous space by the eye of the geographer, it was also positioned and fixed within a homogeneous temporal structure that charted, through the clock and calendar, the historical progress (or backwardness) of such totalised cultures. Once inscribed into the fixed co-ordinates commanded by a single temporal and spatial frame, the ethnic and cultural diversity of other peoples could then be contained and made transparent.

The totalising vision of the map, with its conflation of geographical and historical, not only divided Europe from its Other but also enabled the formation of national identities as, quite simply, to identify oneself as a member of a community one must first imagine its limits. The mapping of Europe into this single spatial and temporal frame facilitated a sense of national belonging based on the allocation of place to an integrated, homogeneous people, and awarded primacy to the nation-state as the matrix of modernity.[22]

Thus, the belief that Greenwich Mean Time represents merely the scientific measurement of time which, in itself, is somehow free of ideology is completely misguided. GMT rather naturalises a homogenised temporal order that is imposed on the world: a conception of time which presupposes the notion of a single, progressive, linear history that has dominated European thought. The measurement of time by the clock and calendar as a sequence of punctual 'nows' underwrites the measurement of progress of other cultures and sustains the time-lag argument, which provided the justification for colonialism, by which Europe is always advanced, or 'on time', and non-Europe is behind, or 'late'. Only through colonial intervention, it was assumed, could such cultures be raised to the level of modernity that European societies had reached through their own internal rational agency.

Benedict Anderson has argued that the progress of the nation as an 'imagined community' is charted along this same line of historical continuity and self-identity. 'The idea of a sociological organism moving calendrically through homogeneous empty time,' he states, 'is a precise analogue of the idea of the nation, which is also conceived as a solid community moving steadily down (or up) history.'[23] In other words, homogeneous time is shared time; shared by a unified, cohesive society with a common history, culture and identity. It is, of course, Anderson's conception of the 'meanwhile', the punctual present of homogeneous empty time, that defines the worldwide celebrations for the new millennium and the grand opening ceremony of the Millennium Dome at 00hrs, Jan 1, 2000 (GMT).

New Labour, New Britain

New Labour has predictably capitalised on the popular view of the inception of the new millennium as a watershed of renewal, claiming it as a defining moment for New Britain, as an opportunity to make Britain a 'young country' again and to regain its position at the helm of modernity and progress. Chris Smith, Secretary of State for Culture, Media and Sport, has stated: 'The millennium is a turning point in history. It marks the point at which Britain with its proud past meets a Britain with new confidence in the future.'[24] In fact, New Labour's analysis of what is wrong with Britain is based on the rather simple premise that since the loss of its empire, Britain has been falling behind. Peter Mandelson, formerly Minister without Portfolio responsible for the Dome, writes, 'The continuing myth of Britain's world power status, perpetuated by the Falkland's War, has delayed acceptance of our destiny in Europe and reinforced resistance to the need for modernisation.'[25] Whereas Thatcherism represents the climax of a period of *regression*, the last spasmodic twitches of a dying empire and a desperate attempt to hold onto old values, the creation of New Britain involves leaving certain of these behind and forging ahead to the nation's true destiny, or self-realisation. In the words of Tony Blair: 'I want a new Britain that is true to itself – true to its history, true to its character and gifts, and above all true to its future. That is the only way to regain our sense of direction and fulfil the historic destiny of our country.'[26]

The revival of a strong, but new, sense of British national identity is fundamental to New Labour's communitarian One Nation vision, and its projection is the rationale behind the Dome at Greenwich. By restoring national pride and forging a 'new moral purpose' for the nation, it is argued that old social conflicts will be overcome and everyone will work together, 'on the same team', for the common good.[27] The appeal for a new patriotism befitting an inclusive society draws on the commonplace distinction between benign nationalism and xenophobia. Blair proclaims, 'In the end I am simply a patriot. I believe in Britain, but it is an enlightened patriotism ... based not on narrow chauvinism but on the right values and principles.'[28] The wrong values and principles, of course, belong to the bad patriotism of Thatcherism which for all its flag-waving, Blair claims 'spent 16 years tearing apart the fabric of our nation.' 'Enlightened patriotism', on the other hand, rests on the belief that national identities need not be exclusionary; that as Blair says, 'Pride in my country is not the same as hostility towards others', but to the contrary, has a strong integrative function. Furthermore, this is seen to represent the true patriotism of the nation as it constitutes 'the reassertion of one-nation ideals based on Britain's enduring values - social unity, common purpose, fairness, and mutual responsibility.'[29] In other words, the core moral values of New Labour's one-nation vision are claimed to be synonymous with those lying at the very heart of British national identity, and New Labour is construed as the 'people's party' not only because of its one-nation consensual and inclusive politics, but also because it reflects the true essence of Britishness itself.

Although New Labour's 'enlightened patriotism' appeals to a revival of old British values, its emphasis lies on the importance of modernising nationalism and national identity. Just as the politics of the old Left and New Right are rendered obsolete for a post-industrial, globalised, diverse society, so is that traditional British nationalism based on pride in empire and rooted in the belief in a single, homogeneous national identity. Enlightened patriotism, rather, is 'a patriotism born not of nostalgia but of an understanding of the changing nature of the world [...] A new Britain for a new world, finally breaking free of our imperial shadows.'[30] Whilst New Labour ideology claims to reflect this 'new era' of British society, in which a new sense of national community is understood to have emerged (i.e. signalled by New Labour's election victory and the spontaneous public emotion displayed at Diana's funeral), it at the same time claims to define it, and determines to reshape identity and society to fit it. New Britain is simultaneously a state of affairs based on the social analysis of the Third Way and a utopian vision of a 'young country' that New Labour promises to create.

New Labour's projection of New Britain, is thus on the one hand an attempt to reflect the new realities of a transformed society, yet on the other, an attempt to rebrand British national identity. Mark Leonard's report from Demos, the influential London think-tank, entitled *Britain™: Renewing Our Identity*, is essentially an argument for the commodification of national identity, offering a mixture of grand visions and practical suggestions for marketing British identity abroad, based on the premise that 'it is possible to manage identity systematically'. Contesting the nationalist myth that constructs Britain as the result of '1,000 years of unbroken continuity', Leonard argues that it was invented as recently as the eighteenth century, but that the old narratives of that invention can no longer be applied to contemporary Britain.[31] Therefore, he maintains, if Britain is to get ahead the old narratives of national identity must be reinvented or rewritten.[32] Defining this identity has, however, appeared to be problematic, judging from the difficulties organisers of the Dome have had in finding the formula to prove the reality of One Britain and please all of the people at the same time.

The reinvention of Britain as a 'hybrid nation', and the celebration of cultural and ethnic diversity is, of course, crucial to the formulation of an inclusive New Britain. Celebrating hybridity for its marketing potential, Leonard declares, 'Britain is the least pure of European countries, more mongrel and better prepared for a world that is continually generating new hybrid forms.'[33] As evidence of this he points to a foreign presence in those most British of institutions, the House of Windsor and Marks and Spencer, and underlines the marketing potential of hybridity by reminding us that Indian cuisine is one of Britain's largest exports. In accordance with New Labour's One Nation ideology, Leonard confidently describes Britain as 'the home of happily co-existing subcultures' and, punning on the successful Benneton advertising campaign, suggests the slogan 'United Colours of Britain' for marketing this image abroad.[34]

A major pursuit of the New Labour government, the task of marketing Britain abroad has resulted, amongst other things, in the institution of Panel 2000 at the Foreign and Commonwealth Office, the staging of the much criticized Powerhouse::uk exhibition and, of course, the Millennium Dome. A number of large companies, like British Airways,[35] have followed suit by creating new brand identities to reflect a new Britain, and the British Tourist Authority replaced the old Union Jack with a new, more dynamic graphic design. Furthermore, to promote Britain's so-called 'creative industries', 2000 examples of British innovation and design will be selected as Millennium Products, and the Design Council has hosted a series of workshops to think up images that define the best of British. The suggestions have been many and varied, including one design consultant's image of three sheep: 'Sheep 1: a sheep on the hillside, evocative of our national heritage, traditions and landscape – our inherent strengths as a nation. Sheep 2: the Damien Hirst sheep pickled in a tank, showing the radical, avant-garde side of British culture and creativity. Sheep 3: the genetically engineered Dolly, symbolising British leadership in innovation, science and technology.'[36]

All this emphasis on marketing and rebranding unsurprisingly increased the widespread critique of 'Cool Britannia' as merely hot air and hype. The response has been to underline (like the Demos report) the importance of basing these new narratives on empirical truths. At a press conference for the launching of Panel 2000, Robin Cook downplayed marketing strategy and emphasized empirical reality: 'The job of the Foreign Office is to ensure that the national identity that Britain projects abroad is a positive one. This is not, therefore, an exercise in rebranding or in creating an image; rather, it is about projecting the truth about our identity. Our task is to promote what Britain really is – a modern Britain, but one firmly rooted in its traditions and in its heritage.'[37] Defending the empirical truth of these constructed narratives of national identity, Cook here beats a sudden retreat to the organic metaphor of roots and essentialised, ethnically defined identities.

Despite the emphasis on New Britain and new British identity, the importance of national continuity has been repeatedly stressed. Although Blair may have spoken of 'breaking free of our imperial shadows', pride in imperial Britain is encouraged, as are certain old stereotypes of Britishness:

> We live in a new age but in an old country. Britain won two world wars. We had an empire and formed a commonwealth. We invented the sports that the rest of the world now plays; we gave the world some of the finest literature, art and poetry. We are proud of our history, but its weight hangs heavy upon us. Why? Because it has left us far too long defining ourselves as a nation not by what unites us but by what divides us.[38]

Imperial history, then, 'hangs heavy' not because of a guilty conscience but simply because, like the rest of modern British history, its glory is tainted by the existence of social conflict and the lack of cohesion. And though insufficient for the demands of today's world, pride in Old Britain and its past achievements is considered necessary. Asserting the need for increased creativity and innovation, Blair actually laments the disappearance of what he see as the spirit of adventure that characterised British imperialism: 'We are no longer a country', he states, 'that, in the words of the opening to *Star Trek*, wants "to boldly go". We are less adventurous, daring, forward-looking. Yet our history is all about being outward-looking, imaginative, clever.'[39]

Whilst it could be argued that the old British values of justice, liberty, tolerance, and fair play that New Labour promotes can be shared by ethnic minorities and therefore provide the foundation for an inclusive British identity, it should be remembered that these same values legitimised imperial Britain's civilising mission, and that although ethnic minorities are not excluded from sharing these values, they are certainly excluded from sharing in Britain's glorious past. Furthermore, as the Stephen Lawrence case has shown, there are many who believe they will not experience fair play and justice in Blair's New Britain.[40] The irony here is that all the government's emphasis on newness and the rebranding of identity for a diverse New Britain has resulted in a resurgence of the old stereotypes of white ethnicity, perhaps most evidently in the appearance of the British Bulldog in New Labour's election broadcasts.

The liberal, multicultural ideal of cultural diversity or pluralism, however, clearly belongs to New Labour's inclusive One Nation ideology, and New Labour has committed itself to pursuing the principle of racial equality. Whilst this commitment has been seen to waver when there have been votes to be gained (e.g.,

Peter Mandelson's campaign tactics at the Saddleworth and Littleborough by-election which played on paranoias about immigrants),[41] a greater problem concerns the implication of the homogenising of 'the people' under New Labour's unifying discourse of social inclusion for ethnic minorities, and for minority groups in general.[42] Despite New Labour's promotion of diversity and pluralism, the obscuring of differences amongst those who are included means that the overriding vision of multicultural New Britain is essentially a homogeneous one, resting on a denial of the incommensurability of cultural difference. Blair has stated, 'We seek a diverse but inclusive society, promoting tolerance within agreed norms.'[43] But the question to be asked is agreed by whom? The assumption of achieved consensus, and the existence of shared values and interests, means the question of who determines the norms of decent, or 'fair', conduct is left entirely unaddressed. Moreover, the focus on the individual's duty to integrate and adhere to perceived common norms ('rights come with responsibilities') leads to the further question of how collective political demands can be made and on whose terms. New Labour may encourage the strengthening of ethnic communities, but only as long as they are integrated into society as a whole and as long as their pursuit of collective interests coincides with those of the wider national community. Whilst ethnic minorities are not excluded from One Britain, the demand becomes one of assimilatory inclusion. The limits of multicultural New Britain are clear enough: cultural diversity is acceptable, and even appreciated, but only as long as it does not create political conflict, and thereby undermine the shared values and aims of 'the people'.

A United Kingdom(e)?

The positioning of the Millennium Dome on the Prime Meridian at Greenwich serves to illustrate the transition pronounced by New Labour from Old to New Britain, where the Royal Observatory and Greenwich's other historic attractions represent the nation's illustrious past, and the Dome, the nation's new future. The linking together of these two supposed national 'eras', of past and future greatness, by the Prime Meridian reaffirms the notion of Britain as

Edward the Confessor had built Westminster Abbey. By late morning Michelangelo had shown us unimaginable beauty. Sir Walter Raleigh brought back the potato just in time for lunch. Shakespeare wrote sonnets in the afternoon, and the Earl of Sandwich invented the sandwich around teatime. Florence Nightingale and later Mother Theresa showed us the power of compassion. Logie Baird invented the television in time for the evening news and in the few minutes before bedtime we've seen a man on the moon, the fall of the Berlin Wall and the end of Apartheid. Imagine what we can do tomorrow.[49]

The Eurocentric perspective offered here of the last one thousand years is truly astounding, and it is clear that celebrating the millennium on these terms is equivalent to celebrating Britain's role in the history of European domination.[50] The self-congratulatory belief in progress and the achievements of Western civilisation expressed in the final phrase 'Imagine what we can do tomorrow' underlines with a flourish the ideology behind the millennium celebrations, in which the Dome itself is no less than a theme-park of New Labour-style nationalist pedagogy.

Shortly after coming into office, the New Labour government relaunched the Dome project, promising that it would be 'the finest exhibition the world has ever seen' and 'a beacon to the world'. Yet in sharp contrast with the early confidence of such pronouncements, there has continued to be a great deal of speculation and controversy surrounding the actual contents of the Dome (inviting, perhaps, an easy analogy with New Labour spin and policy). Organised around the theme 'Time to Make a Difference', the main exhibition will consist of fourteen zones which, focusing on the themes of education, work, health, leisure, communication, community, finance and the environment, appear to broadly match government policy areas.[51] This, of course, suggests that the exhibition inside the Dome will indeed function as a vehicle for New Labour propaganda.

The presentation of an inclusive, harmonious and united 'hybrid Britain', as New Britain has been dubbed, of 'happily co-existing subcultures' has, of course, been a priority for organisers of the Dome in deciding on the contents, and has also been at the centre of controversy.[52] This is most obviously being attempted in one of the most publicised zones of the Dome, the 'Faith' zone.

Here we are informed that '[t]he formative influence of Christianity in the history of the western world will be recognised as will the presence of other religious beliefs'. Again, it will be shared values and the 'setting aside of difference' that is emphasised as visitors are invited to '[e]xperience a moment of peace and reflect on our deepest common beliefs'. But perhaps the most interesting zone in this context is the zone on British national identity, called 'Self-portrait', which will invite people to '[d]ecide what being British means for all our futures'.[53] This zone is being planned as a 'celebration of all things British' and will exhibit objects nominated by the general public precisely for their Britishness. Whether this exhibit will comprise objects other than the traditional stereotypes of Britishness (from red double-decker busses to Shakespeare) remains to be seen – although it is, of course, also likely to contain objects and images that are also seen to reflect and define New Britain.

Whatever its final contents, the Dome itself can be seen to epitomise the problems of multiculturalism: as an exhibition of 'hybrid Britain', the cultural objects or images chosen to represent minority groups are collected and contained under the hemisphere of the Dome on zero degree longitude. In other words they are assimilated into the homogeneous time of the nation and into the single linear narrative of national development and progress that is traced from the days of empire. Furthermore, the commodification of these multicultural identities represents, one could argue, a museumisation of culture, which only adds to the totalising structure of the Dome. Thus, like the Royal Observatory, the Dome has its own panoptic function. Jonathan Glancey has pointed out that historically domes have been the preferred monuments of dictators: 'Dictators and their architects', he writes, 'have chosen domes because domes represent the last word in control. A dome settles over people placed inside and below it like a Victorian glass bowl does over stuffed animals. The circular form of a dome is like a trap. Which way do you turn to find the way out?'[54] Whilst it may appear that, for ethnic minorities, the choice is between exclusion or assimilatory inclusion, their diasporic presence within the nation space always already de-synchronises the national narrative of a homogeneous people moving along a single path of linear progress. In the same way, it should be noted that whilst the Prime Meridian at Greenwich divides East from West and attempts to establishes a panoptic centre of space and time, it also splits and divides the metropolitan centre itself, and thereby reveals the instability of such constructions.

In order to debunk the linear narrative which underpins the millennium celebrations it is necessary to consider the presence of different temporalities within the nation-space. This, however, does not mean that one can simply point out, as many critics have done, the fact that different cultures have their own calendars - for instance, that on the Jewish calendar the year 2000 is actually 5760, or according to the Muslim calendar, 1421.[55] Such arguments only point to the fact of calendrical accident - a fact that is well-rehearsed in all discussions of when the new millennium actually begins, i.e. in year 2000 or 2001. Moreover, the formulation of calendrical alternatives simply leads back to the totalising and homogenising ideology that is inherent in the construction of time lines. Whilst they can be seen as cultural assertions that do question and challenge the Western naturalisation of time and the understanding of the millennium as a universal celebration, they do not move beyond the notion of a single temporal frame. Rather, it is necessary to explore the multiple, disjunctive temporalities within the nation that do not conform to the symbols of contemporaneity set up by the nationalist time-frame, and which contest the historicist view of the nation as a self-identical, united subject progressing towards its destiny along the line of homogeneous time.

Notes

1. See, for example, the numerous publications of the Center for Millennial Studies at Boston University.
2. Stephen Jay Gould's recent book, *Questioning the Millennium* (London: Jonathan Cape, 1997), is currently one of the most popular of these.
3. At the time of writing, the Dome is still an unfinished project.
4. See, for example, Mark Leonard's article 'Rebranding Rationale', *Newsweek*, 6 July 1998. The connection between Britain's millennium celebrations for year 2000 and these anniversaries (the Union Jack [1701], the Great Exhibition [1851], and the Festival of Britain [1951]) tends to be made without recourse to the debate on the arbitrariness of calendrical

calculations i.e. whether the millennium actually begins in year 2000 or 2001. Of course, it is precisely the calendrical 'coincidence' of these anniversaries with the celebrations planned for year 2000 that is used to reinforce the conceptualisation of the millennium as a national event. For Stephen Jay Gould, the debate over when the millennium actually begins is an issue of elite vs. popular culture. New Labour does not, however, appear to have made use of the opportunity of labelling year 2000 the 'people's' millennium.

5. Rachel Sylvester, 'Dome on target and will be envy of world, says Blair', *Daily Telegraph* 25 Feb. 1998; David Lister, 'Unveiled: Blair's theme park for the new Millennium: PM promises Greenwich extravaganza will be the envy of the world', *Independent* 25 Feb. 1998.
6. Cited in Sylvester.
7. Kristen Lippincott, *A Guide to the Old Royal Observatory: The Story of Time and Space* (Kent: Addax, n.d.) ii.
8. This is the subtitle of Charles Jennings's book *Greenwich: The Place where Days Begin and End* (London: Little, Brown, 1999).
9. Harold Spencer Jones, *The Royal Observatory, Greenwich* (London: Longmans Green, 1944) 1. See also the three volume set by Eric G. Forbes, A. J. Meadows and D. Howse, *Greenwich Observatory* (London: Taylor and Francis, 1975).
10. Jan-Willem Broekhuysen, 'Preface', in Derek Howse, *Greenwich Time and the Longitude (Official Millennium Edition)* (London: Philip Wilson, 1997) 9.
11. A number of suggestions were put forward for a neutral prime meridian (including Jerusalem, the Great Pyramid at Giza, the Azores and Faeroe Islands, and Bering Strait), but these were highly impracticable as there were no principal observatories at these locations.
12. See Meadows, *Greenwich Observatory* 2: 75. Howse notes that 'the North American railroads had adopted a standard time system based on the Greenwich meridian only eighteen days before the invitations [for the 1884 Washington Conference] were sent out' (134). When the final vote on the second resolution to fix the prime meridian at Greenwich was taken, San Domingo was the only country to vote against. This was explained as a protest 'on the occurrence of the disagreement produced by the proposal of the Delegates of France, a nation renowned for being one of the first in intellectual progress', and anticipating the acceptance of the seventh resolution (on the principle of decimal angles and time) put forward by France, it was stated, 'That day will be saluted with a cordial *hosanna* by the republic of San Domingo, which is always ready freely to give its assent to the progress of civilisation' (cited in Howse 137).
13. Howse 149-50, 140.
14. See Dava Sobel, *Longitude: The True Story of a Lone Genius Who Solved the Greatest Scientific Problem of His Time* (London: Fourth Estate, 1996).
15. See, for example, Beryl Platts, *A History of Greenwich* (Newton Abbot: David and Charles, 1973), Clive Aslet, *The Story of Greenwich* (London: Fourth Estate, 1999), and Jennings. Platts states that it was from Greenwich,

Chaucer's home for over a decade, that he 'was able to watch the Becket pilgrims pouring over Blackheath to Canterbury' (93).

16. Cited from the dust jacket to Jennings.
17. See, for example, Aslet's long and somewhat melodramatic description of Lord Nelson's funeral procession at Greenwich at the beginning of his book, *The Story of Greenwich.*
18. Sobel 169.
19. Joan Anim-Addo's *Sugar, Spices and Human Cargo: An Early Black History of Greenwich* (1996), which traces the lives and conditions of slaves, servants and the black settler population of Greenwich from the sixteenth to the eighteenth century is an exception to the rule. Writing with the concerns of Greenwich's contemporary black community in mind, her short history of 'black' Greenwich and its connection with the anti-slavery campaign offers a valuable insight into the historical diversity of this community and demands recognition for their neglected, or forgotten, past.
20. José Rabasa, *Inventing America: Spanish Historiography and the Formation of Eurocentrism,* (Norman: U of Oklahoma P, 1993) 191.
21. David Harvey, *The Condition of Postmodernity,* (Oxford: Blackwell, 1995) 252 (his emphasis).
22. From conversations with Prem Poddar.
23. Benedict Anderson, *Imagined Communities: Reflections on the Origins and Spread of Nationalism* (London: Verso, 1991) 26.
24. Chris Smith, 'Get Ready for Britain's Millennium Bonanza', Department for Culture, Media and Sport, 25 March 1998 <www.coi.gov.uk>.
25. Peter Mandelson and Roger Liddel, *The Blair Revolution: Can New Labour Deliver?* (London: Faber, 1996) 9.
26. Tony Blair, *New Britain: My Vision of a Young Country* (London: Fourth Estate, 1996) 287.
27. Blair, *New Britain* 71.
28. Cited in *The Independent* 11 Nov. 1997.
29. Blair, *New Britain* 72, 259, 299. William Hague has attempted to counter the reputation of Conservative jingoism and xenophobia with 'patriotism without bigotry'.
30. Blair, *New Britain* 268.
31. Mark Leonard, *Britain™: Renewing Our Identity* (London: Demos, 1997) 10, 24.
32. The six 'stories' Leonard proposes as 'a toolkit for a new sense of identity' are Britain as a 'global hub', a 'hybrid nation', a 'creative island', a 'silent revolutionary', a 'nation of fair play' and 'open for business', and these narratives, or 'trademarks' are offered as a neat package to be marketed abroad (62).
33. Leonard 56.
34. Leonard 56.
35. British Airways is also the sponsor of the Millennium Wheel, or 'London Eye'. The Chief Executive of British Airways, Bob Ayling, is also Chairman of the New Millennium Experience Company.

36. Jeremy Myerson, 'Designs on Britain's Future', *Independent on Sunday* 29 March 1998.
37. Robin Cook, 'Panel 2000: Opening Statement by the Foreign Secretary', Foreign and Commonwealth Office, 1 Apr. 1998 <www.fco.gov.uk>.
38. Blair, *New Britain* 64-65.
39. Blair, *New Britain* 251.
40. Because this case not only foregrounds race crimes, but also addresses the issue of institutionalised racism within the British police forces, the Stephen Lawrence affair has become the major symbol of troubled race relations in contemporary Britain, thus undermining the narrative of multicultural Britain's 'happily co-existing subcultures'. Whilst racist thugs and supporters of the BNP can easily be represented as an aberration from normal 'decent' society, the exposure of institutionalised racism in one of the pillars of society brings all government and state institutions into question and reveals the pervasiveness of racial tension in Britain.
41. See *New Statesman* 29 Nov. 1995.
42. For a critique of New Labour's discourses of social inclusion and exclusion see Ruth Levitas, *The Inclusive Society? Social Exclusion and New Labour* (London: Macmillan, 1998).
43. Tony Blair, *The Third Way: New Politics for the New Century* (London: Fabian Soc., 1998) 12.
44. One of the Dome's attractions will be The Greenwich Pavilion. Built outside the structure of the Dome by the meridian line, this will house an exhibition on the story of time and Greenwich.
45. Cited in Anthony Bevins, 'You Must Love My Dome, Orders Mandelson', *Independent* 24 Feb. 1998.
46. Here it may be interesting to note that for France's own millennium celebrations the Eiffel Tower has been renamed as the 'Worldwide Observatory of the Year 2000'. The French celebrations will also feature the 'Green Meridian' project, in which a line of trees are planted across the country along the Paris meridian.
47. Alastair Irvine, *The Battle for the Millennium Dome* (London: Irvine News Agency, 1999) 79; Mark Reddy cited in Celia Hall, 'The Dome's New Britannia Logo is a Woman with a Past', *Daily Telegraph* 6 June 1998. The choice of this logo has been controversial as it was earlier used to advertise pharmaceutical products by Roche.
48. Cited in Patrick French, 'Is There Any Longer Such a Thing as a National Identity?', *Daily Telegraph* 16 May 1998.
49. Cited in 'A Thousand Years in a Day – Imagine What We Can Do Tomorrow', *NME* 15 May 1998. This advert ran only through January 1999. The recent advertising campaign for the sale of tickets to the Dome continues to be based around the slogan 'One amazing day', and the phrases 'a 1000 years in a day' and 'Imagine what we can do tomorrow' feature on the Millennium Experience website <www.dome2000.co.uk>.
50. Parodying the Millennium Experience advert, Ziauddin Sardar offers instead an 'alternative history of the last millennium': 'After returning from

narrative frameworks which accompany the concept. And there are strong narratives involved. One of my presumptions concerning globalization is that it fills out a gap left over by the fall of the older, great narratives. Another presumption is that the task prescribed to the concept is so huge that its use immediately involves a debate over the abuse to which it can lead.

The old world of universalism and particularism

Before examining the meaning and use of globalization, it could be of interest to compare the term with other, older world concepts, that is, concepts used to describe phenomena on a global scale. I shall restrict myself to two concepts, universal history and civilization, as they appear in two paradigmatic works, Francis Fukuyama's *The End of History* and Samuel P. Huntington's *The Clash of Civilization*.[2] In a way, these two works delineate a traditional horizon within which Western thought since the Enlightenment has coped with the world. Fukuyama's imitation of 18th-century rationalism presents a wonderfully clear picture of a universalist position in actual use, and Huntington's concept of civilization is an equally clear demonstration of a culturalist position used to describe the world situation.

Fukuyama's universalism is based on a Hegelian version of a philosophy of history. History is the process through which mankind fulfils its struggle for freedom. In Fukuyama's modernized version of Hegel the struggle for recognition is fulfilled by the invention of a liberal democracy based on the universal standards of liberty and equality. Capitalism as a process of rationalization lends a helping hand to this end. But only democracy can end History because only this form is truly universal. Capitalism is linked to the Hegelian narrative as a weaker form of universalism in as much as it is part of a universal direction, that is, economic modernization.[3] But because capitalism allows for all sorts of non-universal regimes democracy is needed to direct it in the right universal way.

Fukuyama inscribes his universalism in an optimist narrative in contrast to a post-1945 pessimistic mood that he sees as a general trend in Western thinking. In the opening of his book he bluntly states that '[a]s we reach the 1990's the world as a whole has not revealed new evils, but has gotten *better* in certain distinct ways.'[4] We have to remind ourselves today that Fukuyama's optimism itself was part of a triumphal optimism prevailing in the first years after 1989. Into this optimistic, universalist narrative, Fukuyama inserts all kinds of world events such as the fall of authoritarian regimes, the appearance of nationalist and fundamentalist movements, the role of UN and NATO, Third World under-development etc. All of these are placed on either side of a main fault line between democracy and culture located respectively in a post-historical world and a historical world: 'For the foreseeable future, the world will be divided between a post-historical part, and a part that is still stuck in history.'[5] Democracy belongs to the post-historical world where History (with a capital letter) has fulfilled its mission. In this universal world (or universal civilization) all conflicts, all hopes will be formulated within a democratic imagination. No other alternatives are any longer available. Culture, on the other hand, forms the historical world, a world 'riven with a variety of religious, national, and ideological conflicts.'[6] Culture, in Fukuyama's view, is particularistic and essentialist. In its political manifestation, it takes the form of nationalism and fundamentalism.

Fukuyama's reformulation of the traditional dualism between universalism and particularism leads to a two-world model conceived along the meta-temporal lines of History. The main difference between Fukuyama and other temporal perspectives, such as modernization theory and development theory that deal with three worlds, is that he is capable of setting an end to development. But also Fukuyama stays within the temporal perspective handed over by Western rationalism.

Fukuyama has been met with severe criticism for ethnocentrism. Admittedly, in his more empirical statements he comes very close to conflating the post-historical world with the West, but it would be unfair not to acknowledge his effort to distinguish the position of mankind from its cultural manifestations in the West and elsewhere (even though he only treats the question of universal practices superficially).[7]

The other pole in the traditional horizon is marked by Huntington's paradigm of the clash of civilization. For Huntington the only perspective that can explain the changing world order is cultural. He locates the states of the world in large cultural units or civilizations defined by traditional cultural criteria such as ethnicity, language, religion and ways of life,[8] and he supports this culturalist approach with a simple anthropological claim about people always being tempted to divide themselves into us and them.[9]

Huntington's approach is not only culturalist, it is emphatically anti-universalist. In his frontal attack on universalism, he aims at both globalization (understood as the claim of a progressive homogenization of the world) and the idea of the universal, both of which he assembles in a notion of 'universal civilization'. His central claim is almost the complete opposite of Fukuyama's: 'The concept of a universal civilization is a distinctive product of Western civilization.'[10]

Huntington seeks to refute all claims of globalization by pointing to the existing cultural diversity. From his point of view globalization and its universalist ideology is seen as Westernization, and the reactions as defensive cultural responses against a form of cultural imperialism. Consequently, there are neither universal values nor global homogenisation, but a clash between civilizations. In his denunciation of universalism as Western cultural imperialism, Huntington apparently joins a traditionally third world critique (tiersmondism) of Western dominance.[11] But his purpose is only to create a separation between 'the West and the rest' in order to place the West as the best by attaching all the positive values to the Western world. In the tiersmondist approach Western civilization is treated as having a global power. Any talk of globalization will, in this view, be reduced to imperialism. Serge Latouche, a French economist and anthropologist, has tried to formulate an idea of globalization as Westernization. To do this, he has to evacuate the cultural content of the West which then becomes like 'a machine, impersonal, soulless [...] masterless' and 'uncontrollable'. Westernization is precisely the reproduction of this model which can be reproduced because it is 'transhistorical and non-spatial'.[12] To turn the West into a machine makes it easier to identify global economy (and its social consequences) as

Western, but at the cost of emptying the West completely, so that it becomes difficult to see any sign of the West being a civilization. But the political purpose is obvious: globalization is the fault of the West.

Huntington cannot disregard all ideas of a general process of modernization. He introduces modernization into his scheme of civilization as an underlying, almost structural movement in the development of all societies related to 'industrialization, urbanization, increasing levels of literacy, education and social mobilization'. But when he at the same time states that 'modern cultures' are as diverse as were 'traditional cultures', he places culture at the fundamental level thereby staying on safe cultural grounds in order to claim that the 'West [was] the West long before it was modern.'[13]

Huntington represents the particularist and relativist pole in the traditional horizon. This perspective is conceived along a spatial logic where world events can only be seen as located in different places. Even modernization, which is viewed as a general, structural trend, can only materialize in different civilizations. The culturalist pole thus delineates a position where time is subordinated to space, so to speak, in complete opposition to Fukuyama's temporal perspective where space can only be perceived as a difference in time.

The positions outlined by the works of Fukuyama, Huntington and Latouche stays within the semantic and discursive field covered by the traditional concept of civilization. On one side we have a universal civilization described in a temporal perspective, on the other side we have a Western civilization which is expressed either in a purely cultural framework (Huntington) or in a more economical form as Western capitalism (Latouche).

McWorld vs McJihad – a simple formulation of globalization

By coining the conceptual couples McWorld and McJihad in a book bearing this title, Benjamin Barber has done much to popularize the concept of globalization.[14] In his view, globalization manifests itself both as a universal sphere driven by pure economic market logic and as an ideology, a globalism, through which the market logic expresses itself. It is this sphere and its ideology that he subsumes under the now highly popular term McWorld.[15] The term, of course, refers to McDonald, the burger chain, as a useful metaphor for the link between a global market and a cultural homogenization (McDonald connoting both food culture and the world of Disney). McWorld is a world consisting of 'trade', 'capitalism', 'market' and 'corporations'. It has its proponents and its ideology or world view which, in Barber's caricature-like depiction, presents the future as a

> busy portrait of onrushing economic, technological and ecological forces that demand integration and uniformity and that mesmerize peoples everywhere with fast music, fast computers, and fast food - MTV, Macintosh, and McDonald's - pressing nations into one homogeneous global theme park, one McWorld's tied together by communications, information, entertainment, and commerce.[16]

Concentrated in this passage we have all the main ingredients of Barber's concept of globalization. It is first of all a concept that can link and concentrate - one is tempted to say homogenize - different fields (technology, economy, culture) into one. The main feature of globalization as the phenomenon signified by the concept happens to be the actual homogenization of the world, which takes the form of the market subverting culture with the help of communication technology. The core meaning is then that globalization is global economy dominating all other spheres,[17] and even more important, that the world of globalization can be described as uniform. Economy links up with technology, which immediately points to communication technology. From this chain of connotations, one can easily move on to more ontological questions concerning the constitution of reality, where McWorld becomes 'a kind of virtual reality, created by invisible but omnipotent high-tech information networks' which demands a new concept of space, cyberspace, in order to be described, 'McWorld's chilly new cyberspace',[18] in Barber's dramatic narrative. Even though Barber's cyberspace is only very loosely connected to any social reality (the concept is disconnected from the different dimensions of communication) its introduction points to the need of giving space a new meaning. For Barber cyberspace indicates that '[y]ou are nowhere. You are everywhere. Inhabiting an abstraction.'[19] One might object that this definition comes close to becoming meaningless. One could, of course, also contend that all spaces have an abstract or rather symbolic dimension. The democratic community, which plays the role of an authentic space in Barber's narrative, must also be seen as an abstraction, or as it has become trendy to say, an imagined community. But these contentions aside, the point made by Barber is that cyberspace is something outside traditional space, a purely symbolic space (nowhere) used to perceive of the world as such (everywhere). But because not even Barber can escape the spatial, he turns cyberspace into a world, McWorld.

In Barber's very pessimistic narrative McWorld fills out the role of a negative universalist civilization. In this way he takes up a traditional critique of modernity developed in Western thinking from the late 19th century. But contrary to Huntington, he does not seek refuge in a Spenglerian version of civilization. Another negative pole he places in his story of a 'world (that) has been sent spinning out of control' is McJihad. Through McJihad he depicts a world haunted by 'retribalization' and a 'balkanization of nation-states in which culture is pitted against culture'.[20] This clash of cultures and within cultures is seen as a revolt against the globalization of McWorld. But at the same time, the particularism of McJihad is part of globalization. As Barber states it, the linkage between the forces of the two worlds is 'deeply dialectical', whereby is meant that they strengthen each other in a pattern of cause and effect.[21] This pattern produces the actual world disorder which is the main theme in Barber's global diagnosis. Squeezed between the destructive forces of McWorld and McJihad, Barber finds the democratic nation based on pluralism, legalism and collective responsibility. The main threat to democracy lies in 'the denationalizing practices' which follow from the negative forces of the two worlds.[22] The theme and concept of denationalization appear to be part of the semantic field of globalization. Denationalization functions as a transitory concept in a reconceptualization of the nation. Contrary to others, Barber does not propose the *postnational* as a concept attached to globalization, perhaps because

way of coping with this on a conceptual level is to invent a new non-spatial space, cyberspace. Another more traditional way is to upgrade the concept of the nation to a global scale as proposed by Edgar Morin: 'Il nous faut [...] lier concentriquement nos patries familiales, régionales, nationales, européennes, et les intégrer dans l'univers concret de la patrie terrienne.'[32] Morin's idea of a global *patrie* based on a concentric expansion of the concept of *patrie* allows the transfer of an ethical dimension (patriotism) to the global level. The world thus becomes a place defined by the responsibility and solidarity of everyone. And the barbaric sides of globalization can be encountered by a global policy of civilization. As Morin states, we must 'civilize the world'.[33] Even though Morin formulates his proposal in a very French-style universalism he certainly captures a trend in the globalization debate, one that was also formulated by Coca-Cola in the famous slogan: 'We are the world'. Of course, when formulated by Coca-Cola, the *we* in the phrase is simultaneously a global actor in McWorld and mankind as such. Morin's global patrie is conceived much along the same lines as Barber's squeezed democratic nation, the only difference being that the latter due to his (American) communitarianism cannot imagine how the barbarity of McWorld can be civilised.

Globalization as a relation between the local and the global

Whereas McWorld designates a world outside the nation and thereby creates a conceptual fault line between the two, Morin thinks concentrically. But they are both strongly anchored in a traditional perspective of national spaces. Others have tried to get out of the conceptual prison marked by the nation. This has been done by reformulating the relation between the global and the local. First of all, the purpose of introducing the local is to criticize any simple definition of globalization as a uniform process of homogenization. Even if an idea of homogeneity has to be accepted - without which it would be hard to conceive of a global level at all - the reactions or the interpretations of the global influences will differ from culture to culture, it is claimed. The contention of the important role of the local is part of an optimistic narrative which goes against the different pessimistic end-of versions (end of the nation, end of democracy, end of the welfare state and so forth) presented by Barber, Bauman, Huntington and others. 'The local strikes back' could be the title of this optimistic story, which is formulated not in end-terms, but in post-terms. As I shall show, post-modernism plays a crucial role in the story.

The story of the local is typically framed within a cultural discourse where reactions to global influences are viewed as everyday life interpretations and constructions of meaning. The subject in this discourse is not anonymous forces, systems or corporations, as it was the case in McWorld, but rather everyday people.[34] Globalization is in general investigated through culture, so that global culture on one hand will mean the homogenization of meaning and on the other hand the different meanings of this meaning. The simplest way of introducing the local is to see it as a setting for responses to the global. This form stresses the active role of the global and the defensive, passive role of the local. The global will typically be related to negative terms like 'penetration' and 'threat'.[35] Taking this point further, Bauman talks about 'localities [that] are losing their meaning-generating and meaning-negotiating capacity'. In Bauman's bleak perspective, the losing localities are furthermore placed in a social frame of top and bottom where the losers happen to be 'those at the bottom', the 'localized' rest separated from 'the extraterritorial elite'.[36] Through the double separation of global–local and top–bottom, Bauman depicts a world divided between a local and disempowered underclass and a powerful global elite. This description can then 'explain' 'neo-tribal and fundamentalist tendencies', Barber's world of McJihad, as the (almost legitimate) response of the disempowered. This way of relating globalization to the separation between a disconnected or rootless (and ruthless) elite and a localized rest in the form of a slumbering monster of fundamentalism seems to be extremely popular because it can unite and explain different phenomena such as the success of right-wing movements in Western Europe, genocide in Bosnia, religious fundamentalism in Iran, anti-EU tendencies within the member countries so forth in a simple form.

Any view of the local involves a consideration of the dualism or the dialectics between the two levels. In Baumans's type of global action-local response framework, localization merely becomes an effect of globalization: 'An integral part of the globalization process is progressive spatial segregation, separation and exclusion.'[37] (This obviously leaves open the question of the status of existing forms of localities. Bauman simply dismisses this question by inscribing the global–local relation in a post perspective, for example 'after the nation state'.

Bauman's pessimistic outlook is countered by those who confer a more active role to the local. Instead of placing the local at the mere receiving end of globalization it becomes a setting for an active re-elaboration of global influences. First of all, contrary to Bauman, responses are not viewed in a uniform way, but as 'selective responses of relevant collective actors'.[38] National cultures as well as other entities such as regions or civilizations can be relevant actors. Secondly, responses are not simply echoes, but 'continue to deform and reform, blend, syncretize and transform, in various ways', as Featherstone puts it.[39] This perspective on the global–local is framed within a paradigm that Ulrich Beck calls the both–and paradigm in opposition to a more traditional either–or paradigm.[40] Both–and indicates that we have to think of globalization as both global and local, which involves a lot of different both–and connections: both centralization and decentralization, both homogeneity and pluralism, both multiculturalism and fundamentalism, and so on.

The active role of the local is related to its interpretative capacities (at least if local is a question of culture). A simple but still inevitable way of stating the role of the local is to stress the fact that all influences have to be experienced and interpreted by specific people somewhere. This methodological 'localism' is strongly emphasized by John Tomlinson when he claims that globalization as time-space compression 'has to be understood in terms of a transformation of practice and experience which is felt *actually within localities*'.[41] This general restating of the local as an interpretative space is typical for the cultural approach on globalization contrary to the more instrumental perspectives which mainly focus on the anonymous (and often technological) forces of the global. There is, however, an inherent risk here of completely eliminating the global level by claiming that it is made up of different localities.[42] Any theory of globalization must therefore involve an idea of a global level whether as transactions, connections or as horizons and consciousness.

A way of perceiving the cultural capacity of localities is to focus on their power to reformulate traditional concepts and ideas of the local. Featherstone speaks of a rediscovery, re-emergence and re-enactment of identity and rituals.[43] But rediscovery does not mean the return of the old (which is the way fundamentalism is often explained). Rediscoveries are consciously constructed within a framework acknowledging the global. People know that rediscovery is re-construction. In that sense they are post-ethnic and postnational.[44]

Hybridity

The power to reconstruct is equally a power to mix and blend. A whole vocabulary of blending and mixing accompanies this view of the local: indigenization, syncretization, multiculturalism, third cultures, hybridity. Two popular catchwords seem to capture the general meaning of this vocabulary: hybridity and postmodernism. Jan Nederveen Pietersee has proposed to see the process of globalization as fundamentally a process of hybridization.[45] Hybridization is defined as 'the ways in which forms become separated from existing practices and recombine with new forms in new practices'. Instead of treating the global–local as a distinct relation, Pietersee introduces a whole panoply of possible combinations operating in different specific spheres. The result is a dramatic increase in the possible combinations or 'hybrid, which is precisely what globalization means for Pietersee. Hybridity is at work everywhere. Local spaces turn into 'hybrid spaces', that is, spaces characterized by combination such as the 'cities of peasants' in Latin America.[46] But how does the concept of hybridity fit into the global–local framework? In a limited view of hybridity it can be seen as a sort of 'third culture' functioning as an outpost within the local. Third cultures have a 'relative autonomy and [a] global frame of reference [which] necessitates that they take into account the particularities of local cultures.'[47] The new concept of *glocalization* comes close to this understanding of hybridity. Glocalization was introduced to describe the local targeting of the marketing strategies of global firms.[48] Glocalization is to some degree a twist on the well-known slogan: 'Think globally and act locally.' Global firms have to act globally and think locally in order to sell their products in different cultural localities. Third cultures could, of course, also be the global elite so castigated by Bauman and others.

Even though the concepts of third cultures and glocalization were introduced to grasp the relation between the global and the local, they mark a tendency towards separating the two levels from each other. The 'glocalizers' and the members of the hybrid third culture are posited at a distance from the local. The more radical point made by Pietersee is that hybridity works at all levels. In order to analyze hybridity we need, he claims, a new concept of culture adapted to the phenomenon of global culture. As it happened with the concept of the nation, the concept of culture comes under fire in the debate over globalization. Pietersee proposes to view culture as a translocal process of hybridity in opposition to a traditional concept of culture as territorially bound. One could argue here, however, that most cultural theorists would subscribe to this new concept. The interesting aspect of Pietersee's new concept is that it is not delocalized. Translocality functions in a locality, but installs what he calls 'an outward-looking sense of place'. What is meant by this is most likely a sort of reflexivity towards hybridity, that is, an awareness of the possibility for combinations (in the same way as Featherstone's 'postnostalgics'). Pietersee, however, pursues the combinatory logic inscribed in his concept of hybridity by shifting the focus from the elements combined (which would still be identifiable as in the idea of the multicultural) to the different modes of combination. He ends up establishing an infinite space of combinations, an infinite chain of 'hybridizations of hybrid cultures' which resembles the idea of cyberspace.[49] By this operation he ultimately seems to erase any notion of the local.

At first glance Pietersee's hybridization represents a figure of thought in direct opposition to Huntington's geo-cultural civilizations. But if we look closer we can see that they both posit themselves within a relativist paradigm - Huntington in a traditional nationalist relativism, Pietersee in a postmodernist second order relativism which argues for an infinite relativization of the relative. In this confrontation Pietersee has the upper hand because he can range Huntington among the nostalgic responses to globalization.

Globalization in time

The concept of *postmodernism* is intimately linked to hybridization. 'Postmodernists champion the local, diversity, difference, and heterogeneity, and sometimes claim that globalization itself produces hybridity and multiplicity', it is claimed.[50] Postmodernism is here mainly perceived as a critical paradigm that reflects on recent epistemological and social changes in the world. Its criticism is directed against 'the universalist claims of the metanarratives of the Western enlightenment'.[51] But the concept also contains a temporal meaning as a specific phase in the history of modernity, a phase precisely characterized by fragmentation and hybridity.[52]

Featherstone places the postmodernist paradigm within 'a shifting global balance of power' weakening the cultural hegemony of the West. It might seem a paradox that in describing a new historical situation characterized by a clash between Western and other foundational values Featherstone comes pretty close to a Huntingtonian diagnosis, and also comes to the same conclusion on the relative status of Western values: 'It may well be that what we consider to be the substantive cultural responses and experiences of modernity likewise can be relativized to the Western particularity.'[53] But whereas Huntington speaks of civilizations in a traditional cultural discourse, Featherstone prefers to speak of global modernities eliminating any question of historical disjunction (*Ungleichzeitigkeit*).[54] And by ranging the differences within the same concept of modernity the latter keeps a minimal rim of universalism since all cultures can be set in the same context.[55]

Featherstone creates a direct link between postmodernism and globalization. His argument runs as follows: Globalization produces a situation of hybridity leading to a dismantling of Western cultural hegemony. Postmodernism is a theoretical reflection on this new situation. Featherstone can thus claim that 'globalization produces postmodernism'.[56] Leaving aside the tautological dangers involved in this claim, it can rightfully be asked what happened to the temporal meaning of postmodernism. The answer seems to be that it has been eliminated. Featherstone argues strongly in favour of leaving the temporal tyranny of the concept of modernity. He thus proposes to privilege a spatial view of modernity: 'We need, he says, to ask the question of the spatial dimension of modernity, or where is modernity? [...] in terms of the spatial relationship of the non-West to the West.'[57] This is precisely the question asked by postmodernism, according to him. Maybe Featherstone would claim that he only adds a spatial perspective to the temporal, but it is hard to find any considerations of time and history in his treatment of globalization.

Featherstone's spatial perspective is not so radical as the one involved in the notion of cyberspace. Or to put it differently, Featherstone inscribes cyberspace in a clash of cultures.[58] He therefore does not have the same possibility as, say a Virilio, to let historical time disappear in instantaneous interchanges.[59]

A way of keeping a temporal perspective is to locate globalization within *modernity*. I am aware that modernity is just as much a contested concept as globalization. But it seems to be generally agreed that modernity characterizes a specific period in history or at least a historical process of transformation.[60] If globalization, therefore, is located within modernity it can be recaptured by historical time. One simple way of doing this is simply to claim that globalization is modernity writ large. Anthony Giddens thus claims that modernity is 'inherently globalizing'.[61] Consequently, the different features of globalization such as time-space compression can be given a history, or at least be situated within a loose historical frame of the transition from traditional to modern society.[62]

Another more radical way of historicizing globalization is proposed by Roland Robertson, who places globalization in a long history beginning with a 'germinal phase' in the early fifteenth century and taking off between the 1870s and the mid-1920s, the latter phase being made to correspond with the early thematization of the problem of modernity. The present time can then be viewed as a phase of 'accelerated globalization'. He even proposes to read the whole of world history, including the different historic empires, as sequences of 'miniglobalization'.[63] The obvious inherent risk of this approach is to empty the meaning of globalization. If globalization is identified with all forms of inter-civilizational exchanges or with all kinds of world images, it can be said to have been around always. Robertson does not claim this, but his description of the newness of the truly global phases of globalization is formulated in very general terms, like when he speaks of the world moving from 'being merely "in itself" [...] to the possibility of being "for itself"'.[64]

History, however, can also be used in an argument against the concept of globalizations. Globalization sceptics such as Paul Hirst and Grahame Thompson claim that history bears witness to periods of higher levels of global (which for them is solely economic) interdependence than the present, and furthermore that internationalization and regionalization would be more correct conceptualizations of the phenomena covered by the concept of globalization.[65] One immediate objection to this dismissal of globalization must be that the concept of internationalization is fixed in a traditional perspective of interchange between identifiable entities that is unable to grasp any autonomy of the world in-between.

The historical perspective reinserts globalization in a temporal scheme but without reducing historical time to a universal civilization process. Globalization and modernity are still viewed within a polyphonic framework, whether directly linked to a global logic of hybridity or taking the form of non Western voices.

Globalization as a discourse – a second order globalization

Globalization is typically defined as a multiform phenomenon of flows and exchanges. In the cultural approach to globalization the focus is more often on the semantic and discursive dimensions of the flows and exchanges. One of the most prominent contributions to the analysis of this dimension is given by Roland Robertson. Robertson treats globalization as the different ways 'quotidian actors, collective or individual go about the business of conceiving of the world'.[66] All the different statements about the world make up a *global field* of discourses on the world. The global field is thus an analytical concept of globalization that intends to capture the discursive structures of globe talk. Robertson detects different reference points in the global field, such as national societies, individuals, mankind and the world system, which indicate the basic ways in which the world can be conceived. These points must inevitably be related to each other. An individual perspective of the world might clash with a national one. A national perspective might certainly conflict with the perspective of mankind. The confrontations between the different points are seen by Robertson as 'relativizations' or 'challenges' to the stability of particular perspectives.[67] The aforementioned confrontation between a particular nation and mankind can be viewed both as a challenge to the national perspective (as it occurs in human rights policies) and to the universalist perspective (as it occurs in the criticism of cultural imperialism).

Part of Robertson's global field is constructed around an axis of universalism and particularism. Contrary to many globalization theories, Robertson's theory of global discourse thus emphasizes the close connection between the universal and the global. Furthermore, he does not see the axis as constituted of opposed poles, but as a relational field where the two dimensions penetrate into each other whereby we get a twofold process of 'the universalization of particularism and the particularization of universalism'.[68] What at first glance might seem like a vertiginous play on words actually introduces a new perspective on the global–local. Particularization of universalism focuses on the local cultural interpretations of global influences including the negative responses in the form of fundamentalism, while the universalization of particularism captures such aspects as the global spreading of Western ideas (for example nationalism). The important point made by Robertson is that the two processes are interconnected. As an example we can point to the phenomenon of European nationalism exported to the rest of the world through European world hegemony, but that also had to be adapted to the local cultures.

The axis of universalism and particularism presents a general structuring of the global field. Too general, perhaps. Even if Robertson allows for a difference within universalism between a moral pole around mankind and a political pole around the world system of societies, one needs to ask whether the global is not much more than universalism.[69]

Robertson relates his discussion of global discourses to the question of ideologization. 'Globe-oriented ideologies' or 'images of world order' are normative discourses proposing an ordering of the world. Robertson structures the different ideologies around the classical sociological concepts of *Gesellschaft* and *Gemeinschaft*.[70] *Gemeinschaft* ideologies of the world view the world through community concepts. One way of doing this is to imagine the world as a community towards which every human being has a responsibility. Edgar Morin's global *patrie* would certainly fall under this ideology. *Gesellschaft* ideologies, on the other hand, conceive of the world as a system, for example in political, economic or environmental terms. Robertson primarily focuses on cosmopolitan ideologies of world government. But as pointed out by Ulrich Beck, globalism (which is the term he uses for ideologies of the global) can also be about the economic system. Beck goes so far as to claim that globalism mainly is an ideology of reducing globalization to world economy and world market. Even though this seems an unfounded limitation, Beck clearly points out the ideological effect of ideology: 'Sie [die Ideologie] verfährt monokausal, ökonomistisch, verkürzt die Vieldimensionalität der Globalisierung auf eine, die wirtschaftliche Dimension.'[71] Here ideology is not only about the normativity of world images (as Robertson tends to claim), but also about the closing of the global field. Beck also emphasizes that normativity, mainly in its negative form, is what world order should not be. He writes about different ideological colorings of protectionism (black, green and red).

In parts of the globalization debate we are presented with a high level of conceptual awareness. We might even speak of a second order globalization where the debate concentrates on the semantical and discursive aspects of globalization. As an example we can take Beck's effort of conceptual ordering. He proposes to make a difference between globalism, globality and globalization.[72] Globalism is the ideological closing of the field. Globality defines the existential condition of living in a world society characterized by the totality of exchanges transcending the national state borders. To this more phenomenological definition we might add

cultures, which can easily be told in a pessimistic way (Huntington). The new master narrative of globalization can be a pessimistic story about the power of a rootless, global elite, growing standardization and so forth. But it can also be told optimistically as a world of increasing hybridity transcending the old mental prisons of culture and nation.

The problem with the new master narrative is that it is built around a concept that is highly ambivalent. Globalization can be used and abused in many different ways. It can have the abusive function of cancelling thinking. When Barber, for example, introduces the monster of McJihad in his story it becomes a very easy way of explaining by escaping the complex field of fundamentalism, nationalism, ethnicity and so on. Another abusive function is the cancelling of political action. When political representatives justify a specific political choice, or rather lack of choice, with reference to globalization what we have is an elimination of politics. This is precisely what Ulrich Beck points out when speaking of globalism as an ideology.[77]

Globalization has to be treated as a concept and a discourse with structures of their own. One of the characteristic features of the global discourse is the existence of several competing poles of enunciation. In this way the contested character of the concept of globalization is built into the discourse.

Notes

1. Ulrich Beck, *Was ist Globalisierung? Irrtümer des Globalismus – Antworten auf Globalisierung* (Frankfurt: Suhrkamp 1998) 44.
2. Francis Fukuyama, *The End of History and the Last Man* (London: Hamish Hamilton, 1992); Samuel P. Huntington, *The Clash of Civilizations and the Remaking of World Order* (New York: Simon and Schuster, 1996).
3. Fukuyama treats 'modernization theory' in general as the last version of a universal history in Western thinking (68).
4. Fukuyama 12
5. Fukuyama 276.
6. Fukuyama 276.
7. Within the field of international relations he discusses the role of the UN and NATO (Fukuyama 280-83).
8. The idea of using the concept of civilization to designate large cultural units goes back to 19th-century Europe. For an overview of the historical

meanings of civilization, see Jan Ifversen, 'The Meaning of European Civilization: A Historical-Conceptual Approach', *European Studies Newsletter* 1.2 (1998).

9. Huntington 32.
10. Huntington 66.
11. For a critique of tiersmondism from a universal point of view, see Alain Finkelkraut, *La défaite de la pensée* (Paris: Gallimard, 1987).
12. Serge Latouche, *The Westernization of the World: The Significance, Scope and Limits of the Drive towards Global Uniformity* (Cambridge: Polity, 1996) (originally published in French, 1989) 3-4, 51.
13. Huntington 68-69. The argument has the advantage of countering the culturalist argument as it is expounded, for example, in the idea of Asian values where modernization refers to specific cultural values, but it leaves open the question of how then to explain modernization as different from Westernization.
14. Benjamin Barber, *Jihad vs. McWorld: How Globalism and Tribalism are Reshaping the World* (New York: Ballantine, 1995).
15. In the Danish newspaper articles on globalization that I have looked through, 'McWorld' appeared as the most popular synonym of globalization.
16. Barber 4.
17. Ulrich Beck rightly terms this view on globalization 'World market metaphysics' (196).
18. Barber 26-27.
19. Barber 99.
20. Barber 5, 4.
21. Barber 18.
22. Barber 7.
23. Postnationalism belongs to the group of temporal concepts with the prefix post, like post-industrialism, postcolonialism, postmodernity. The theme of the end of the nation state is strongly represented in the narratives on endings, cp. Jean Guéhenno, *La fin de la démocratie* (Paris 1993), translated as *The End of the Nation State* (Minneapolis: U of Minnesota P, 1995).
24. Barber 7, 279.
25. David Held, A. McGrew, D. Goldblatt and Jonathan Perraton, *Global Transformations: Politics, Economics and Culture* (Cambridge: Polity, 1999) 15.
26. John Tomlinson, *Globalization and Culture* (Cambridge: Polity, 1999) 3.
27. Manuel Castells, *The Information Age: Economy, Society and Culture*, vol. 3: *The End of the Millennium* (London: Blackwell, 1998) 370; Zygmunt Bauman, *Globalization: The Human Consequences* (Cambridge: Polity, 1998) 139.
28. Pierre Lévy, 'Skriften, der aldrig slutter', *Information* (Denmark) 27 Mar. 1998: 12.
29. Tomlinson 2.
30. Tomlinsion 107.
31. Marc Augé, *Non-lieux: Introduction à une anthropologie de la surmodernité* (Paris: Seuil 1992).

32. Edgar Morin, 'La pensée socialiste en ruine', *Le Monde* 21 Apr. 1993: 2.
33. Morin 2.
34. This way of thinking is strongly influenced by a traditional dualism in Western thinking between system and human life which can be found in the splitting of Gesellschaft and Gemeinschaft, or in a Habermasian version as the split between system and life world.
35. In the Danish newspaper articles on globalization that I have examined, 'threat' appears to be the most common qualification of globalization.
36. Baumann 2-4.
37. Baumann 3.
38. Roland Robertson, Globalization. Social Theory and Global Culture (London: SAGE, 1992) 60.
39. Mike Featherstone, *Undoing Culture: Globalization, Postmodernism and Identity* (London: Sage, 1995).
40. Beck 54.
41. Tomlinson 9.
42. This thinking is at the center of the globalization skeptics. A good representative of the skeptics is Anthony Smith, who claims 'that the quest for a global culture and the ideal of cosmopolitanism are continually subverted by the realities of power politics and by the nature and features of culture' (Anthony Smith, Nations and Nationalism in a Global Era [Cambridge: Polity, 1995] 19). He ends his book by concluding that 'the nation and nationalism provide the only realistic socio-cultural framework for a modern world order' (159).
43. Featherstone 98.
44. Frederick Buell is thinking along these lines in his analysis of tendencies towards a 'nationalist postnationalism' ('Nationalist Postnationalism: Globalist Discourse in Contemporary American Culture', *American Quarterly* 50.3 [1998]: 548-91). Mike Featherstone sees the post phenomenon as a form of cosmopolitan and almost ironic distance towards cultures among middle class groups of 'post-nostalgics' and 'posttourists' (99).
45. Jan Neederven Pietersee, 'Globalization as Hybridization', *Global Modernities*, ed. M. Featherstone, S. Lasch and R. Robertson (London: Sage, 1995) 45-68.
46. Pietersee 49, 51.
47. Featherstone 91.
48. Robertson 173-74.
49. Pietersee 61, 64.
50. Douglas Kellner, *Globalization and the Postmodern Turn* (1998) <www.geis.ucla. edu/courses/ed253a/dk/glo>.
51. Featherstone 78
52. Consumer culture and media representation have been typical areas for postmodernist studies of fragmentation.
53. Featherstone 83.
54. It could be argued that Huntington's idea of different forms of modernization very much resemble Featherstone's modernities.

55. Tomlinson makes the reasonable objection that even modernity in the plural preserves a reference to the same. A more radical solution would be to drop it totally (65).
56. Featherstone 114.
57. Featherstone 147.
58. One reason for this is Featherstone's close affiliation to postcolonial theory.
59. Paul Virilio, *Cybermonde: La politique du pire* (Paris: Seuil, 1996) 14.
60. Alan Swingewood sums up the different meanings of the concept of modernity in three points: (1) Modernity as a literary-aesthetic concept; (2) modernity as a sociological-historical category; (3) modernity as a structural concept dealing with the transformation of whole societies (*Cultural Theory and the Problem of Modernity* [London: Macmillan, 1998] 140).
61. Anthony Giddens, *The Consequences of Modernity* (Cambridge: Polity, 1990) 64.
62. The temporal perspective also appears in the different efforts periodize modernity, e.g. as late modernity.
63. Robertson 59, 58, 54.
64. Robertson 55.
65. Held et al. 5-7.
66. Robertson 26.
67. Robertson 29.
68. Robertson 100.
69. I have discussed this in more detail in a paper, 'European Values and Universal Values' delivered at the conference *The Asian Values and Vietnam's Development in Comparative Perspectives*, Hanoi, 24-26 Mar. 1999 (forthcoming).
70. Robertson 78-83.
71. Beck 26.
72. Beck 26-31.
73. Robertson 78.
74. Beck's proposal for a conceptual order bears a resemblance to the different meanings historically attached to the concept of civilization. Civilization can both mean a condition of living in a civilized society and a historical civilizing process. And one could certainly also speak of civilization as an ideology. One major difference from globalization is, however, that it is much easier to have civilizations in the plural. For the different historical meanings of civilization, see Jan Ifversen, 'Begreber, diskurser og tekster omkring civilisation', *Diskursanalysen på arbejde*, ed. Jacob Torfing (Copenhagen: Roskilde Universitetsforlag, 2000).
75. Held et al. 14-20.
76. Held et al. 25, 27-28.
77. Beck 26.

Fear amidst Plenty: The Duality of Economic Optimism at the Close of the 20th Century

Jamsheed Shorish

The anticipation of the millennium has been brought into focus by two widely disparate phenomena: on the one hand, the juggernaut of the United States economy rolls into its 9th year of expansion, bringing with it huge increases in the value of publicly traded firms while keeping consumer prices relatively stable, and unemployment at a near historical record low. The Asian economic crisis has appeared to run its course as well, allowing for modest recoveries in the Far East. And Europe has enjoyed a recent surge in both output and consumption, thanks largely to the enormous consumer demand from the U. S. This would seem to imply that in America and Europe at least, there is considerable optimism about future economic trends in the face of the millennium date change. It appears that in the minds of consumers, businesses and the government, the 'real' effect of the date movement from 19's to 20's is practically nil. This is precisely because the date change is simply 'all in our head', and has no direct impact on the world economy (excepting such publicity stunts as the Millennium Dome project of the U.K., which may be seen as a form of advertising, albeit of gargantuan form).

On the other hand, during the course of 1998-99 there has been a clear increase in the variability of consumer confidence regarding the date change. For example, although most of the Wall Street pundits show no signs of dismay over, for example, the 'Y2K Bug', they have still valued companies whose sole existence is to eradicate the bug in the millions of dollars. This is despite the fact that (1) such companies will by definition cease to exist within the

Fins de Siècle/New Beginnings, ed. Ib Johansen, *The Dolphin* 31, pp. 240-54.

ISBN 87 7288 382 0; ISSN 0106 4487.

next year or two (pending completion delays on current projects), and (2) the consensus has indicated that the Y2K bug will not greatly affect banking and other financial systems, at least in the United States and Western Europe. In general, the trend has been for individuals, and consumers in particular, to look upon any object of high technology with a certain trepidation, as though the usually infallible electronic laws will somehow let us down. This uncertainty has spread to the point that many individuals appear to take the possibility of catastrophic (or at least irritating) failure of high technology almost for granted.

Just ask anyone if they're willing to fly on New Year's Eve, or even use an elevator – indeed, many hotels and other businesses have indicated that in the changeover from December 31, 1999 to January 1st, 2000 they will shut down elevator service 'just in case'. While this may be seen simply as prudence in the face of uncertainty, the news is replete with examples of not so 'rational' behavior. We have all heard the rumors of households stocking up on cash in the face of a potential cash machine crash (a sort of virtual run on banks). In the more extreme cases, households have stockpiled food and water for the moment when, so they say, cities will be unable to provide such necessities following January 1st. And for the first time in nearly 40 years, bomb shelter-type structures are being built in backyards, in order to be safe from, well, something insidious that will assuredly happen after the next four months. Attempting to infer their opinions from their actions, it appears that for these individuals their confidence in anything modern or 'high-tech', from cash machines to transportation of necessities to cities, has reached an all-time low. After all, we can see that they are willing to sacrifice income today as insurance against catastrophe tomorrow – certainly their expectations of the magnitude of the impending disaster must be very high.

From the foregoing stylized assessment of the Western economic outlook we are able to identify, roughly speaking, two points of view regarding the real economic impact of the Millennium changeover. Rather tritely we may divide these views into an 'Optimist' camp and a 'Pessimist' camp. The rationale for identifying and comparing these two camps is that we are faced with two very different (and highly divergent) attitudes towards the upcoming change, while at the same time we appear to have nearly the same kind of information on hand in each camp. That both of these attitudes may co-exist is not surprising given the plethora of individual variation within any given population to start with; one need only consider the old 'glass half-empty' vs. 'glass half-full' anecdote to underscore the notion that people who see the same thing, and who possess the same information, may nonetheless come to very different conclusions.

But what is of interest is the *degree* to which these two attitudes toward the millennial date change diverge, due in no small measure to the very uniqueness of the event. Comparable differences of opinion say over the outcome of a football game, or which number will win the lottery, or who will be the next President, have precedents that are more or less common knowledge. We've seen football games won and lost in the past, we've all (or nearly all?) lost at the lottery, and Presidential elections have come and gone on a quadrennial basis. The millennial date change is different: not only will all of us only experience this change once, we are also a very small subset of the planet's population throughout history who have experienced such a date change in their own calendar system. Although this characterization smacks of hyperbole, the point is simply that there is no previous experience that most of us can hearken back to which will placate our imagination and prevent it, in some cases, from going wild. In the economics parlance, the date change is a foreseen exogenous shock, which defines a possible 'regime shift'. In this case, the regimes are the twentieth and the twenty-first centuries, and the question to be answered is: will this change be continuous, or discrete?

The Optimist camp opts for a continuous change: things are going to continue the way they've gone in the past, so why worry? Put another way, there's simply too much inertia from the previous century to lead to a cataclysmic collapse of the information society. In contrast, the Pessimist camp believes that there is somehow a dependence of the structure of the economy upon the date change itself – it is as if the society has hard-wired real variables, or more realistically the interactions between real variables, to the calendar date. If the Optimist camp is correct, then nothing will happen during and immediately after the changeover.[1] The fundamental determinants of the economy will continue in the same path they've recently taken, and consumer confidence will thus be unshaken. If the Pessimist camp is correct, then real variables that determine the economy will substantially change after New Year's Day, and in a fashion which may be very hard to predict.

We could, of course, simply adopt a 'wait-and-see' attitude. The millennial date change will either change the path of real variables like inflation, unemployment, income, stock market indices, etc in a discontinuous fashion (so that the date change is correlated with a regime shift), or nothing substantive will occur to these variables when the changeover occurs. From the perspective of traditional economic theory there is not much to add. By definition the regime change is unique – therefore it is nearly impossible to predict what effect on the economy the changeover will have. However, this kind of 'laissez-faire' approach to the millennial date change ignores one crucial issue: that both of these viewpoints, the Optimist and the Pessimist, themselves generate actions from the individuals which affect the real variables in an economy, *before the date change actually occurs*. Pessimists who stock up on necessities (or cash) drain available inventories of such goods, while those who, for example, invest their pensions in mutual funds with an eye to 'cashing in' during the next 5-10 years are banking future consumption upon their Optimism. The stakes of the game are in fact quite large – as one example, the Internet companies which have sprouted up on the eve of the date change to do battle with the 'Y2K bug' have resulted in transfers of wealth on the order of billions of U.S. dollars, as stock market investments over the two years prior to the advent of Y2K itself.

To explore the causes of this difference of opinion, and at the risk of embarking upon a tangent which has less to do with the millennial date change, but more to do with its impact upon economic behavior, let me introduce the notion that this divergence in opinion as evidenced in the Optimist vs. Pessimist dichotomy is not just limited to this once-in-a-lifetime-event. Rather, it is the case that more and more, rather than less and less, difference in opinion about the future of the real variables in the economy, the so-called 'economic fundamentals', is evidenced between the economic professionals (academics, private and government economists, etc.) who make policy recommendations and the general population which takes these fundamentals and uses them in making decisions about consumption, investment, marketing, retirement, etc. The key point here is that the policy recommendations that the professionals usually give, which are based upon continuous changes in the economy and are hence usually Optimist in nature, rarely imply the same actions as those actually taken by the individuals in the economy who are more skeptical, more risk-averse and inherently more Pessimist.

There is in economics today a general trend to place very restrictive structure upon individual and collective economic behavior in order to make predictions about such behavior in general. Central to this thesis is still the notion that one can treat economic behavior (e.g. consumer choices, investment, etc.) as if it were the simple (usually linear) superposition of individually rational behavioral choices, where individuals behave according to an axiomatic framework of behavior. This approach has its roots in Classical economics prior to the First World War, and its resurgence and considerable mathematization in the 'neoclassical' paradigm has made it the standard theory of economic behavior for the last 30 years. In a review of John Coates's *The Claims of Common Sense: Moore, Wittgenstein, Keynes and the Social Sciences*, John Davis argues this point within the context of John Maynard Keynes and Ludwig Wittgenstein's revolt against the Classical paradigm:

> [T]he old deductivist Cambridge that Keynes and Wittgenstein sough to escape appears to have made a full recovery in the post-war rise of the neoclassical formalism that currently dominates contemporary economics [...]. One measure of this is how axiomatic choice theory has itself acquired the status of being a canonical notation.[2]

In axiomatic choice theory, individuals follow extremely rigid logical rules when making economic decisions. It is usually assumed that they are extremely proficient (usually perfect) at implementing these rules. In addition, under the theory individual decisions made by each economic participant, or 'agent', do not greatly affect the decisions and expectations of those around them.

What has resulted is an evolution of the language of economic behavior away from the 'animal spirits' of Keynes and toward e.g. 'rational expectations', 'perfect foresight' or 'rationalizable preferences/strategies/equilibria'. The focal point of this analysis is usually that it allows a reasonably straightforward definition of an 'equilibrium', or steady-state, rest state, place of rest, etc. which is considered the 'natural' tendency of the economy. The concept of equilibrium, like its counterpart in the natural sciences, is then a perfectly reasonable goal for any economic model of behavior to express, since any economy appears to move in a continuous fashion along 'equilibrium paths'. It is thus within this setting that the Optimist interpretation may be strongly supported.

Analytically, the esteemed position of equilibrium analysis owes itself to classical mathematical techniques as applied to an economic population. When economists maximize utility, they are optimizing conservative systems. These systems most often need to be homogenized in order for the technique to be applied. Differences between individuals are ignored, or are assumed to spread out over the population more or less evenly. This type of smoothing of the population, which relegates heterogeneity to the 'intractable' or 'needlessly complex' rubbish bin, leads to a steady-state characterization where trends are constant and growth is stable. Smoothing also implies that economic agents are informed enough to make consistent decisions when faced with similar economic situations. They must be able to assess the uncertainties of the world quickly and without cost, and they must know 'all relevant information' when engaging in economic decisions. This ensures that the resulting decisions are both optimal, in the sense that the person could not have done better once the uncertainties are resolved (i.e., there is no regret), and also stable with respect to these uncertainties. To put this another way, the economic agent should not, in the conventional analysis, add any uncertainty to the real economic situation *simply by virtue of the decision-making process that they undertake*. By strictly enforcing these assumptions on economic behavior, economic and financial science as applied to the economic population generates a language which is predisposed to steady-state, smooth analysis and which is ill-equipped to deal with the richness of real economic behavior.

Coexisting with this specialized language is the 'conventional wisdom' of the economic populace, which leads to the type of economic behavior and decision-making that economists are attempting to explain. Buy low, sell high. Renegotiate mortgages when interest rates are low. Listen to what the bankers say about, for example, the U.S. Federal Reserve's interest rate decisions. Buy bicycles for your children, because they'll enjoy riding. Buy insurance for one's house and car, but buy lottery tickets and gamble on the outcome of football matches, or horse races. Try to guess what others are thinking, and then out-guess them. Provide a steady income. Save for retirement. Buy a car when you see one on TV. Never buy a dishwasher 'on principle'. Individuals are notoriously loath to give up such 'mantras' even in the face of changing economic conditions. And it is the reliance upon these mantras, these rules of thumb, which leads to problems for formal economic analysis. This type of decision-making cannot easily be couched within the aforementioned axiomatic theories of behavior.

Economic analysis has struggled to explain such common occurrences as providing for one's children (requiring a theory of 'altruism' which does not fit the conventional axiomatic choice theory), impulse spending (requiring a theory of short-term irrationality, which implies that once 'cooler heads prevail' there could be regret in one's decision), and principled purchasing (the statement 'I don't believe in dishwashers', for example, must in conventional theory imply a marginal preference for hand-washing over automatic washing, which ignores the possibility that even were dishwashers free of all costs some individuals would still refuse to use one). A realistic economic environment is replete with rules of thumb which individuals use in place of the careful optimizing assumptions presented by standard neoclassical analysis. These rules of thumb typically allow the user to confront a dizzying array of uncertainties by utilizing relatively few decision-making tools, rather than having to optimize on a case-by-case basis. And in many cases, an individual may knowingly discard potentially useful information in order to be able to make a decision with the least amount of discomfort. For example, the expression 'don't tell me, I don't want to know' implies that there is a cost to acquiring (potentially adverse) information in excess of its potential use in decision-making. Rules of thumb are generated in extraordinarily complex and uncertain environments which cannot be modeled, or even approached, in the conventional fashion.

This difference in the assumed complexity of the environment, and the resulting difference in decision-making processes and descriptive languages, is not limited to the final consumer of economic goods. Even sophisticated, large corporations use 'rules of thumb' generated from years of experience in the industry, but which defy normal optimization principles. Profit, to take an archetypal example, may be quite a different *normative* concept from its theoretical expression. The usual 'marginal benefit/marginal cost' analysis is often inappropriate when, for example, it is applied to a firm whose employees have all known each other for years, and are quite unwilling to 'adjust the optimal level of labor' in order to gain marginally more revenue. To an economist, such complicated interdependency as that embodied in the statement that employees have 'known each other for years' is relegated again to a form of altruism, or a limited type of irrational behavior. Rather than being explored as the foundation for economic interaction, it is nearly always studied as a 'special case' of economic behavior.

Naturally, this dismissal of what the real world appears to offer has itself reflected upon what individuals consider the role of the economist to entail. There is a general feeling among the populace that economists are 'Voodoo' charlatans, espousing dark and quite possibly satanic rituals for saving the economy, while perhaps driving it further into chaos. Due to the poor track record of conventional Optimistic models in explaining real world phenomena, most people tend to believe that economists are simply giving advice in order to earn a return at the expense of those who know less. And the language of academic economists reinforces this - in most cases, the basic economic concepts are quite unintelligible when heard by laymen's ears.

But Voodooism and poor predictions aside, is this difference in the expression of economic concepts necessarily a bad thing? Is it not true that a physicist will use a different language to explain a ball's influence under gravity than, for example, a football player might? It is certainly the case that phrases such as 'minimal energy state' or 'conservation of momentum' might not enter into the vernacular of the layman when describing physical processes. But – and this is the key difference – in economics what we are describing is the behavior of the economic *person* as a thinking and reasoning economic *agent*, which should be performing the very tasks that we as economists model in order to analyze them! In order to arrive at an economic conclusion at the individual level, economists must model how individuals think about economic decisions. If they do not think as economists assume they do, then the resulting conclusions regarding the optimal economic decision will not be the same for the economist as for the person. Such an 'observer/observed' dichotomy does not exist in physics – particles do not need to be modeled as 'thinking' when they minimize an energy level, while economic agents must be modeled as thinking when they perform economic decisions such as maximizing utility.[3] At some level, then, what the individual feels are the important characteristics of economic decisions should be the same as those characteristics that the economist uses to predict such decisions, even if the language used to express the characteristics is different from that used in everyday experience. But the different languages, unfortunately, all too often speak of different things.

One way out of this incompatibility of language is to say that economic agents only behave 'as if' they are following the complicated precepts of academic economic analysis. They are still rational (and hence, the language used by economists to describe the real world remains valid), but this rationality need not be taken at face value because there is something unconscious in our behavior forces us to be rational. This interpretation of economic behavior is indicative of a recent trend to redefine the restrictive assumptions of neoclassical theory:

In the face of considerable evidence from psychologists demonstrating that the [axiomatic choice] theory does not accurately describe individuals' actual decision-making behavior [...], leading proponents of the theory now increasingly say that it is best interpreted as a normative rather than descriptive account of choice, or one that is scientifically preferred, thus canonical – a theory of choice that individuals ought to obey if they are to be regarded as rational [...][4]

Economic models are, after all, just that: models or abstractions of the real world which are designed to only capture those salient features of the environment which are truly important for economic decision-making and their resultant outcomes. Regardless of what language economic agents are using to describe their situation, so the argument goes, the model still captures their behavior in a realistic fashion. Their behavior is now considered to be precisely along the 'as-if' lines given by the model! For example, a common 'as-if' interpretation of the standard optimization assumption imposed upon economic agents is that the process of maximizing utility is similar to that of a dog catching a Frisbee. We know that the dynamics of the dog running, jumping and catching the Frisbee between its jaws is characterized by a complicated second-order partial differential equation. Yet we also know that the dog is not actually solving a partial differential equation consciously – the dog behaves 'as if' it is solving such a system of equations.

May we give the same unconscious behavior to economic agents as a whole? That is, is it true that each and every one of us is unconsciously optimizing our utility, given our budget constraints, every time we purchase groceries, or buy an ice cream, or pick up a stuffed animal that our child might like? Are impulse purchases in some subtle sense 'rational'? In general I think it is fair to say that human beings are both more overt in their decisions and also less complex, even unconsciously, in their computational tasks. We do not appear to be running an unconscious program during all economic decisions – instead, we seem to take the rules of thumb and the colloquial language we are exposed to in our daily lives, and use it to make our economic decisions over a relatively short time horizon, i.e. 'as the problems arise'.

To relegate these types of optimization processes, based upon axiomatic theories of behavior, to unconscious behavior is to make it either purely instinctive, or instinctively *learned*. Consider an analogy between such instinctive economic learning and the learned behavior of bipedal motion, which is usually acquired while young, but from then on becomes part of the unconscious act of moving. According to a theory of instinctive *economic* learning, maximizing utility, forming optimal portfolios, smoothing consumption across time etc. must be characteristics which are initially learned (through trial and error etc.) but are then more or less 'automatic' after a certain amount of time has gone by.

This does not appear to be a realistic description of individual behavior. To continue the analogy, the learning of bipedal motion has the underlying unconscious action of using muscles to remain stable under motion. This is *completely* unconscious - the body attempts to remain stable and the muscles automatically act to stabilize. Perhaps in the early stages of walking a baby might overcompensate, and it is this degree of compensation that must be learned. But the overall tools at the child's disposal are 'optimized' unconsciously. The same inherent set of optimization tools is not, I think, naturally at the disposal of economic agents. Learning how to be happiest in one's decisions, without regret, does not appear to be a learned trait using some 'pre-optimized' fundamental processes. For if this were true, an individual would unconsciously know for a fact that, say, three hamburgers and a coke is the absolutely perfect balance of goods for a restaurant lunch, dictated by a long-ago-learned relative weight between a little more enjoyment from a little more hamburger and a little less enjoyment from a little less coke. For the so-called 'marginal analysis' to hold true, economic agents must have compared in the past the smallest changes in each good in order to come up with the bundle of goods which is 'best'. In the strong form of the analysis, furthermore, these comparisons must have been performed on an infinitesimal scale because the neoclassical marginal analysis, by definition, does not allow for indivisible goods!

It may be wise at this point to close this lengthy 'digression' and return to the earlier motivating observation: individuals appear to be viewing the approaching millennium date change with no small divergence of opinion. Where does the preceding analysis fit in? We have identified the standard academic nomenclature with its origins in the analytical foundations of modern economic theory. That is, the currently held language used by academic economics is one of stability, optimization, and 'the absolute best that one can do under the circumstances'. In some sense, it is hopelessly Optimist. Carried to its natural conclusion, the current neoclassical paradigm repeatedly predicts that, for example, developing countries ought to be able to optimize themselves out of poverty. Optimal contracts can always be written for optimal debt relief. Everyone knows how to form *the* correct expectations about the future, and those expectations may be framed in a stable and often linear fashion. To keep the model as 'clean' as possible, there is no room for a richness of diversity – the conclusion is almost always a stationary equilibrium with continuous changes. The models say so, because the models cannot say anything else.

In contrast, the underlying economic world is more like a seething mass of information overload. The cultural heterogeneity that most economic systems possess, and the sheer number of cross-connections, feedback effects, 'know thy neighbor' social interactions, etc. all lead to an entanglement of overlapping decisions which cannot be added together linearly, much less optimized down to the individual level. This implies, among other things, that if you listen to those individuals around you, and you condition your own actions upon what they say, then it does not necessarily matter what (qualitatively) the truth 'ought' to be. Which means that the millennium change, as innocuous as it seems, may actually hold the portent of real economic change. For if individuals *believe* strongly enough in its importance, then they will take economic decisions based upon that importance, regardless of the irrationality of such decisions when framed in the standard conventional paradigm.

In fact, one may study simple models of complex, irreducible economies built in this fashion, where expectations may dominate 'right thinking', and conclude that the millennium change may indeed usher in a period of instability which can change the real fundamentals of the economy. The primary vehicle for such change, which has been recognized as an important component of government policy for many years (although it is still an economic modeling 'black box'), is *consumer confidence*. In a sense, the previous discussion has been about how (or even whether) to model and interpret consumer confidence. In an Optimist system the linkages between economic agents are usually weak if non-existent, and there is no way for consumers to influence each others' confidence through news or gossip, purchasing decisions, or a common culture. Since these linkages are absent, there is no possibility for instabilities to magnify and propagate through the population simply because others believe it might occur.[5]

If such instability were nonetheless observed, conventional economic analysis would usually relegate the source of the instability to a 'shock to the system' which is assumed to be unexplainable. This might be interpreted as a temporary shock, in which case it is simply passed off as a temporary blip on the serene path of stability. Or it might be interpreted as a permanent shock, which occurs 'for some reason' and has changed the preferences of the population. Even in this case, however, the situation is usually rationalized as a one-time jump from one equilibrium to another, with the same type of optimizing behavior associated with both equilibria. The shock is by definition completely unexplainable. This is because, as summarized earlier, the underlying models cannot predict much variation away from equilibrium without an external disturbance. The accommodation of such permanent changes, or permanent shocks, usually requires a different model assuming different fundamentals.

But in a way this seems like cheating. A true characterization of the underlying fundamentals should be able to adjust itself to movements both temporary and permanent. Moreover, the sources of such movements must be identified within the model - after all, the model is supposed to encompass all relevant sources of economic meaning to be ascribed to an economy. It is a strange situation indeed when most macroeconomic models currently in use by Western nations for government policy need to posit a purely unknown (or even worse, unknowable) outside influence in order to achieve results which even weakly correspond to the real world. As argued earlier, a more realistic model need not be horribly complicated, or necessarily be so open-ended that 'anything is possible'. Rather, such a model must encompass the language and the culture of the population it is designed to imitate, in order to represent the heterogeneity of that population in a concise and predictable fashion.

It certainly appears that in order to accomplish such a feat, one must be willing to drop (1) linearity (and a healthy dose of analytical tractability), (2) perfect rationality, and (3) a full or axiomatic characterization of individual decision-making. Although economics would like (with good reason) to tout itself as the closest thing to a natural science that the social sciences has, it has repeatedly tossed out the baby with the bath water in its quest to quantify economic behavior under the most restrictive behavioral assumptions. Ironically, it has not generally followed its natural science counterparts in developing more realistic models of natural behavior within inherently complicated environments. Recent advances in fluid dynamics, for example, have been utilized to explain the extremely complicated behavior of many, many particles all interacting in a nonlinear fashion. We see some of this work trickling down to economics and particularly finance, but not enough. Rather, economics has taken the tack that 18th-century conservative systems analysis is the most internally consistent method of modeling human behavior. The mathematical representation of this underlying thesis has become ever more complicated, to encompass the seemingly endless 'special cases' that the real world brings to 'extend' or 'refine' the approach. A fundamental challenge of this approach to economic behavior is now on the horizon.

In view of conventional economic modeling's poor (some might say 'dismal') explanatory and predictive power it is clear that some deeper modification of both the economic foundation and the methodology is necessary. Happily enough such work is already underway, as more and more tools that can be used to analyze heterogeneity become available. Paradoxically, it appears that in order to get a better perspective upon such intangibles as language and culture one must venture even further into the realm of technical complexity. This is because the more complicated the world becomes, the more complicated become the tools which are used to sort and organize the world into something we can understand. Simply from a modeling perspective, I would argue that a movement away from linearity and linearization is definitely required, and a move firmly toward complex systems analysis and inherent non-linearity, where higher-order terms and nonlinear linkages are prevalent, is crucial. It appears that to 'stay the course' in current academic economics is to foster a continuing divergence of expectations between the 'science' and what, for lack of a better term, must still be labeled 'reality'. It is clear that we really don't know what people think - and that contrary to standard Optimist analysis, this is a source of constant 'surprise'. The divergence of opinion regarding the millennium change is perhaps one of the more overt symptoms of a long-standing illness in economic analysis.

Notes

1. 'Immediately after' might be as long as six months after the millennium date change, allowing for any potential underlying adjustments to make themselves felt in real economic variables.
2. John B. Davis, 'Common Sense: a Middle Way between Formalism and Post-structuralism?', *Cambridge Journal of Economics* 23 (1999): 504.
3. Note that the observer/observed dichotomy in quantum physics, as exemplified in the 'Schrödinger's cat' uncertainty paradigm, is different than this dichotomy in economics. In the former case, the measurement of a physical phenomenon may lead to a change of state, so that the observer cannot help but influence the phenomenon under scrutiny. In this sense the 'observer' alters the outcome of the 'observed', perhaps changing it to a state which would not have existed if the observer had not been present. In the latter case, the observer is not directly influencing the economic phenomenon, but is imposing a modeling procedure upon normative grounds that individual economic participants must obey for modeling to be viable. This includes procedures for thinking, learning, information processing, etc. Hence, the 'observer' dictates the modeling behavior of the 'observed'. The observer/observed dichotomy in the sense of quantum physics has, however, made its appearance in economics in the so-called 'Lucas critique', in which Nobel laureate Robert E. Lucas noted that an economist's statistical models may be incorrect by virtue of the fact that agents themselves use these models in their own decision-making, thus changing the environment under study.
4. Davis 504.
5. This is known in the economics literature as 'sunspot' behavior, because the behavior is as if people have decided to condition their actions upon a purely random event like sunspot activity, instead of upon solid economic 'fundamentals'.

Linguistic, Mental and Biological Laws

Anjum P. Saleemi

The relationships between brute physicality, the biological, and mental events and entities have become extremely important issues that are being subjected to rigorous investigation at the turn of the millennium. There is a particularly huge gap between the biological and the mental. Though an issue of contention throughout the last millennium, it has now acquired proportions that are both puzzling and exciting. It probably will not be wrong to say that this issue is going to become the centerpiece of multidisciplinary research and of a search for the unity of knowledge. Indeed, to some extent it has already has become so, and is currently perceived by many, I think correctly, as the biggest challenge there is to test the limits of human knowledge, a challenge that the next century and the millennium just cannot afford to ignore or bypass. As is well known, it was Descartes who posed it in a form that sharpened its formulation and increased its depth, starting the process that converted what appeared to be an intractable mystery into a problem worthy of serious and intensive examination.

For a long time, at least going back to the days of Descartes, the mind-body problem, re-christened in this century the mind-brain problem by writers such as Noam Chomsky, has remained an outstanding unresolved item on the research agenda of many human sciences. Indeed, it is notable that writers like Ray Jackendoff perceive a further conflict between different versions of the mind, the so-called mind-mind problem.[1] This paper intends to spell out an overarching but speculative framework primarily covering the mind-body/brain problem alone, substantially in respect of natural language.

Fins de Siècle/New Beginnings, ed. Ib Johansen, *The Dolphin* 31, pp. 255-63.

ISBN 87 7288 382 0; ISSN 0106 4487.

The contents of the paper are organized as follows. The introductory short section is followed by a relatively longer catalogue of the problems in question, coupled with some discussion. A much longer section then attempts to sketch an ontological picture which I think is an appropriate starting point for putting together a coherent science of human nature.

The Overall Ontological Picture

The array of problems foreshadowed above is indeed wide-ranging, to the extent of being nearly all-inclusive, hopefully non-trivially so. The levels of reality incorporated in the framework in question, exhibiting my interpretation of the work of the philosopher John Searle,[2] is represented below (*Fig. 1*) in the shape of concentric circles, depicting an ontological cross-section and the temporal dimension of time (perhaps one should say 'the arrow of mental time').

Evidently, the diagram purports to be materialistic in a broad sense, as it locates what is currently known to be tangible right at the heart of the whole matter. It does not, though, imply reduction as naively conceived to be the ultimate aim.[3] Instead, a two-way interplay of both reduction AND expansion is conceived as the right way to the resolution of the puzzles, a point that has often been made by Chomsky.[4] The view adopted can be taken to be physicalist in another obvious sense too, most probably correctly, insofar as matter as understood in the physical sciences today is likely to retain its centrality of the universe of being. What is thus envisioned is a unified framework, or at least an eventually unifiable one. To borrow a phrase from the subtitle of Searle's most recent book, it seems to be the only way of doing 'philosophy in the real world', that is, philosophy that can ultimately mature into or manage to earn an empirically credible way of pointing to plausible directions of research, without being too narrow in its conception of what is empirical, as is the case in the hitherto successful branches of physical sciences, or to predict constructs as being tractable or intractable (cf. Chomsky's by now familiar distinction between problems and mysteries) rather intuitively. Progress should be made wherever and whenever it can be made,

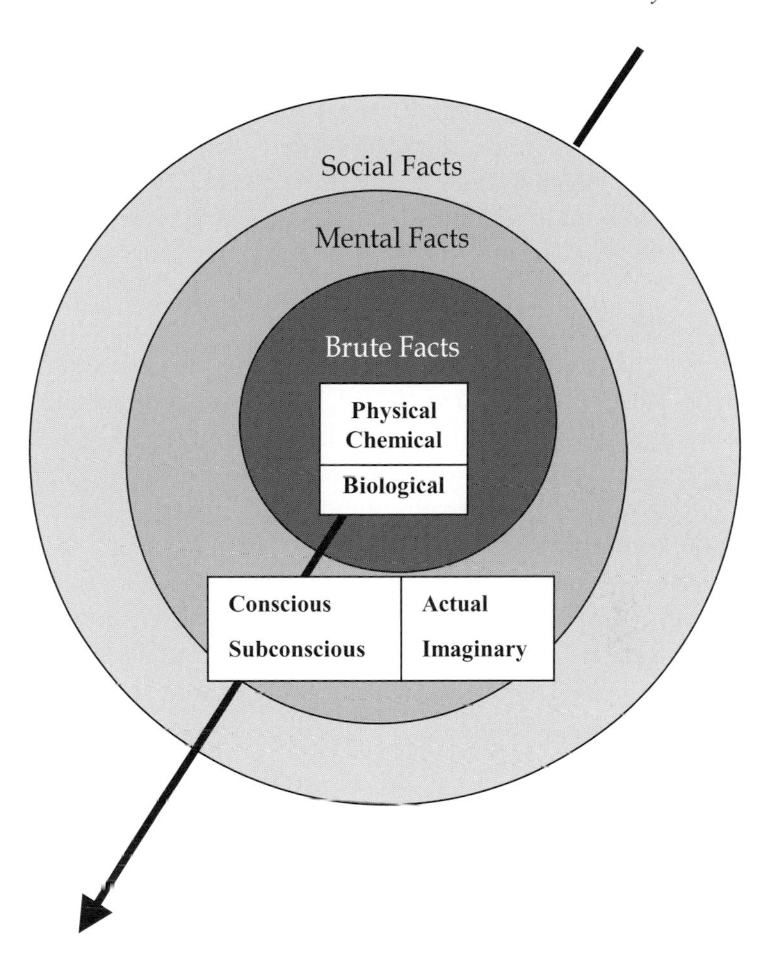

Fig. 1: Ontological Space-Time

in the hope that in the foreseeable (or, if we are not lucky enough, very distant) future, the presently non-existing inter-linking mechanisms, or even presently missing levels, will finally emerge.

The next issue, of course, is how to proceed further assuming the usefulness of such a holistic ontological view. It is to this question to which I turn to in the following pages.

Some Examples and Discussion

It appears self-evident to some (for example, me!) that cause-and-effect relations of some simple kind are hardly going to disappear. Most certainly, though, some or most of them will increasingly attain a more elaborate shape. Without throwing overboard whatever advantages simplicity offers, the possibility of a two-way network of upward and downward causation might turn out to be inevitable. Perhaps at this stage a more specific illustration is in order.

Let us consider natural language, in fact only a particular one, namely English, as the case in point. The immediate causation of a linguistic rule (that of English or otherwise) underlying the corresponding elements of linguistic behaviour, has to be bodily, i.e. largely neurological. (I do not even want to touch upon the question of whether these rules have their origin in biological evolution, social progress, or both.)

To return to concrete exemplification, I propose to describe the rule of Affix-hopping in English, going back to half a century.[5] A simplified outline of the rule under discussion is as follows. Consider the following fairly common English data that show the complexity of the maximal verbal sequence in the language:

(1) The dog was well trained.
(2) The man trained the dog.
(3) The man has trained the dog.
(4) The man may have trained the dog.
(5) The man may have been training the dog.
(6) The dog was trained (by the man).
(7) The dog has been trained (by the man).
(8) The dog may have been trained (by the man).
(9) The dog may have been being trained (by the man).

As these intriguing data reveal, English affixes do not consistently appear attached to the same words. In fact, depending on the complexity of the verbal sequence, verb and the relevant tense, aspect and voice affixes often appear in different places, detached from words to which they are logically speaking grammatically and semantically related. Consider the most complex sequence, i.e. example (9), which is passive and contains the maximum number (that is, five) of verbal elements in English. The deep, logical relationships already pointed out are those depicted in (10), that may be accounted as the underlying structure of (9).

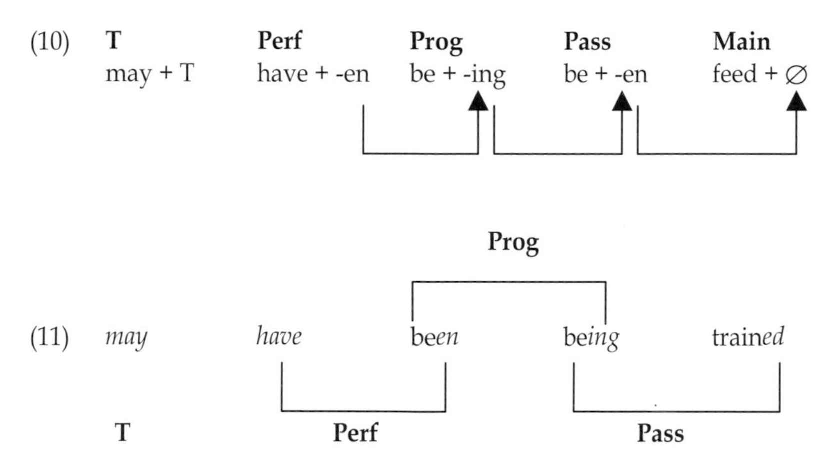

The transformation of the underlying input to the actually uttered phonological output, shown in (11), is considered to be mediated by transformational rules, so that the logical sequence changes into the spoken output. This process is schematized in *Figure 2*.

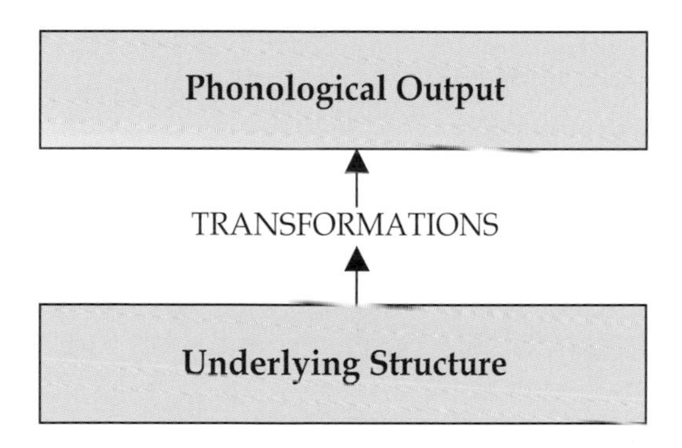

Fig. 2: 'Deep' and 'Surface' Levels of Syntax

The rules governing the relevant part of English syntax can be listed as follows, and a summarized formulation appears in the grey box that follows.

- The English (finite) clause has a shrinking and expanding backbone whose building blocks are auxiliary verbs and the related grammatical affixes.
- *Tense, Perfective, Progressive,* and *Passive* (see examples 6-9) affixes target and land on the nearest verb to the right.
- *Pass* aux appears to the immediate left of the main verb.
- A grammatical affix must be realized as a word or as part of one; it cannot stand on its own and be manifested phonologically.

> ***Affix-Lowering:*** **When an Affix^1 has to move, it takes the shortest step to move to the site originally occupied by Affix^2. As a result Affix^2 gets kicked downstairs a step lower, dislocating Affix^3, and so on, until the very last verb (i.e., the main verb) is reached.**

What saves the split elements into a deteriorated, chaotic system is the array of mechanisms employed above, and more importantly, the assumption that somehow these mechanisms (the categories, transformations, etc.) are mental counterparts of a neurological substratum. Under no stretch of imagination can this core aspect of English syntax be explained in terms other than those that do not involve the notion that the mind is ultimately a biological organ, as Chomsky has always stressed. However, for writers like Searle the rules of the aforementioned kind are not enough. He wants linguists to develop theories that integrate syntax, semantics, speech acts, and intentionality. His picture of the brain is that of an organ that is first of all conscious, and only afterwards other things, perhaps peripherally so.

Let us also have a brief look at the extremely interesting bogy language phenomena. Some recent research suggests that non-verbal communication and gestures are even less under voluntary control that verbal communication.[6] They seem to be more like autonomous reflexes that have naturally joined hands with much later evolution of language. If such a view gains greater credibility, then they would appear to be much closer in nature to what Searle calls 'the gut brain' (of course as opposed to the really intentionally-driven brain). Given this contrast, where does verbal communication, and the rules arguably responsible for its structural and computational aspects belong in *Figure 1*? Could it be that some of such rules are more intentional than others, and there are others which are totally impervious to any conscious control or mere memory-driven manipulation? Does the linguistic chain of causation work in both and 'outward' and an 'inward' fashion, cutting across the boundaries (provisionally) adopted in *Figure 1*? Finally, if language is indeed a multi-faceted set of phenomena, how do we find out which is which, and how does language function smoothly to the extent that it does? A possibility is (in the first instance) to try to find out those linguistic mechanisms that are inherently determined by neurological mechanisms. In more concrete terms, for a rule like Affix-hopping to be able to work as it does, among all sorts of speakers (young and old) who have no conscious access to its intricacies, regardless of how exactly they are formulated, there has to be a serious mind–brain linkage, probably a very complex one. The brain, or related parts thereof, have to be able to be at least structurally compatible if not custom-designed for language. Thus, hypothetically, there must be in the least two kinds of mechanisms - mental ones (call them M) and corresponding neurological ones (simply abbreviated in *Figure 3* below as N). This minimalist view of the mind-brain should look like this:

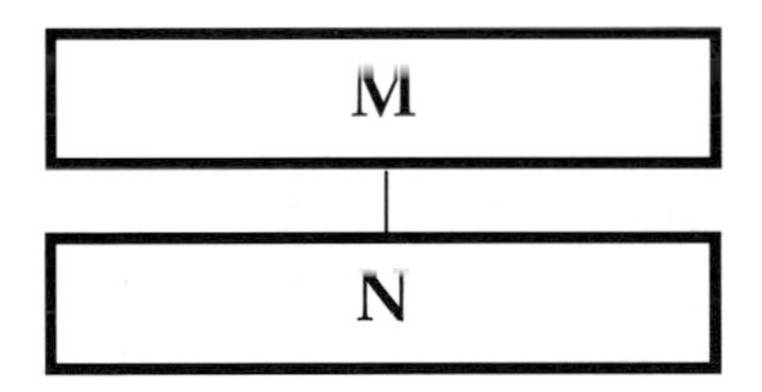

Fig. 3: Mind and the Neural System

This figure possesses only two boxes representing two kinds of entities, belonging to the two innermost circles in *Figure 1*, with no claim at completeness and a gaping hole in between. Such gaps, however, are not unknown in the most successful physical sciences: they exist between quantum theory and relativity, molecular biology (specifically genetics) and ethology, micro- price-auction economics and macroeconomics pertaining to aggregate economic behaviour, to name only some prominent examples, all of which, interestingly, offer parallels to Roger Penrose's points about the large-scale and the small-scale physics.[7] Setting the seeming generality of these problems aside, what specific strategies should be devised to enable researchers working in different fields and different levels within each to be able to mutually interact meaningfully?

I believe the greatest obstacle to finding the missing linkages is a non-existent theory of information processing and storage in the brain. Knowing the neuro-chemical and neuro-anatomical correlates is undoubtedly useful, but not sufficient. Constructs of the mental sort appear reducible to neither supply of chemicals nor neural topology. To know where the mental information is (if we are lucky enough to know that in the first place!) is to know (also) how and at what kind of most likely yet undiscovered level(s) mental rules are encoded. Human mental information is arguably primary and intentional, not derivative or ultimately reliant upon an external programming intentional agent as in the case of artificial machines. If linguistic rules are simply stored in the memory and not 'hard-wired', the acuteness of the problem does not decrease. Yet, assuming the doctrine of the unity of sciences, the mind and the brain, the mental and the neurological levels, have to be interdependent.

In short, perhaps it is time to abandon a narrowly empirical/ physical view of the brain, and instead try to reconstitute mental phenomena increasingly tangibly. This of course is easier said than done, but an awareness of the possibility will certainly deter us from remaining confined to self-constructed cells within the reigning academic orthodoxy. Some progress has indeed been made in recent years, but not enough to dispel worries such as mine, The challenge posed is so gigantic, nothing less than a large-scale, multi-disciplinary and concerted effort (remember the Manhattan Project?) is going to begin to yield some insightful results. If the mind–brain enterprise is worth the bother at all, vast amounts of human and material resources will be required, since the big picture being advocated may not ever emerge out of piecemeal efforts and gradual accretion of small disconnected discoveries. When it comes to unearthing the mind-brain secrets, the time for doing small-scale science might be fast becoming a tale of antiquity. Needless to remark, any combined work, though necessarily expensive, is going to save resources at the end of the day, and reduce unnecessary duplication of effort. Perhaps it is time also to take others' disciplines seriously – I mean anything from quantum theory of consciousness to empirically grounded and rigorous philosophical thinking. As Searle has often pointed out, the brain is merely about the size of a soccer ball, but it remains the biggest black hole in the science of human scientific endeavour, and likely to remain so for a long time to come. E. M. Forster is well known for having said, 'Only Connect'. The big question is: 'Can we?'

Notes

1. See references and discussion in Anjum P. Saleemi, 'Skinners's Razor and the Varieties of Mentalism', *Text in Education and Society*, ed. Desmond Allison and others (Singapore: Singapore UP and World Scientific, 1998).
2. See, for example, John Searle, *The Construction of Social Reality* (New York: Free P, 1995) and *Mind, Language, and Society: Philosophy in the Real World* (London: Weidenfeld and Nicolson, 1999).
3. See Jerry Fodor's classic treatment on this issue in the first chapter of *The Language of Thought* (Cambridge, MA: Harvard UP, 1975).
4. For example, Noam Chomsky, 'Language and Nature', *Mind* 104 (1995): 1-61
5. Noam Chomsky, *Syntactic Structures* (The Hague: Mouton, 1957).
6. See the ably summarized account in Laura Spinney, 'Body talk', *New Scientist* 2233 (2000): 30-33, and the references cited therein.
7. Roger Penrose, *The Large, the Small and the Human Mind* (Cambridge: Cambridge UP, 1997).

Part Six

The 1990s/2000

Ends, Idiocy, Beginnings

No Ground to Stand On

Graeme Thomson

I. NO GROUND TO STAND ON

La terre

(Ramassons simplement une motte de terre)

Ce mélange émouvant du passé des trois règnes, tout traversé,
tout infiltré, tout cheminé d'ailleurs de leurs germes et racines, de
leur présences vivantes: c'est la terre.
Ce hachis, ce pâté de la chair des trois règnes.

Passé, non comme souvenir ou idée, mais comme matière
Matière à la portée de tous, du moindre bébé; qu'on peut saisir
Par poignées, par pelletées.

Si parler ainsi de la terre fait de moi un poète mineur, ou
Terrassier, je veux l'être! Je ne connais pas de plus grand sujet.

Comme on parlait de l'Histoire, quelqu'un saisit une poignée de
Terre et dit: «Voilà tout ce que nous savons de l'Histoire Universelle.
Mais cela nous le savons, le voyons; nous le tenons: nous l'avons
Bien en mains.»
Quelle vénération dans ces paroles!

Vous aussi notre aliment, où se préparent nos aliments. Nous
Campons là-dessus comme sur les silos de l'Histoire, dont chaque
Motte contient en germe et en racines l'avenir.

Voici pour le présent notre parc et demeure: la chair de nos
Maisons et le sol pour nos pieds.
Aussi notre matière à modeler, notre jouet.

Il y en aura toujours à notre disposition. Il n'y a qu'à se baisser
pour en prendre. Elle ne salit pas.

Fins de Siècle/New Beginnings, ed. Ib Johansen, *The Dolphin* 31, pp. 267-89.

ISBN 87 7288 382 0; ISSN 0106 4487.

On dit qu'au sein des géosynclinaux, sous des pressions énormes, la pierre se reforme. Eh bien, s'il s'en forme une, de nature particulière, à partir de la terre proprement dite, impropre ment appelée végétale, à partir de ces restes sacrés, qu'on me la montre! Quel diamant serait plus précieux!

Voici enfin l'image présente de ce que nous tendons a devenir.
Et, ainsi, le passé et l'avenir présents.
Tout y a concouru: non seulement la chair des trois règnes, mais l'action des trois autres éléments: l'air, l'eau, le feu.
Et l'espace, et le temps.

Ce qui est tout a fait spontané chez l'homme, touchant la terre, c'est un affect immédiat de familiarité, de sympathie, voire de vénération, quasi filiale.
Parce qu'elle est la matière par excellence.
Or, la vénération de la matière: quoi de plus digne de l'esprit?
Tandis que l'esprit vénérant l'esprit ... voit-on cela?
- On ne le voit que trop.

Preamble

Let us simply pick up a clod of earth:

I might speak of beginnings and of what has brought me to begin, but lightly, placed in parenthesis, as it were, as all first causes must be. Picking up Ponge quite by chance one day, tired of rooting around for material to compose this seminar on the question of the millennium or on the *fin de siècle,* at any rate on the business of endings and beginnings and what it is, if anything, that marks them, a subject on which I had nothing major to add, nothing to show or prove, yet felt inclined to speak anyway, though quietly, almost in an embarrassed murmur, as befits one with no grounds for speaking, no ground to stand on, who is in a continual state of trespass.

I might therefore speak of invitations such as the one which brought me here, a form of generosity or temporary inclusion, or that which Ponge extends in the above parenthesis that cups it lightly as though in two hands, and holds it, offers it to us.

In this way we could say that (at least) the invitation 'holds', although at the same time it remains suspended above the earth it both invites us to pick up, and by this very gesture (with our acceptance, with our help) accomplishes itself.

> You don't have to be learned, to know or be familiar with a particular area, but to pick up this or that in areas which are very different. This is better than the 'cut-up'. It is rather a 'pick-me-up' or 'pick up' – in the dictionary = collecting up, chance, restarting of the motor, getting on to the wave-length; and then the sexual connotation of the word. (Deleuze and Parnet 10)

Let us consider how a particular community (of sympathetic readers, of gatherers of clods of earth) are hereby invited, summoned and thus themselves 'picked up' in this moment of accepting the invitation that has been, is being, will be extended to them for as long as this invitation holds, which is to say, for as long as there are clods of earth, (or books of Ponge?) for them to pick up. We, for I naturally speak as one of them, for whatever reason, on whatever grounds, feel ourselves inclined to accept Ponge's invitation. I suspect it is precisely this 'inclination' which causes us to bend down to pick up a clod of earth, or perhaps I should say, *une motte de terre*, considering for the moment whose soil we are trespassing on.

The gesture is infinitely repeatable and yet different each time it is repeated, depending on atmospheric conditions, the quality and type of earth, the particular traversals and crisscrossings, both marked and unmarked, of the place which constitutes its buried history or indeed that of the unearther. It is what passes between unearther and unearthed. It is the gesture by which I take part of the ground from under my own feet.

Les mottes et les choses

We can say of Ponge's earth, both terrestrial and textual, that it 'gives' in all senses of the word. We are no longer or not yet on solid ground, but on earth that can be picked up in clods, handfuls, shovelfuls, or to use Ponge's word, in *mottes*, that are curiously friable, that threaten to decompose and yet somehow hold together, that maintain a certain material consistency which 'holds' by being 'held' but which cannot be 'grasped' (since it continues to give: its giving is a form of resistance to the grasp).

The *motte* itself is a sample, a fragment, of a mélange, sample of an earth that has been trampled and traversed by many and is permeated and crisscrossed by numerous seeds and roots; or we might say, a *mélangue* consisting of the seeds and roots of numerous *mots*. What is more in the roots and seeds which traverse it are interred further fragmentations and decompositions: a burial mound, and yet a castle (structure and its absence) motes, a motet, tomes, a totem. The *motte* never stops decomposing and thus enters into new compositions - with death, with the 'least baby' of the poem who is traversed by conflicting forces of individuation (the castle of the Lacanian ego?) and molecular multiplicity (Lucretian motes), with music. The *motte* is traversed by motifs, which we could also say, following the logic of traversal, are 'if-words' (mot/ifs), suggesting chances for new lines and blocs of composition.

We can therefore say that Ponge composes with the earth and its forces by means of a breakdown, a decomposition of elements which then enter into new concatenations that combine sense and non-sense rather than cause and effect. The poem and the earth pick up from each other the multiplicity which can never be fully grounded, either in time or space, since it contains heterogeneous times and spaces, encounters which it repeats in every encounter with it, every encounter that adds to it its own time and space. Yet at the same time this multiplicity can only ever be given or picked up as a sample, a fragment, a 'motte' that is not nor ever can be 'the whole story', but is, rather, uncountable.

Thus Ponge begins not from what would be an object of knowledge, nor even from an 'object' but from an encounter. Between language and earth. Between something and nothing. And yet we might define this encounter, as that which does not count and upon which we cannot count. Ponge is fascinated by the insignificant, the almost nothing which he prefers to nothing, since nothing would return us to the pure negative and the illusory significance of the absolute. For Ponge art becomes this 'almost nothing', piecemeal, fabricated from a mélange of bits and scraps.

In this sense, in the consideration it affords to the insignificant, his work may be compared to that of the land artist Richard Long, many of whose pieces are literally 'unremarkable'.

I suppose my work runs the whole gamut from being completely invisible and disappearing in seconds, like a water drawing, or dusty footprints, to a permanent work in a museum that maybe could last forever. The planet is full of unbelievably permanent things, like rock strata and tides, and yet full of impermanence like butterflies or the seaweed on the beach, which is in a new pattern every day for thousands of years. I would like to think my work reflects that beautiful complexity and reality.

Long's is an art which voluntarily merges with or fades into the insignificant (of permanence or impermanence) an art which has nothing to say and says it, to borrow John Cage's formulation. Much of Long's oeuvre denies the existence of an oeuvre proper, surviving as no more than a meagre trace of its former presence, (for example a map of composed of a few arrows indicating the direction of the wind in 'Wind Walk'); of some works there is no trace left at all, save those which Long carries with him in memory. In working 'with earth' and the elements, Long enters into a becoming with it. Thus Art and life permeate each other and become an inseparable continuum. However, it is no longer a question of 'making one's life a work of art,' but rather of getting to what Blanchot calls the 'worklessness' of both. Here the encounter which constitutes art as an event takes refuge in its insignificance, in its partiality. We could say that this event, as multiplicity, is guaranteed by its tendency to decompose, to fall to pieces, to not amount to much.

In a sense the work of both Ponge and Long, and with them we could cite many others, indicates an approach to art, to earth and to the event which resists and refuses the catastrophic loss of history and the event much spoken about by Baudrillard who had already shrugged off the millennium in a text of the mid-eighties, 'The Year 2000 has already happened'.

We are truly 'liberated' in all senses of the word, liberated to such an extent that we have left, through speed (the accelerated metabolization of our societies), a certain space/time, a certain horizon where the real is possible, where the event is possible, because gravitation is still strong enough so that things can think themselves, return to themselves, and thus have some duration and some consequence. A certain slowness (that is to say, a certain speed, but not too much) a certain distance, but not too much, a certain 'liberation' (energy of rupture and change), but not too much, are necessary to produce that sort of condensation, of significant crystallization of events that we call history, that sort of coherent deployment of causes and effects that we call the real. (35-36)

In speaking for some presumed all, Baudrillard attempts to undo the movement he describes by the very act of naming it. His universalizing notion of history is governed by an already presumed *significance* of events and their interrelation. In the acceleration of his own thought, in its apocalyptic eagerness, he somehow fails to realize that the event is never 'given', but must be constructed or at least seized, picked up in the form of an encounter with what gives, which has nothing to do with history, which is in a sense against history and which effectively and affectively takes place behind its back. But the event is by nature self-effacing, vulnerable, unrecognizable. This secrecy, the fact that it concerns only a minority, is part of the event's strength, for what is preserved in it is the possibility of an encounter. History as Baudrillard says may have become its own Hollywood-style special effect, but 'the possibility of the real' always remains in the way by which things and ourselves 'give' in the space of such an encounter.

Towards a minor/miner life

Si parler ainsi de la terre fait de moi un poète mineur, ou
terrassier, je veux l'être! Je ne connais pas de plus grand sujet
(Ponge 158-59)

Is there the chance that this 'return to earth' as the possibility of that which 'gives' might be extended from the natural to the cultural field in its exasperating materiality, insignificant fragments of which might subsist as regenerative traces in composite assemblages. Deleuze and Guattari explain the conditions of minor literature as:

[...] the deterritorialization of language, the connection of the individual to a political immediacy, and the collective assemblage of enunciation. We might as well say that minor no longer designates specific literatures but the revolutionary conditions for every literature within the heart of what is called the great (or established) literature. Even he who has the misfortune of being born in the country of a great literature must write in its language, just as a Czech Jew writes in German, or an Ouzbekian writes in Russian. Writing like a dog digging a hole, a rat digging its burrow. And to do that, finding his own point of underdevelopment, his own patois, his own third world, his own desert. (18)

Yet we can see that the ongoing standardisation of *cultural* practices and means of production, an effect of globalisation which extends from the record industry to academic publishing, tends to ensure that, whatever 'subject position' we speak from, we all end up speaking the same language, and whatever exceeds or breaks with that language is eventually brought back safely within its bounds.

However, what Deleuze and Guattari offer me here is not simply a description which places 'minor literatures', but a call to arms, an invitation to a more general 'minorization' of material practices in line with Long's art/earth/life continuum, one which may deterritorialize or displace our own particular relation to the 'major language' of culture *tout court*, rather than return it to the special effect of its historicity. A gesture of resistance which would necessarily only be partial, local and voluntarily in/significant.

Playing for real

Play is sometimes amusing, but it can also be deadly serious, since it questions the necessity of creation. Play may help us to shirk fundamental issues; it may go to the very heart of the truth, and of our own uneasiness, by revealing the huge accumulation of culture with which we are more or less bound to live, and indeed to 'compose'. playing with this culture means trying to abolish its influence by making it quite clear that one has mastered all its mechanisms – even the most perverse. (Boulez 356)

Play in the sense Boulez intends here, resembles the 'bored' game of the absolute master, who has seen and done it all and who pushes the pieces of culture around the table for his own amusement. Such play, for which we could substitute the word 'postmodernism' has by now exhausted itself. But we might ask, where can the spirit of play emerge in one who knows the rules. Play can only proceed by not knowing how to play, by not knowing how to proceed. It is necessary therefore that we extract from culture what is most unrecognizable in it, proceeding as though we did not speak the language of culture, in the manner of Ponge's 'least baby', reaching for the elemental earth blindly, as though we did not know what it was, refusing names, labels, movements, all the ordering and classifying tendencies which regulate our relationship with matter.

We can see this process at work in Lars Von Trier's film *The Idiots* where, following Deleuze & Guattari's lead we might read the 'Dogma' manifesto which informs the film's composition with the emphasis on 'dog'. For here what is important is the irruption of an animal and molecular real into a social organization. Although the idiots are constituted as a group, a group whose aims to disrupt the social fabric are stated both in their meetings and in retrospective interviews, it is finally only *who does not know how to become an idiot*, that is who does not perform the role of the idiot as Oedipal theatre for the gaze and approval of the group and their charismatic leader, who truly succeeds in entering into a molecular 'becoming idiot' .

In this case it is Karin, drawn to the group from the outside, from an ambiguous margin who is inclined, rather than motivated to find an 'inner idiot'. In the end when the group has disbanded, their agenda having collapsed, it is she who goes on becoming idiot in a way that is involutional and contagious, precisely when there is no longer anything in it for anyone except her. In the film's staggering closing scene this imperceptible involution, an un/becoming drool or becoming smear shatters the social organization of the family, as she enters into a new composition between herself and her lost/least baby. It is in its irruption into life, rather than into history, that art 'works' as a kind of stammer in reality, or as Foucault would say, a buzzing, or rippling in discourse, which is non-discursive. The next step in Von Trier's involution, the musical *Dancer in the Dark* , like Jacques Rivette's recent *Haut Bas Fragile* with its return to the Hollywood musical promises another irruption of the non-discursive in the way that song in the musical is always a becoming of speech rather than conceptually separate from it. We generally don't get such irruptions into the discursive field in reality, and when they happen they are allotted a time and a place in the social organization, a performance or dream 'space' in which they can be safely reinserted into the fabric of discourse. But what if people actually started behaving the way they do in a Hollywood musical, or in *Sprechgesang*. We might find them odd, eccentric, a bit mad perhaps. Our perceptual boundaries might be severely shaken. We might be physically disturbed, embarrassed, or perhaps simply uninterested. Or we might find the gesture anachronistic.

Stanley Kubrick's last film *Eyes Wide Shut* is another example of the irruption of the real into a discursive space. Here it is not only Kubrick's death which must be inserted back into the film, and which delineates a 'faultline' in its structure (the non matching cuts that critics have suggested are an indication of the film's incompleteness) but also the Cruise/Kidman couple whose real relationship constantly contaminates the film's fictional space. In this sense it becomes pointless to talk about Cruise's acting because, the film captures an event which goes beyond performance and mask: a certain insistence of the real/unreal as something uncanny. Kubrick makes his actors repeat the shooting of each scene over and over to a point where they have effectively exhausted their acting capacities, and enter into events of a different order. The repetition of the same produces difference, in a chaotic and uncategorizable way, rather like Beckett's Molloy who exhausts and is exhausted by all possible combinations of his sucking stones until he reaches a point where it no longer matters which order he uses. Who cares whether Cruise lives up to his 'role' or not. Kubrick offers us something much more interesting, a breakdown between the real and the imaginary: a non-place where it no longer matters what is art and what is reality, because there are nothing but pure mesmerising effects/affects by which the viewer with his/her eyes wide shut is absorbed. The revelation Cruise undergoes when he sees his costume mask on the bed, a death mask behind which there is nothing but a void is *a revelation in the real* which offers us no possibility of response, save to go beyond it.

This is perhaps Ponge's position in his poem 'The Ultimate Simplicity', a poem about the limits of discourse that suggests how we might go beyond them, by stepping into the in/significance of the event itself. The end of the poem describes the room of Ponge's grandmother who has just died:

> ...Pas
> grand'chose, plus personne: une sorte de scorie, de fœtus, de baby terreux, à qui l'on n'est plus tenté du tout d'adresser la parole, - pas plus qu'au baby rouge brique qui sort de sous le ventre d'une accouchée. (124)

As Ponge says, the corpse is not much to see, one wouldn't address it any more than one would a new born baby. But this 'pas grand chose' is also a step beyond the thing. Just as 'Pas plus' is a step beyond discourse. A step that is also a stop. Derrida has already said much about this but in deconstruction, or at least in its historical effect, it is all brought back safely within the discursive field.

In this sense cinema and the visual arts have much to teach us, since they continue to explore the pedagogical lines of flight that can only occur in partial art/life or user/text assemblages and interfaces, and offer us an invitation to 'unrealize' the world around us in our own way. This is what Godard means in his autoportrait film *JLG/JLG* when he talks about an 'art of living' which culture, 'as representative of the rule', wishes to destroy. As in the case of Richard Long, such an 'art of living' does not offer us any ground to stand on, for it is also an 'art of dying' as well as a 'dying art', a composition that enters into a dialogue with its inevitable decomposition, an art of failure that preserves the possibility of an encounter. The art of living as a line of flight is not a question of escape, for as Baudrillard says, culture has already reached escape velocity, but an act of sympathy, of 'staying behind' to deal with the im/material wreckage. 'Behind' not in a temporal sense, but in what we could call the subterfugal sense of 'behind the scenes' or 'behind one's back' where the spotlight of history is not yet, or no longer, looking.

Questions are generally aimed at a future (or a past). The future of women, the future of the revolution, the future of philosophy, etc. But during this time, while you turn in circles among these questions, there are becomings which are silently at work, which are almost imperceptible. (Deleuze and Parnet 2)

Works Cited

Jean Baudrillard. 'The Year 2000 Has Already Happened'. *Body Invaders*. Ed. Arthur and Marilouise Kroker. Montreal: New World Perspectives, 1987.

Pierre Boulez. *Orientations*. London: Faber, 1986. 356.

Gilles Deleuze and Félix Guattari. *Kafka: Towards a Minor Literature*. Minneapolis: U of Minnesota P, 1986.

Gilles Deleuze and Claire Parnet. *Dialogues*. London: Athlone, 1987.

Richard Long. 'Fragments of a Conversation VI'. *Walking in Circles*. London: Thames and Hudson, 1991.

Francis Ponge. *Selected Poems*. London: Faber, 1998.

II. NO GROUND TO STAND ON: FROM PONGE'S EARTH TO RUSHDIE'S QUAKE

Ramassons simplement une motte de terre:

Ponge was born in 1899 and entered the earth in 1988. This would be his centenary. I checked the web to see if anything had been organised to celebrate it. My search engine told me something was being put on at the Pompidou, but when I tried to go there I ended up at a site called

Not found.

From daybreak it is evident in France – even though woven in corners – and in a marvellously confused language – that the spider is at one with her web.

```
Suspendu, sans contexte à ses propres décisions -
Dans l'expectative à son propre endroit
```

(Ponge, The New Spider/*La Nouvelle araignée*)

If you go to Ponge's tomb all you will find of him is a name and two dates, Francis Ponge 1899–1988.
Birth and death are what is beyond us, beyond our reach.

The 'beyond' is neither a new horizon, nor a leaving behind of the past... Beginnings and endings may be the sustaining myths of the middle years; but in the *fin de siècle* we find ourselves in the moment of transit where space and time cross to produce complex figures of difference and identity, past and present, inside and outside, inclusion and exclusion. For there is a sense of disorientation, a disturbance of direction, in the 'beyond': an exploratory, restless movement caught so well in the French rendition of the words *au-delà* – here and there, on all sides, *fort/da*, hither and thither, back and forth. (Homi K. Bhabha, *The Location of Culture*)

I couldn't help noticing how the dates matched, as though one was just a different mélange of the elements of the other, as though one generated the other, contained its seeds and roots as well as the route that short-circuited them. The fact that Ponge's age at death (89) could be extracted from his birth date (1899), his end from his beginning. What was the chance of this coincidence. No matter, it was like a secret, a trace that nobody would notice, least of all Ponge himself, that could never have any meaning beyond the fact that it subsisted.

Matière à la portée de tout, du moindre bébé...

Voici enfin l'image présent de ce que nous tendons a devenir.
Et ainsi, le passé et l'avenir présents. (Ponge)

Normally when we pick up the earth it is only to dig, for some thing, or some reason, we don't think about the fact that what we have unearthed in the gesture is earth itself. Earth uplifted. Volatised.

Une motte de terre.

I should like to limit myself to a single word, kept pure and alive in its absence, if it weren't that through that one word, I have all the infiniteness of all languages to bear. (Maurice Blanchot, *The Writing of the Disaster*)

Looked up motte *in the dictionaries. It gave me: a mound with a castle keep, a clump of trees in prairie country, a burial mound.*

Broke it down to mote, mot which gave motto and thus 'murmur' from the Latin root. Do I say it as I hear it, murmur it in the mud?
Mixed it up giving motet, totem.

The earth is our plaything, our clay for modelling. (Ponge)

The Man who fell to Earth

When Ponge entered the earth in 1988, I was in Canada. It was the time of the Satanic Verses *affair. Images of the burning book were all over the media. I picked it up for the first time in December, in a shop in Toronto railway station. While I was waiting for the train to Manitoba, I read the first few pages.*

'To be born again,' sang Gibreel Farishta tumbling from the heavens, 'first you have to die. Ho ji! Ho ji! To land upon the bosomy earth, first one needs to fly. Tat-taa! Takathun! How ever to smile again, if first you won't cry? How to win the darling's love, mister, without a sigh? Baba, if you want to get born again....' Just before dawn, one winter's morning, New Year's day, or thereabouts, two real, full-grown, living me fell from a great height, twenty-nine thousand and two feet, towards the English Channel, without benefit of parachutes or wings, out of a clear sky.

'I tell you, you must die, I tell you, I tell you,' and thusly and so beneath a moon of alabaster until a loud cry crossed the night, 'To the devil with your tunes,' the words hanging crystalline in the iced white night, 'in the movies you only mimed to playback singers, so spare me these infernal noises now.'

Gibreel, the tuneless soloist, had been cavorting in moonlight as he sang his impromptu gazal, swimming in air, butterfly-stroke, breast-stroke, bunching himself into a ball, spreadeagling himself against the almost-infinity of the almost-dawn, adopting heraldic postures, rampant, couchant, pitting levity against gravity. Now he rolled happily towards the sardonic voice. 'Oh, Salad baba, its you, too good. What-ho old Chumch.' At which the other, a fastidious shadow falling headfirst in a grey suit with all the jacket buttons done up, arms by his sides, taking for granted the improbability of the bowler hat on his head, pulled a nickname-hater's face. 'Hey, Spoono,' Gibreel yelled, eliciting a second inverted wince, 'Proper London, bhai! Here we come! Here we come! Those bastards down there won't know what hit them. Meteor or lightning or vengeance of God. Out of thin air baby. Dharraraaammm! Wham na? What an entrance, yaar. I swear: splat.'

Out of thin air: a big bang, followed by falling stars. A universal beginning, a miniature echo of the birth of time...the jumbo jet *Bostan*, Flight A1-420, blew apart without any warning, high above the great, rotting, beautiful, snow-white, illuminated city, Mahagonny, Babylon, Alphaville. But Gibreel has already named it, I mustn't interfere: Proper London, capital of Vilayet, winked blinked nodded in the night. While at Himalayan height a brief and premature sun burts into the powdery January air, a blip vanished from the radar screens and the thin air was full of bodies, descending from the Everest of the catastrophe to the milky paleness of the sea.

Who am I?

Who else is there?

I put the book down and got on the train. The journey across the frozen wastes of Ontario took 30 hours. I passed the time talking to a school-teacher from Thunder Bay. On arrival in Manitoba, I was collected by a friend. When we got back to her house, it was all over the TV news, the Lockerbie bombing, just 12 short miles from where I lived.

...not only books but also copies of books have their fates.

The disaster ruins everything, all the while leaving everything in tact. It does not touch anyone in particular; 'I am not threatened by it but spared, left aside. It is in this way that I am threatened; it is in this way that the disaster threatens in me that which is exterior to me – an other than I who passively become other. There is no reaching the disaster. Out of reach is he whom it threatens, whether from afar or close up, it is impossible to say: the infiniteness of the threat has in some way broken every limit. We are on the edge of disaster without being able to situate it in the future. It is rather always already past, and yet we are on the edge or under the threat, all formulations which would imply the future – that which is yet to come – if the disaster were not that which does not come, that which has put a stop to every arrival. To think the disaster if this is possible, and it is not possible in so much as we suspect that the disaster is thought) is to have no longer any future in which to think it. (Maurice Blanchot, *The Writing of the Disaster*)

One of the titles you commonly find at airport bookshops these days is an anthology of transcriptions of Black Box recordings taken from air disasters. I wonder who buys these books. I hang around the shop hoping to meet them, find out what's in it for them, whether they are arrivals or departures.

But more than this what I really wonder about is the black box in the cockpit, whether the pilot and co-pilot are aware of it, silently going about its business of taking down everything they say. I wonder if they are conscious of this little bank vault buried under the instrument panel where each word is deposited for safe-keeping, and that is the first thing the rescue teams look for among the debris when a plane falls out of the sky.

Like a holy book that you wouldn't normally bother to pick up, except in case of death, catastrophe or the end of the world. Or a black book that's got your name in it somewhere. Or a burning book that refuses to be consumed.

'There is no explosion except a book.' A book: a book among others, or a reference to the unique, the last and essential *Libre*, or, more exactly, the great Book which is always one among others, any book at all, already without importance or beyond important things. 'Explosion,' a book: this means that the book is not the laborious assemblage of a totality finally obtained, but has for its being the noisy, silent bursting which without the book would not take place (would not affirm itself). But it also means that since the book itself belongs to burst being – to being violently exceeded and thrust out of itself – the book gives no sign of itself save its own explosive violence, the force with which it expels itself, the thunderous refusal of the plausible: the outside in its becoming, which is that of bursting. (Maurice Blanchot, *The Writing of the Disaster*)

The aircraft cracked in half, a seed-pod giving up its spores, an egg yielding its mystery. Two actors, prancing Gibreel and buttony, pursed Mr. Saladin Chamcha, fell like titbits of tobacco from a broken old cigar. Above, behind, below them in the void there hung reclining seats, stereophonic headsets, drinks trolleys, motion discomforter receptacles, disembarkation cards, duty-free video games, braided caps, paper cups, blankets, oxygen masks. Also – for there had been more than a few migrants aboard, yes, quite a quantity of wives who had been grilled by reasonable, doing-their-job officials about the length of and distinguishing moles upon their husbands genitalia, a sufficiency of children upon whose legitimacy the British Government had cast its ever reasonable doubts – mingling with the remnants of the plane, equally fragmented, equally absurd, there floated the debris of the soul, broken memories, sloughed-off selves, severed mother tongues, violated privacies, untranslatable jokes, extinguished futures, lost loves, the forgotten meaning of hollow, booming words, *land, belonging, home.* Knocked a little silly by the blast, Gibreel and Saladin plummeted like bundles dropped by some carelessly open-beaked stork, and because Chamcha was going down head first, in the recommended position for babies entering the birth canal, he commenced to feel a low irritation at the other's refusal to fall in plain fashion. Saladin nosedived while Farishta embraced air, hugging it with his arms and legs, a flailing, overwrought actor without techniques of restraint. (Salman Rushdie, *The Satanic Verses*)

We call this plane, which knows only longitudes and latitudes, speeds and haecceities, the plane of consistency or composition (as opposed to the plan(e) of organization and development). It is necessarily a plane of immanence and univocality. We therefore call it the plane of Nature although nature has nothing to do with it, since on this plane there is no distinction between the natural and artificial. However many dimensions it may have, it never has a supplementary dimension to that which transpires upon it. That alone makes it natural and immanent[...] It is a geometrical plane, no longer tied to a mental design but to an abstract design. Its number of dimensions increases as what happens happens, but even so it lose nothing of its planitude. It is thus a plane of proliferation, peopling, contagion; but the proliferation of material has nothing to do with an evolution, the development of a form or the filiation of forms. Still less is it a regression leading back to a principle. It is on the contrary an *involution*, in which form is constantly being dissolved freeing times and speeds.
[...] So the plan(e) – life plan(e), writing plan(e), music plan(e) – must necessarily fail for it is impossible to be faithful to it; but the failures are part of the plan (e) for the plan(e) expands or shrinks along with the dimensions of that which it deploys in each instance (planitude of *n* dimensions). A strange machine that is simultaneously a machine of war, music and contagion-proliferation-involution. (Gilles Deleuze & Félix Guattari, *A Thousand Plateaus*)

When the Fatwa was announced Rushdie in his defence summoned the idea of the 'death of the author' as part of literature's ongoing project of modernity. These were not his opinions. Meanwhile, politicians spoke in defence of freedom of expression. But it was not a question of freedom of expression. It was as Rushdie said, a question of relativity, of the author washing his hands of his creation.
Paradoxically the fatwa, in pronouncing 'the death of the author' in the sphere of the real, had the effect of a rebirth.

When you think about it, Salman Rushdie is a pretty baleful name to have to carry around with you. In Italian salma means 'corpse' . Salman - a man who is at the same time a corpse. A dead man, or rather, a man in a rush to die.
While I was an exchange student at the University of Massachusetts, Rushdie visited a friend of his, a professor of cultural studies at nearby Hampshire College, who apparently advised him not to publish the book, warning him of the dire consequences. Rushdie went ahead, despite his friend's warning.

Such a passage through symbolic suicide is at work in every act worth the name – after an act, I'm literally 'not the same as before'. In this sense we could say that the subject 'undergoes' the act ('passes through' it) rather than 'accomplishes' it; in it, the subject is annihilated and radically reborn (or not) i.e. the act involves a kind of temporary eclipse, *aphanasis,* of the subject. Which is why every act worthy of this name is 'mad' in the sense of radical *unaccount-ability:* by means of it, I put at stake everything, including myself, my symbolic identity; the act is therefore always a 'crime,' a 'transgression,' namely of the limit of the symbolic community to which I belong. The act is defined by this irreducible risk. In its most fundamental dimension, it is always *negative,* i.e. an act of annihilation, of wiping out – we not only don't know what will come out of it, its final outcome is ultimately even insignificant, strictly secondary to the NO! of the pure act. (Slavoj Žižek, *Enjoy your Symptom*)

Now, however, time, having no further use for me, is running out. I will soon be thirty-one years old. Perhaps. If my crumpling, over-used body permits. But I have no hope of saving my life, nor can count on having even a thousand nights and a night. I must work fast, faster than Scheherazade, if I am to end up meaning - yes, meaning - something. (Rushdie, *Midnight's Children*)

How many of us feel, these days, that something that has passed us too quickly is ending: a moment of life, a period of history, an idea of civilization, a twist in the turning of the unconcerned world. A thousand ages in Thy sight they sing in St. Thomas's Cathedral to their no-doubt non-existent god, are like an evening gone; so I might just point out O my omnipotent reader that I have been passing too quickly too. A double speed of existence permits only half a life. (Rushdie, *The Moor's Last Sigh*)

Up there in air-space, in that soft, imperceptible field which had been made possible by the century and which, thereafter, made the century possible, becoming one of its defining locations, the place of movement and of war,

But even if the formless ground or the undifferentiated abyss is made to speak with its full voice of intoxication and anger, the alternative imposed by transcendental philosophy and by metaphysics is not left behind: beyond the person and the individual, you will discern nothing...Nietzche's discovery lies elsewhere when, having liberated himself from Schopenhauer and Wagner, he explored a world of impersonal and pre-individual singularities, a world he then called Dionysian or of the will to power, a free and unbound energy. These are nomadic singularities which are no longer imprisoned within the fixed individuality of the infinite Being (the notorious immutability of God), nor inside the sedentary boundaries of the finite subject (the notorious limits of knowledge). This is something neither individual nor personal, but rather, singular. Being is not an undifferentiated abyss, it leaps from one singularity to another, casting always the dice belonging to the same cast, always fragmented and formed again in each throw. It is a Dionysian sense-producing machine, in which nonsense and sense are no longer found in simple opposition, but are rather copresent to one another within a new discourse. The new discourse is no longer that of the form, but neither is it that of the formless: it is rather that of the pure unformed...As for the subject of this new discourse (except that there is no longer any subject) it is not man or God, and even less man in the place of God. The subject is this free, anonymous and nomadic singularity which traverses men as well as plants and animals independently of the matter of their individuation and the forms of their personality. (Gilles Deleuze, *The Logic of Sense*)

As the plane touches down, Ormus cama's head starts pounding. There is something about this England in which he has just arrived. There are things he cannot trust. There's a rip, once again, in the surface of the real. Uncertainty pours down on him, its dark radiance opens his eyes. As his foot alights upon Heathrow, he succumbs to the illusion that nothing is solid, nothing exists except the precise piece of concrete his foot now rests upon. The homecoming passengers notice none of this, they stride confidently forward through the familiar, the quotidian, but the new arrivals look fearfully at the deliquescent land. They seem to be splashing through what should be solid ground. As his own feet move gingerly forward, he feels small pieces of England solidify beneath the. His footprints are the only fixed points in his universe. He checks out Virus: who is untroubled, serene. As for Spenta Cama, her eyes are fixed on the crowd of waving greeters high above. Trying to pick out a familiar face, she has no time to look down. Never look down, Ormus thinks. That way you won't see the danger, you won't plunge through the deceptive softness of the apparent into the burning abyss below.

Everything must be made real, step by step, he tells himself. This is a mirage, a ghost world, which becomes real only beneath our magic touch, our loving footfall, our kiss. We have to imagine it into being from the ground up. (Rushdie, *The Ground Beneath her Feet*)

By God if I ever cracked I'd try to make the world crack with me. Listen! The world only exists through your apprehension of it, and so it's much better to say it's not you that has cracked - it's the grand canyon. (F. Scott Fitzgerald, *The Crack-Up*)

His horror, his sense of foreboding, of wrongness and impending doom - cracks in the world, abysses, the four horsemen, all the anachronistic apparatus of millenarian eschatology - is increased by the knowledge of his own involuntary gift of visions, the holes in the real that manifest themselves to show him another reality, which he resists, though it beckons him to enter; for entry would feel - he knows this - very like insanity. Can it be this visionary madness, the thing he most fears within himself that's most in tune with his new world. (Rushdie, *The Ground Beneath Her Feet*)

While I was piecing this together, the earthquake in Turkey was on the news nearly every day. I almost stopped. It seemed like bad taste. But it was once again the meeting of writing and disaster. What is it about Rushdie, I thought, that he's so in tune with events. Pointless to dwell on the chaotic mess of this conjunction.

The apparent motive, the principal motive was, of course, single. But the crime was the effect of a whole list of motives which had blown on it in a whirlwind (like the sixteen winds when they twist together in a tornado, in a cyclonic depression) and had ended by pressing into the vortex of the crime the enfeebled 'reason of the world.' [...] And then he used to say, but this a bit wearily, 'you are sure to find skirts where you don't want to find them.' A belated Italian revision of the trite 'cherchez la femme.' And then he seemed to repent, as if he had slandered the ladies, and wanted to change his mind. But that would have got him into difficulties. So he would remain silent and pensive, afraid he had said too much. What he meant was that a certain affective motive, a certain amount or, as you might say today, a quantum of affection, of 'eros', was also involved even in 'matters of interest', in crimes which were apparently far removed from the tempests of love. Some colleagues, a tiny bit envious of his intuitions, a few priests, more acquainted with the many evils of our times, some subalterns, clerks, and his superiors too, insisted he read strange books: from which he drew all those words that mean nothing, or almost nothing, but which serve better than others to dazzle the naive, the ignorant. (Carlo Emilio Gadda, *That Awful Mess on Via Merulana*)

Back at the Orpheum in the winter cold, alone and bereft, I hug myself and shiver while my white breath hangs in the air, I'm sitting out on the roof in my hat and coat with my hands over my cold-stung ears, trying to conjure up Vina sunbathing naked in the height of summer, Vina stretching her body and turning to me with a lazy, faithless smile. But it's too cold and anyway the racket is everywhere, there's no escape from the war of meanings, the white air is full of words.
Diachronically speaking, this is an event in history, to be understood within time as a phenomenon with certain linear antecedents, social, cultural, political. Synchronically, however, all versions of it exist simultaneously, collectively forming a contemporary statement about art and life ... its importance lies in the random meaninglessness of the death... her radical absence is a void or an abyss into which a tide of meanings can pour... she has become an empty receptacle, an arena of discourse, and we can invent her in our own image as once invented god... no possibility of the phenomenon fizzling any time soon because the phase of exploitation has now set in, the shirts bearing the last photograph, the commemorative coins, the mugs, the tackiness, her old school mates selling their stories, her army of casual lovers, her entourage, her friends... these are multiplier effects, she's caught in an echo chamber and the noise bounces round and round getting boomier, fuzzier, less distinct...it's just noise now. (Rushdie, *The Ground Beneath Her Feet*)

So, the veneration of matter: what is more worthy of the spirit?
Whereasspirit venerating spirit ... do we see that?
- We see all too much of it.

(Ponge)

Earthworks:

This text is a slightly abbreviated version of the written part of a multi-medial 'theory' performance, which also involved the use of film and music. The resulting conjunction of, and dialogue between, these various elements was in no way predetermined, though the general idea was to stage a suggestively catastrophic millennium scene. Throughout the performance a tape-recorder played a voice recording of Jean Baudrillard's essay 'The Year 2000 Has Already Happened' read simultaneously in English (by myself) and Italian (by Silvia Maglioni) to provide a contra-puntal background 'ambience'.

For this section, rather than listing the works buried in the textual rubble, I have decided to list the (absent) music and film sources used during the actual event.

Films

Idioterne. Dir. Lars Von Trier. Denmark 1998.
Deux ou trois choses que je sais d'elle. Dir. Jean Luc Godard. France 1967.
Germania anno zero. Dir. Roberto Rossellini. Italy/West Germany, 1947.
JLG/JLG. Dir. Jean Luc Godard. France.
Zabriskie Point. Michelangelo Antonioni. USA, 1969.
Caro Diario. Dir. Nanni Moretti. Italy 1994.
2001: A Space Odyssey. Dir. Stanley Kubrick. US 1968.

Music

Olivier Messiaen. *Quatuor pour la fin du temps*.
Gavin Bryars. *After the Requiem*.

Notes on Contributors

Michael Böss is Associate Professor in the Department of English at the University of Aarhus. His publications include *Den irske verden: Historie, kultur og identitet i det moderne samfund* (Samleren, 1997).

Jan Ifversen is Associate Professor at the Centre for European Cultural Studies, University of Aarhus. His publications include his dissertation *Om magt, demokrati og diskurs diskuteret i lyset af den franske revolution* (Aarhus University, 1997).

Ib Johansen is Associate Professor in the Department of English at the University of Aarhus. His publications include articles on Blake and Poe and *Sfinksens forvandlinger: fantastiske fortællere i dansk litteratur fra B. S. Ingemann til Per Højholt* (Aalborg University Press, 1986).

Cheralyn Mealor is a postgraduate student at the Department of English, Aarhus University.

Sylvia Mikkelsen is a graduate of the Department of English, Aarhus University, where she has since taught courses on authors including Emily Dickinson and James Joyce.

Richard North is Reader in English at University College London. His publications include *Heathen Gods in Old English Literature* (Cambridge University Press, 1997).

Per Serritslev Petersen is Associate Professor in the Department of English at the University of Aarhus. His publications include articles on literary pedagogy, Shakespeare and modern drama.

Norman Ravvin is Chair of Canadian Jewish Studies at Concordia University, Montreal. His academic publications include *A House of Words: Jewish Writing, Identity, and Memory* (McGill-Queen's University Press, 1997). He also publishes fiction.

Robert Jensen Rix is completing a PhD thesis on William Blake at the University of Copenhagen.

Anjum Saleemi is the author of *Universal Grammar and Language Learnability* (Cambridge University Press, 1992).

Jamsheed Shorish currently holds a research position in microeconomics at the Institute for Advanced Studies in Vienna.

Graeme Thomson teaches English Studies in the Psychology Department of the University of Turin. He writes regularly on contemporary literature and critical theory for *L'Indice dei libri del mese*. He has published articles on authors including Charles Dickens and Don DeLillo, and has translated several contemporary Italian plays. He is currently researching the representation of music in contemporary fiction.